GOOD MORALS

AND

GENTLE MANNERS.

FOR

SCHOOLS AND FAMILIES.

ALEX. M. GOW, A. M.

VAN ANTWERP, BRAGG & CO.,

137 WALNUT STREET, *CINCINNATI.* 28 BOND STREET, *NEW YORK.*

ECLECTIC PRESS:
VAN ANTWERP, BRAGG & CO.,
CINCINNATI.

PREFACE.

The author of this work believes that the subjects of good morals and gentle manners are unequaled in importance by any that can be imparted in the public schools, either for intellectual discipline or practical utility.

He believes that the true happiness and real usefulness of each individual, and of every community, depend largely upon the application of the principles of virtuous living.

He believes fully in the wisdom of the proverb, that we shall "*Train up a child in the way he should go; and, when he is old, he will not depart from it.*"

He believes that moral and social training do not result from hearing little moral stories, or from reading goodish little books.

He believes that training implies discipline, and that while little books and stories afford amusement and entertainment, they alone are not sufficient to educate children in the duties of morality and politeness.

He believes in teaching by parables, especially when accompanied by such direct and practical applications of truth as are exhibited in the "Proverbs" and the "Sermon on the Mount."

He believes that moral lessons, which are taught in anticipation of temptation, are more profitable than those which follow the commission of crime; that a boy just convicted of stealing is not in the best frame of mind to receive his first lessons upon honesty.

He believes that moral instruction should be given as regularly, systematically, and practically as instruction in any other department of science, and that its postponement to the latter part of the college course is unwise and unphilosophical.

He believes that all schools should be places of true refinement and elegant culture, and that when they are not, they must be nurseries of vulgarity.

He believes that much of the vandalism exhibited in many of the higher institutions is due to the lack of good moral culture in the lower ones.

He believes in Sunday Schools, but doubts whether the teaching of one hour, of one day in seven, if ever so valuable, can counteract the evil influences of the remaining six days of the week.

He believes, religiously, in the fundamental principles of our American system of government, as the best adapted to the American people, and that the permanence of this system depends upon the intelligence and virtue of the citizens.

He believes that, "*Righteousness exalteth a nation; but sin is a reproach to any people;* and that a nation's sins are but the aggregate reproaches of the individuals who compose it.

He believes that the principles of our government must be taught constantly and thoroughly to promote true patriotism.

He believes that the self-control necessary for the good citizen must be based upon the principles and practice of a good school; for a school is but a state in miniature.

He believes that the gentleman and lady must be distinguished by good manners, and that good manners are the outgrowth of good morals.

He believes that educators generally appreciate the necessity of regular instruction in morals and manners as an important auxiliary in the government and discipline of the schools; but he is not aware of any systematic text book on moral and social law which is adapted to the use of grammar and intermediate schools, and of families. Therefore he has prepared this manual. If it meet with the acceptance which the importance of the subject demands, he will feel that he has not written in vain.

EVANSVILLE, IND., 1873.

TABLE OF CONTENTS.

PART I—MORAL LAW.

PART II—MUNICIPAL LAW.

PART III—SOCIAL LAW, OR POLITENESS.

MORAL LAW.

CHAPTER I.

"He that walketh with wise men, shall be wise."

GOOD SOCIETY.

"What must I do to secure a place in good society?" is a question that often perplexes the minds of the young as they begin to mingle with the world. The answer depends upon what is meant by the term. People differ as to what constitutes good society, and therefore a variety of definitions of it may be given, depending upon the diversity of their views. One supposes good society to be an association of those who are rich and able to afford the luxuries of good living and elegant houses; of fashion and fine dress. Another thinks it consists of those who trace their family name and history back through generations of honored ancestors. Another imagines that official position or prosperous business gives a sure title to good society.

The society of the Good.—While wealth, good family connections, office honorably obtained, and flourishing business are very desirable, yet any of these alone, or all combined, do not make their possessors fit to enter such society and enjoy its benefits, without having some other and better

What is the subject of this chapter? Repeat the text. What question commences the chapter? Why do people differ in their ideas of good society? What is a true definition?

qualifications. The definition *we* shall give of good society is the SOCIETY OF THE GOOD.

People are like birds: they go in flocks, each kind by itself. Those of similar feelings, tastes, and habits associate together. The good prefer to mingle with the good, and the bad are generally found with each other. There is truth in the old proverb, "Tell me the company you keep, and I'll tell you what you are."

The Good.—But who are "the Good?" The answer is: "They who are educated to know, and trained to practice, the rules of good morals and gentle manners." Neither high birth, nor station, nor wealth, nor fashion, nor even intelligence alone can make the gentleman or lady. These proud titles properly belong to those who are "*first pure, then peaceable, gentle, and easy to be entreated, full of mercy and good fruits, without partiality and without hypocrisy.*" To be a lady or a gentleman is a high distinction, and worthy the study of every one who possesses an honorable ambition. There is not a boy in the land so poor, nor a girl so humble, who may not aspire to the knowledge which will secure this enviable superiority. That it is a most important study, all who reflect upon the subject must admit, since it enables us to be good and to do good. Not a day passes in the company of others, in which we are not called upon to practice the lessons of morality and exhibit our knowledge of good manners. These lessons in goodness and politeness are necessary, if we would enter good society; for they are practiced only in its circles. Counterfeit gentlemen and ladies are as common as counterfeit money; if there were no value in good currency, nobody would take pains to imitate it; so, if there were no real men, gentle-men, there would be no shams.

Why are people like birds? Who are "the good?" Why may we tell a man's character by his company? What are the characteristics of a gentleman? Who may learn to be a gentleman? Why should we study this subject? Who are counterfeit gentlemen and ladies?

The King of Men.—The Scottish poet, Burns, gives his idea of "the king o' men" in the following extract:

"What tho' on hamely fare we dine,
  Wear hoddin* gray and a' that,
Gie fools their silks, and knaves their wine,
  A man's a man for a' that;
For a' that and a' that,
  Their tinsel show and a' that,
The honest man though e'er sae poor
  Is king o' men, for a' that.

"Then let us pray, that come it may,
  As come it will, for a' that,
That sense and worth, o'er a' the earth,
  May bear the gree† and a' that;
For a' that and a' that,
  It's coming yet for a' that,
That man to man the warld o'er
  Shall brothers be for a' that."

Since the principles and laws of morality form so important a part of a good education, we shall offer such helps in these pages as will afford instruction upon this subject, and at the same time teach those rules and maxims of politeness, which will enable the student to enter the society of the good with ease and comfort to himself, and with the approbation of his friends.

Our suggestions, we trust, will also be profitable to the family and the school, since that which is of such special advantage to the individual, can not fail to be desirable where numbers are closely united.

*Humble. †May bear the victory.

Who is described as the king o' men? Give the idea of the poet in his or in your language. What is the object of this book? What advantage to the individual may be derived from this study? What benefit to the family and school? Why?

CHAPTER II.

"Keep thy heart with all diligence; for out of it are the issues of life."

HABITS.

Illustration.—"A young man in Waltham, Mass., was very feeble, but not sick. He was advised by his physician to set out upon a journey on foot, but was cautioned not to walk at any time till exhausted. He began his journey in the morning, and, with short exertion and frequent rest, he walked three miles on the first day, and was fatigued. The next morning, to his surprise, he felt more vigor and courage to go on, and started again. He walked on that day in the same manner, and accomplished four miles before night. He thus gained strength and energy day by day, adding little to little, and finally walked to Niagara Falls, more than five hundred miles. After viewing these to his satisfaction, he returned in a much shorter time than he went. But he did not return by a direct course. He visited the interesting places in the neighborhood of his homeward route, and at the end of his sixth week reached home, having walked more than a thousand miles in forty-two days. On the last day he had walked forty miles, and was so little fatigued with the day's journey that in the evening he felt sufficient energy to visit his young friends in the neighborhood."

The successful performance of delightful music, as many school-girls know, is only attained by diligent practice. An accomplished player on the piano-forte will take a new piece of music and play four parts, observing the

---

What does the incident of the invalid illustrate? What is the second illustration?

marks of musical notation, and singing the words at the same time. Another will perform a difficult piece of instrumental music while listening to and perhaps engaging in a conversation. It seems impossible that eyes, fingers, feet, and voice should be brought into such perfect harmony of action, but it is only an illustration of the law of habit. Years of patient practice and diligent study are necessary to secure such results.

Habit defined.—Habit may be defined as a condition of mind or body which results from the frequent performance of an action. Man is called a creature of habit, because all his actions of mind and body are due to repetition. Animals learn to walk, swim, and fly by instinct. Man acquires the arts of walking, swimming, and talking by practice. When a habit is once firmly established it becomes our master, and we rarely have sufficient strength of will to overcome it, although its continuance be condemned alike by reason and experience. We often do its bidding without thought or reflection, not being aware of its influence, and sometimes when we are fully conscious of its power and are desirous of escaping its trammels, our weakness is manifest in our failure.

The boy who was charged with whistling in school denied that he did it, and when censured for untruthfulness, again insisted that he did not, for "it whistled itself." Possibly he was not far wrong, as he meant that he whistled unintentionally and even unconsciously, since the habit had been acquired by a continued practice, and was indulged without any thought or design.

Good and bad habits.—Habits are said to be good or bad, as they are the result of actions that are right or wrong. When we speak of a man of good habits, we

---

Define habit. Why is man called the creature of habit? Is it easy to overcome habits? Why? Do persons always think while performing certain actions? Give an illustration. May the boy have been truthful? When are habits good or bad?

mean that he is a moral man; that is, one who has so long practiced the methods of right thinking, speaking, and acting that he behaves properly from force of habit. A man of bad habits is called an immoral man because he has become confirmed in wrong-doing, and can scarcely act otherwise if he tries. The moral quality of any action is not changed because it has been repeated so often as to become a habit. People often justify bad habits because they find difficulty in overcoming them, but the habitual drunkard who is unable to restrain the appetite that is ruining him and distressing his family, can not say he does no wrong because his habits are bad and it is too late to reform them. Bad habits are the fruits of wrong actions, and wrong actions are always a violation of good morals; but the fact that a man is unable to break the habit is no excuse for the wrong. He began wrong and continues wrong.

Conscience governed by habit.—We have already seen that the minds of men, as well as their physical powers, become subject to the influence of habit. The conscience also may be under the same control. Conscience is defined as the "moral sense," or "that power, faculty, or principle of the soul, which, when the judgment decides on the lawfulness or unlawfulness of our own actions or affections, will suffer pleasure or pain as it is obeyed or disobeyed." When we know the relations we sustain to God and our fellow-man, the judgment will inform us what we ought, or ought not to do, as right or wrong, and the conscience will approve of the decision. This faculty urges us to do right because its performance causes satisfaction, while the doing of wrong causes remorse. Like every other power or sense of body or mind,

---

What do we mean by a man of good habits? Of bad? Is the moral quality of an action changed by its being a habit? May we justify bad habits because they are habits? Of what are bad habits the result? Define conscience. Is conscience subject to the law of habit? What office does conscience perform? Will conscience be strengthened by use?

it is strengthened by proper use and is weakened, or perhaps destroyed, by disuse or neglect. This is a law of our nature.

Anecdote.—A father and son went into a field to steal corn. When they had gone to the middle of the field, the father mounted a stump and looked cautiously around to see if they were observed. The boy whispered: "Father, look up." The tender conscience of the boy was disturbed by this violation of the law, "*Thou shalt not steal.*" He felt that God's command would be broken, and he cautioned his father to look, where, from the habit of stealing, he had not been accustomed to apprehend danger or discovery.

Conscience should be obeyed.—We should always obey the teachings of conscience. It is the highest authority to which we can appeal. If we think an action right, we are under the strongest obligation to perform it; if we feel it is wrong, nothing should induce its commission. If we neglect to listen to the appeal of conscience once, we lose our self-respect; we feel a sense of shame and meanness. If we commit the wrong a second time, its warning voice is not so loud, and finally, after repeated failures to secure attention, it ceases to urge us to do right. The law of habit which enables the conscience to grow each day stronger and more certain in its indications of right, will as surely, if neglected and abused, cease entirely to give its friendly advice. It is a dangerous habit to neglect the kind whisperings of so friendly a monitor.

Character and reputation.—The sum of a person's good and bad habits constitutes his character. The good

---

How does disuse affect it? Give the anecdote. What was the difference between the father and the son? Why should we always obey our conscience? Why do we study the moral law? Is it necessary to educate the conscience? Why? What is the effect of neglecting the appeal of conscience even once? What is the effect of repeated neglect? What is meant by character?

and the bad are mingled together; if the former are in excess, he is said to possess a good character; if the latter are predominant, his character is said to be bad. The term character represents a man as he is. Reputation is the term which expresses the estimation in which he is held by others.

Anecdote.—The following incident will illustrate the value, both of a good character and an unblemished reputation:

Just as the civil war commenced, soldiers were enlisting and going away from almost every home in the land.

A young man had volunteered, and was expecting daily to be ordered to the seat of war. One day his mother gave him an unpaid bill with the money, and asked him to pay it. When he returned home at night, she said: "Did you pay that bill?"

"Yes," he answered.

In a few days the bill was sent in a second time. "I thought," she said to her son, "that you paid this."

"I really do n't remember, mother, you know I've had so many things on my mind."

"But you said you did."

"Well," he answered, "if I said I did, I did."

He went away, and his mother took the bill herself to the store. The young man had been known in the town all his life, and what opinion was held of him the result will show.

"I am quite sure," she said, "that my son paid this some days ago; he has been very busy since, and has quite forgotten about it, but he told me he had that day, and says, if he said then that he had, he is quite sure he did."

"Well," said the man, "I forget about it, but if he ever said he did, he did."

The value of such a reputation is inestimable.

What is meant by reputation? Which is preferable, a good character or good reputation? Repeat the anecdote.

It is not always the case that reputation is founded upon real worth, for some of the best men the world ever saw were neither understood nor esteemed, while some of the basest were reputed the most worthy. Still, as a rule among common men, a man's reputation is based upon a fair estimate of his virtues. If the young acquire the habits which distinguish ladies and gentlemen, if they become "*first pure, then peaceable, gentle, and easy to be entreated, full of mercy and good fruits, without partiality, and without hypocrisy*," their good influence will soon be felt and acknowledged. These virtues are the results of education; for a good education is but little more than the formation and growth of good habits.

Can habits be changed?—Yes; habits may be changed, bad characters may be reformed, and good reputations may be regained, but the processes are sometimes long and difficult. It is easier to avoid bad habits when they are shown us than to correct them after they have begun to control our actions. The habits of an old man are rarely improved. Youth is the time to accustom both mind and body to right methods of life. If wrong practices have been acquired, if bad manners have been formed, if incorrect ideas have been learned, the elasticity of the mind and the hopefulness of the youthful character make a reformation possible. An ancient prophet in reproving the sins of his people, who had long been transgressing, used the following sad but striking language: "*Can the Ethiopian change his skin, or the leopard his spots? then may ye also do good, that are accustomed to do evil.*" If every youth in the land, who has acquired evil ways, were to have as little

---

What habits distinguish the lady and gentleman? What is meant by pure? Peaceable? Gentle? Is a boy who refuses to listen to advice "easy to be entreated?" How are good fruits shown? What is meant by partiality? By hypocrisy? May these virtues be acquired? How? What is meant by a good education? Can habits be changed? What is the period to form good habits? Why are bad habits hard to change? What was the language of the prophet? What does it mean?

chance of reformation as a leopard has to change his spots, then the hope of being and doing good would be truly faint. But fortunately it is not so. Evil habits may be overcome in the same manner they were acquired, that is, by practice.

How shall bad habits be changed?—If conscience tells us that any habit is wrong, it is our duty to change it. There is nothing brave or manly in giving up the hope of reform, or in whining and complaining with a cowardly "I can 't." It is folly to expect to break off in a day the bad habits which have been growing and strengthening for years. The reform can only be accomplished by constant, careful attention, by vigorous resolution, by courageously watching and fighting against the disposition or propensity to do wrong. It is not an easy undertaking. "Avoid the persons, the places, and the thoughts that lead to the temptation, and, on the other hand, frequent the places, associate with the persons, indulge the thoughts that lead away from temptation. Keep busy: idleness is the strength of bad habits. Do not give up the struggle when you have broken your resolution once, twice, or a dozen times. Any failure only shows how much need there is for your increasing efforts. When you have failed to accomplish your desire, think the matter over and endeavor to understand why it was you failed, so that you may be on your guard against the recurrence of the same circumstances." Be honest with yourself, and never suppose you can bear a temptation. Let the daily prayer be, "*lead us not into temptation, but deliver us from evil*," and thus strive to "*Keep thy heart with all diligence; for out of it are the issues of life.*"

How are bad habits overcome? Did you ever hear one say "I can 't?" What does "I can 't" generally mean? What would it be better to say and do? Need we expect to correct bad habits at once? When should the reformation commence? Why not postpone it? Is it easy to correct bad habits? Why? What must be done? Suppose we fail once? Is it well to put ourselves in the way of temptation? Why? Have you any habits that you should correct? If so, what is your duty? How often should you try to correct a habit? Should you give up trying?

CHAPTER III.

"Whoso keepeth the law is a wise son."

LAW.

Law, in its general sense, is defined to be "a rule of action prescribed by a superior power, which the inferior is bound to obey, or suffer the penalties of disobedience." A careful examination of the terms of this definition will assist us in understanding it.

"A rule of action."—A rule of action is an order commanding a course of conduct or principle of living or acting which is uniform and regular in its operations. A rule is some definite, fixed, and certain process. It is not a permission or an agreement to do or not to do a certain thing, but it expresses an obligation to be enforced when not obeyed. The language of a law is not "you may," or "you can," or "you ought," but "you must and you shall."

"Prescribed."—The term prescribed is derived from two Latin words, *pre*, which means before, and *scribere*, to write. Taken literally it means written beforehand. Justice requires that those who are the subjects of a law, shall have an opportunity to know what is required of them, and also what penalties are attached to the neglect of their duty. It would not be right to enforce the penalties of a violated law which the offender did not know, be-

---

What is the subject of Chapter III? Repeat the text. Define law in its general sense. What is necessary that we may fully understand the definition? What is meant by a rule? What is it not? What is the language of a law, you may, or you must? Why?

cause it had never been published. Prescribed, then, means advertised or published, and it is plain that a just and humane law should be so publicly announced that those who are expected to obey it may have no excuse for their neglect, nor cause of complaint resulting from ignorance.

"Superior power."—The next important idea contained in this definition of law is, that the rule of action must be prescribed by a superior power. Nations may make agreements or treaties, which they are in honor and duty bound to perform, but they can not make laws binding each other; for neither party can enforce a lawful obedience. Compliance can only be claimed by a person or a power that has the right to rule, and also the ability to enforce certain penalties for neglect. The subjects of a law-maker are in duty bound to obey the commands of their superior, or suffer the consequences of their refusal or neglect.

"Penalty of disobedience."—The last idea embraced in the definition of law refers to the penalty of disobedience. It would be folly for the superior power to prescribe a rule of action which the inferior could neglect with impunity. It is evident that it must not be left to the free choice of the subject to refuse the prescribed rule of action; for, if obedience is not freely and promptly rendered, there must be a penalty attached to enforce it. The superior power proclaims in every law, obey the rule or suffer the penalty. In short, a law is a rule, prescribed by the superior, to which the inferior must yield submission, or suffer for disobedience.

What does prescribed mean? Why is it right to prescribe a law? What is meant by a superior power? Why can not nations justly prescribe laws to each other? Who only can command obedience? May a child prescribe rules to its parent, or a pupil to the teacher? Why? If the superior has a right to prescribe law, what is the duty of the inferior? What is the last idea in the definition of law? Why is a penalty understood as a part of every law? Suppose the inferior rebels against the law, what must the superior do? State the essential parts of the definition.

The object of law.—The object of law should be to promote the welfare of the subject, whose happiness is secured in proportion as he observes its requirements. Laws are made for protection and not for punishment. If the subject shall disregard his highest good by violating the law, the object of the punishment is to remind him of his duty in such a manner as will prevent the repetition of the offense, and thus secure him, or the community of which he is a member, from future injury. Our highest happiness is found in obedience to all the laws of our nature, and if we fail to secure that highest happiness, it is because we do not fulfill our obligations. We have no right to complain of the penalties we suffer, when we neglect the performance of our duty. So, also, if a person prefers to violate the law, our sympathies should rather be for the injured law than for him, since the law is right and he is wrong. We should always be on the side of truth, justice, and right.

Codes of law.—When a number of laws, relating to any given subject, are classified and arranged in an orderly manner, the collection is called a Code. There are many codes, and they are known and defined by the subjects to which they relate: thus, the code of laws which God has prescribed for the moral government of man is called the MORAL LAW; that for the government of a country is called MUNICIPAL LAW; while that which refers to the several grades of society and their intercourse with each other is known as SOCIAL LAW.

These three systems of laws will occupy our attention in the following chapters, and if thoroughly studied, will assist in preparing the student for an honorable entrance to the best society — the society of the good.

What should be the object of every law? Has any one the right to violate the law? If the law is violated who is to blame if punishment follows? Should our sympathies be given to the law-maker or the law-breaker? Why? On which side should the good be? Is this so in school? What is a code? What are the codes of law to be considered in this book? What is the object of the moral law? Of the municipal law? Of social law? Why should we study all these codes?

CHAPTER IV.

"*My son, forget not my law; but let thine heart keep my commandments: for length of days, and long life, and peace shall they add to thee.*"

THE MORAL LAW.

Moral law defined.—The moral law may be defined as, a rule of action prescribed by God to mankind concerning their duties to him and to each other.

Natural religion.—From the earliest periods of the world's history, among all people, in every part of the earth, mankind have recognized and worshiped a Being, whom they regarded as superior to themselves, possessing attributes of infinite wisdom, power, and knowledge. This being they call God. They derive their knowledge of Him through the traditions of their ancestors and the works of his creation. The following is a sublime description of God as seen through his works: "*He hath made the earth by his power; he hath established the world by his wisdom, and hath stretched out the heavens by his discretion. When he uttereth his voice, there is a multitude of waters in the heavens, and he causeth the vapors to ascend from the ends of the earth; he maketh lightnings with rain, and bringeth forth the wind out of his treasures.*" "*Let*

What is the subject of Chapter IV? Repeat the text. Define moral law. Whom do mankind recognize as their superior? How do mankind generally derive their notions of God? What is meant by tradition? Repeat the beautiful description of God as seen in his works. Who made the world? How does he utter his voice? What do the ascending vapors produce? What would the earth be without rain? Why should all the earth stand in awe of God? Who prescribes laws for the rain, the lightning, and the storm?

all the earth fear the Lord: let all the inhabitants of the world stand in awe of him." He is the "Superior Power," who made us and prescribed the laws by which we are governed. To enable us to understand our relations to him, he has conferred upon us mental and moral faculties, thus making us superior to all his earthly creatures. Other animals possess bodies and bodily powers similar to ours; they are also gifted with a wonderful talent, called instinct, which enables them to preserve their lives, promote their comfort, and increase their kind; but they have no knowledge of right and wrong.

Man's endowments.—The mind of man enables him to perceive and know, by all that is in and around him, that there is a Being superior to himself. He can readily recognize in himself the lord of creation, and yet he feels that there is One who surpasses him immeasurably in all the elements and attributes of greatness. This Creator has conferred upon him a faculty to perceive his relations, reason to reflect, judgment to determine, and a will to execute, and, in addition, an inner sense which enables him to understand right from wrong.

Right and wrong.—Human actions are divided into two classes with reference to their moral quality, the good and the bad. In performing the good, we do right; following the bad, we do wrong. Right and wrong are the subjects of the moral law. Some actions have no moral quality in them, as it can not be said they are either right or wrong. In such cases conscience does not urge us to do or not to do them. Thus, if my inclination leads me to make a call on a friend, I may go to-day, or postpone the visit till to-morrow, as it may suit my convenience, and

---

How is man superior to the rest of God's creatures? What is instinct? Have animals a sense of right and wrong? Why? How does man know there is a Superior Being? How many kinds of moral actions? Has God prescribed good laws for us? Should we obey? Why? What are the subjects of moral law? Are there any actions that have no moral quality? Give an illustration.

whether I go or stay, conscience is silent, since there is no right or wrong in the question. But if my friend is sick, and needs me, and I promised to go at a certain time, I am in duty bound to go. Conscience whispers, "to go is right, to neglect the duty is wrong: therefore go." Conscience not only tells us, but urges us to do right, and its voice should never be slighted.

What are right and wrong?—As persons are differently formed in face and figure, so they are differently endowed with mental and moral powers. There is a dissimilarity in education, in habits of thought, in circumstances of life, in business and social relations, which often makes a vast difference in men's estimates of right and wrong. Men are often unable to see things in the same light, and consequently do not agree in their conclusions. Each believes conscientiously in the correctness of his opinions, and disagrees with the other. What then is the duty of each? It is the duty of every man to follow his own conscientious convictions of right.

Obedience to law.—As God has given each man faculties to perceive, to reason, to judge, and to will, He will hold him, as a moral and intelligent being, accountable for the violation of his laws. We are responsible to God for the use and the abuse of all our powers of mind and body. To arrive at correct conclusions concerning the truth, it is our duty to obtain all the instruction which will enable us to understand our relations to God and man, striving to discover and practice the right. If we violate the laws of health by intemperate eating or drinking, disease, which is the admonition and the penalty, will soon overtake us. If

---

What does conscience say concerning good or bad actions? Are there any two people entirely alike? Do all men agree exactly in their notions of right? What, then, must each man do? Why are we accountable to God for our actions? If we do right what will God do? If wrong? To whom are we responsible for the use of our powers? How shall we learn God's will concerning us?

we transgress the laws of mind, idiocy or insanity may be our punishment; and if we disobey God's moral law, He will as certainly avenge it as He does the infraction of his physical laws.

The penalty for violated law.—If a man drop a lighted match into a keg of gunpowder, the effect of his imprudence is quickly made known by the explosion that follows. If he stick a pin into his flesh, his wounded nerves quickly send his brain a report of the injury. These are the certain and sudden results of violated physical law. But if a boy is passionate, or deceitful, or dishonest, the punishment for these violations of God's moral law may not, and generally do not, immediately follow; but that they will follow at some time is as certain as that the law of right has been violated. It is written that, "*Because sentence against an evil work is not executed speedily, therefore the heart of the sons of men is fully set in them to do evil.*" Because we do not see the execution of God's penalties at once, we are inclined to think that He may not carry out the sentence at all.

The moral law vindicated.—And yet God does sometimes execute the laws of morality in this world, and exact a terrible penalty from those who slight them. The boy who touches, tastes, and handles, when the moral law says, "*Look not upon the wine when it is red,*" gives way to that which may be fearfully punished, as it frequently is, by loss of character, health, friends, and fortune, and finally by the horrors of delirium and a drunkard's grave. He who lies once may become a confirmed liar; he who steals once

---

If we violate natural laws how are we punished? Give an illustration of the penalty of a violated law. Do God's punishments follow immediately? Why are men careless of God's law? What is written in the moral law about the sentence against evil doers? Are the laws of morality ever vindicated in this world? Give an illustration. What may become of him who violates the law which says, "Look not," etc.? What may occur to him who lies once? To him who steals once? Repeat the text.

may become an abandoned thief. This is terrible punishment even in this world.

"*My son, forget not my law; but let thine heart keep my commandments: for length of days, and long life, and peace shall they add to thee.*"

CHAPTER V.

"*All scripture is given by inspiration of God, and is profitable for doctrine, for reproof, for correction, for instruction in righteousness.*"

DUTIES TO GOD FROM THE SCRIPTURES.

Revealed religion.—The light of nature, aided by conscience, was not able to reveal to mankind all that should be known and done with reference to God and human society. God, in his wisdom and love, gave us a written law, that we may know more fully what we are to believe concerning Him and what duties we owe to Him and each other. This code of the moral law is found in the scriptures of the Old and New Testaments, and so beautifully and plainly is it stated, even in a few lines, that no one who fails to learn and practice its precepts can be guiltless. It teaches, "*Thou shalt love the Lord thy God with all thy heart, and with all thy soul, and with all thy mind. This is the first and great commandment. And the second is like unto it, Thou shalt love thy neighbor as thyself.*"

What is the subject of Chapter Fifth? Repeat the text. What is necessary besides the natural law to teach man his duty? Why has God given man the scriptures? What constitutes the moral law? Give a condensed view of man's duty as it is written. What do heart, soul, and mind mean? Why was that made the first and great law? What is the second law?

These commandments are the grand fundamental precepts of the moral law. They are put thus into the fewest words, that they may be more firmly fixed in our minds. From them as primary principles, all knowledge of our duties to God and man may be learned; all that "*is profitable for doctrine, for reproof, for correction, for instruction in righteousness.*" We need to be taught, reproved, corrected, and instructed in what is right, that habits of love, purity, and goodness may be exhibited in our lives.

The great commandment.—What is meant by this "*first and great commandment*"? God demands that we shall love Him with all our powers of affection and reason, judgment and will, and prescribes a method by which we may make our love known. He says, "*If ye love me, keep my commandments.*" Groping darkly by the dim light of nature, we are not left to infer what these commandments are, but God has furnished them to us; and to avoid all errors we are directed to "*search the Scriptures,*" that we may more fully discover his will. He not only asks that we shall love Him, but as an inducement for us to study his word and practice the precepts of his law, He says, "*I love them that love me, and those that seek me early shall find me.*"

Worship.—From the earliest ages to the present, and among all nations, the existence of a Supreme Being has been acknowledged. He has been and is worshiped as an intelligent First Cause, by whom all things exist, and through whose wise supervision they fulfill the designs of their creation. No object in nature has been considered too vast, and none too minute to escape his providential care.

Why are these great laws so condensed? If we follow these rules is it enough? What is it written that the Scriptures contain? Do we need reproof, correction, etc.? Why? What does God demand of us first? How shall it be known that we try to love God? Where shall we find his commandments? How will He repay us for our love? What does He promise? Has God always been worshiped by man?

Mankind have feared Him for his judgments and revered Him for his wisdom and mercy. They have called upon Him as helpless, dependent children, soliciting his paternal guidance. These were the teachings of reason derived from the operation of natural causes, but the Scriptures impart more rational views of praise and prayer. It is written, "*Trust in the Lord with all thine heart; and lean not unto thine own understanding. In all thy ways acknowledge him, and he shall direct thy paths.*" We are told to fear and love; to trust and acknowledge; to call on and praise the Lord. These are the exercises of worship which He has prescribed, and which, if performed aright, He has promised to bless.

Profanity.—We may exhibit our love to God by the constant remembrance of the precept which declares "*Thou shalt not take the name of the Lord thy God in vain; for the Lord will not hold him guiltless that taketh his name in vain.*" The habitual use of God's name and attributes in trivial conversation tends to weaken feelings of veneration toward Him, and to destroy the spirit of devotion which all should cherish. No man of delicate feelings, who loves his wife, will permit her name to be used familiarly and disrespectfully on occasions when there is no necessity for or propriety in alluding to it; so, for a stronger reason, if we love God we should not use his name with improper freedom and levity, nor countenance such a use of it by others.

Profanity is one of the grossest forms of vice, for which there can not be the least apology or excuse. It is not only a perversion of language, but a direct violation of God's special command that nothing can justify. It be-

---

Why have men feared God? Why may they love Him? Repeat the command to trust in the Lord. What does He tell us to do? What is written in the moral law concerning profanity? What effect has it to hear God's name used without veneration? Why can there be no apology for swearing? What is gained by swearing? Is it manly? Is it honorable? Is it necessary? Do the good use profane language?

comes a habit usually in youth, among those who think it manly to be wicked, and is practiced by those who have no command of elegant language and who suppose that to be earnest or emphatic they must be profane. It may be said that they who denounce God's terrible judgments upon their own souls or the souls of others, do not always mean what they say; possibly not in every case, yet as we discovered in Chapter II, no one can excuse the sinfulness of a bad habit by the plea, "I did not think." It is too fearful a crime against God for any such apology. Men must think, "*For the Lord will not hold him guiltless that taketh his name in vain.*"

No gentleman or lady uses profane language, since it is contrary to the law of God and the usages of good society. The most worthless and vile, the refuse of mankind, the drunkard and the vagrant swear. Profanity never did any one the slightest good. No one is richer, wiser, happier, or more esteemed for it. It helps no man's education or manners: it commends no one to good society: it is disgusting to man and insulting to God.

The Sabbath day.—We may also show our love to God by observing the commandment, "*Remember the sabbath day, to keep it holy.*" God, in his supreme wisdom, has ordained that the seventh part of man's time shall be devoted to purposes differing from the ordinary business of the week. Man, as well as the beasts in his service, needs rest. If there were no day especially set apart for repose, he would become so much occupied by the business affairs of life as to forget God. The constant return of the day brings with it the perpetual reminder of his Maker. As a measure of prudence and worldly policy the proper observ-

---

When does it generally become a habit? Is it ever excusable? Do gentlemen and ladies ever swear? Can persons be emphatic without being profane? Do persons always mean what they say in swearing? Why do people swear? In what other manner can we show love to God? Why is the observance of the sabbath day necessary to man and animals? Why does the sabbath day remind man of his Maker?

ance of the sabbath day is of special interest and importance. Those communities or nations that solemnize a seventh day, by abstaining from the employments of other days, exhibit the wisdom of this Divine arrangement in their intelligence, morality, and thrift. On the other hand, those people who neglect to conform to the requirements of the day, or spend it in acts of pleasure seeking and dissipation, are neither virtuous nor prosperous. It may be asked, then, how shall the sabbath, or Lord's day, be observed? We should on that day endeavor to lay aside all unnecessary business, and devote the time to the public exercises of God's worship; to the study of his word; to the improvement of our minds; the culture of our affections, and in acts of mercy and benevolence.

CHAPTER VI.

"*Thou shalt love thy neighbor as thyself.*"

DUTIES TO MAN FROM THE SCRIPTURES.

Who is my neighbor?—God says, "*Thou shalt love thy neighbor as thyself.*" He commands it, and love to Him requires obedience to his law. We should obey it, because our own safety and happiness, as well as our neighbor's, are dependent upon its observance. But the question was asked ages ago, and is often repeated now, "*Who is my neighbor?*"

Is it wise to stop work every seventh day? What advantage have those communities that observe the sabbath? How should that day be observed? Is it for man's good that he observe the day? Why did God prescribe its observance?

What is the subject of Chapter VI? Repeat the text. What reasons are there for obeying this law? When was this question asked before?

The good Samaritan.—A beautiful story is told, in answer to this very question: "*A certain man went down from Jerusalem to Jericho and fell among thieves, which stripped him of his raiment, and wounded him, and departed, leaving him half dead. And by chance there came down a certain priest that way: and when he saw him, he passed by on the other side. And likewise a Levite, when he was at the place, came and looked on him, and passed by on the other side.*

But a certain Samaritan, as he journeyed, came where he was: and when he saw him, he had compassion on him, and went to him, and bound up his wounds, pouring in oil and wine, and set him on his own beast, and brought him to an inn, and took care of him. And on the morrow, when he departed, he took out two pence, and gave them to the host, and said unto him, 'Take care of him; and whatsoever thou spendest more, when I come again I will repay thee.'

"*Which now of these three was neighbor unto him that fell among the thieves?*"

In this story, the national enemy of the wounded man proved himself the kind, loving, liberal friend, while the careless priest, and the proud, rich Levite of his own kindred, haughtily passed by on the other side. Who, then, was neighbor to him that fell among thieves?

Mankind a Brotherhood.—God is our Father: our common Father. For He "*hath made of one blood all nations of men for to dwell on all the face of the earth.*" Mankind is a great brotherhood, differing slightly in form, feature, and color, but essentially the same in having like feelings, affections, duties, and desires. We are not taught in the Moral Law to love our friends, our family, our race, and our color alone; we are commanded to love all men.

Who was neighbor to him that fell among thieves? What is the moral of this story of the "good Samaritan?" What is written in the Moral Law about the brotherhood of man?

It is easy to love those who love us, but it is difficult to obey that law which says, "*Whatsoever ye would that men should do to you, do ye even so to them.*" We desire all men to respect our rights and feelings; we are clamorous for justice and fair play, but have no right to ask what we are unwilling to give. Rights and duties balance each other, and justice demands that we do not claim our rights until we are entirely willing to perform all our duties. Love to our neighbor requires that we shall do nothing to endanger his life, restrict his liberty, offend his person, irritate his feelings, or disturb and destroy his property.

Equality of natural rights.—The only equality that exists among men is the equality of natural rights. Men are unequal in size, physical strength, wealth, intelligence, mental power, and in many other respects, but these differences do not entitle them to put any restrictions upon the intelligence, property, or physical powers of others. Because I am ignorant, my intelligent neighbor has no right to take advantage of me; because I am poor and needy, my wealthy neighbor has no right to defraud me; and because I am weak, my stronger neighbor has no right to beat and impose upon me. God has given me certain powers of body and faculties of mind, and holds me responsible for their use; and it is my duty and right to make the most of them, provided that in using my own, I do not interfere with the equal rights of another.

It will easily be seen that this law of mutual kindness, universally adopted, would prevent quarrels, and take away every cause of dispute. The principle of pure morality requires that, instead of slighting the ignorant, defrauding the poor, and persecuting the weak, we shall,

---

May we treat men unjustly because they are not of our color and race? What is the Golden Rule? If we should go to China or Africa how would we like to be treated? Would we consider it satisfactory for a Chinese to abuse us because we are white? What is the only equality that exists among men? In what are men unequal? What would be the effect among men if the Golden Rule were observed by all?

by our superior wisdom, strength, wealth, and opportunity, give aid and comfort to those who need our care.

Injuries and wrongs.—We learned in Chapter IV, that human actions are divided, with reference to their moral quality, into two classes—the good and the bad; the former being right, the latter wrong. Here then will arise the question, "In what does the right or wrong of an action consist?" The answer to this question will be best ascertained by considering the difference between an injury and a wrong.

Illustrations.—The distinction will be made clear by some illustrations:

First. Two boys climb a tree to procure fruit; one of them ventures upon a small limb, by the sudden bending of which he is thrown down, and, falling, breaks his leg. By this accident he receives an injury, but no blame is attached to any one, for no one is in fault. He has been injured but not wronged.

Second. But let us change the conditions. Suppose the boys, in their anxiety to get the fruit, climb upon the same limb, when one accidentally jars the other, so that he falls and breaks his leg. Here an injury is done, but no wrong, since the boy was not designedly thrown down. He was injured but not wronged.

Third. Let us change the conditions again. Suppose that the boys are ambitious; that A is in a better part of the tree than B, when B attempts to climb over where A is; A, perceiving that it will be dangerous, remonstrates and tells him not to come, as the limb is not strong enough to sustain them. B recklessly disregards the warning and

---

Human actions are divided with reference to their moral quality into how many classes? Give the first illustration in reference to wrongs and injuries. Give the second illustration. What is the distinction between them? Give the third illustration.

continues to advance, when the sudden bending of the limb throws A off, and his leg is broken. Here is a wrong and an injury. It is true that B did not intend to injure A, but by criminal carelessness the injury was done. It will be seen that no one has a right to endanger another's life or property by acts of thoughtlessness or recklessness, and if injury is done our neighbor by our neglect or indifference, it is a violation of the moral law. It is no excuse, under such circumstances, to say, "I did not think," as it is our duty to think, especially when the rights of others are involved.

Fourth. But, changing the conditions again, let us suppose that A was more fortunate than B in gathering fruit, and that B becoming angry, as wicked people sometimes do at the success of their neighbors, shook the tree so violently as to cause A to fall and break his leg. Here is a wrong and a greater degree of guilt, since the injury resulted from envy and passion.

Fifth. With new conditions again: suppose that A is getting the most fruit because he has the most convenient basket and the best part of the tree; that B is envious and wishes A to exchange baskets, which A is unwilling to do. B says that unless A gives him the basket he will shake him off the tree. A refuses, and B carries out his threat, and breaks A's leg. Here is an injury as the result of envy, anger, and malice.

Definitions.—Injury may be defined as a harm or damage done to any one's person, reputation, or property. It may be accidental or intentional. Injustice and wrong are injuries which are the results of evil intentions, recklessness, or indifference. We may inflict an injury without wrong; but

Is any one excusable for negligence? Is it satisfactory to say, in reference to criminal carelessness, "I did not think"? What has God given us mind and conscience for? Give the fourth illustration. What is the difference between the third and fourth illustrations? Give the fifth illustration. What is the difference between the fourth and fifth illustrations? Define injury. How many kinds of injury with reference to its performance? What is a wrong?

we never can commit a wrong without injury to ourselves or to others.

"*Love worketh no ill to his neighbor; therefore, love is the fulfilling of the law.*"

CHAPTER VII.

"*Thou shalt do no murder.*"

HOMICIDE.

Homicide.—The legal definition of homicide is "the killing of any human creature." The distinction between injuries and wrongs, indicated in the preceding chapter, have their application in the discussion of homicide. The idea of taking the life of a human being is shocking to every sense of right and duty. The preservation of life is the very foundation of society; if life is insecure there can be no permanence in the government. Self preservation demands that we make every exertion to preserve the life of our neighbors, and to do this we should study carefully the requirements of the moral law.

There are three degrees of homicide, as defined by the laws of the State: "excusable," "justifiable," and "felonious."

What is the distinction between injury and wrong? Give the concluding text. May we do an injury without wrong? May we do a wrong without an injury to ourselves or others?

What is the subject of Chapter VII? What is the text? What is the definition of homicide? What is one of the important ideas of government? Why should we make every effort to preserve the life of our neighbor? How many degrees of homicide are there?

Excusable homicide.—In the city of Davenport, Iowa, a hardware merchant was handling a gun in his store, when it was accidentally discharged in the direction of the street. By an unfortunate coincidence, a friend who was passing on the pavement was struck by the charge and instantly killed. The killing was not the result of criminal carelessness, recklessness, or malice; it was purely an accident, and although the result was an irreparable injury, there was no wrong—it was "excusable." Homicide is defined to be excusable when "done in self-defense, or in defense of wife or child, servant or property, or by mere accident."

Justifiable homicide.—Homicide is termed justifiable, "to denote that the killing was done under lawful authority;" as when the sheriff executes a man who has been legally convicted and sentenced to death; "or killing a prisoner to prevent his escape, or killing to prevent an atrocious crime." It will readily be perceived that there is no wrong attending justifiable homicide, since the killing is not the result of evil intention or criminal neglect. When the officer executes a convicted criminal or prevents his escape by killing him, he is only performing his official duty, and he does it without malice or even unkindness—the law compels him, and he is justifiable.

Felonious homicide is defined to be "the killing of a human being which proceeds from a depraved, wicked heart, and is done with some degree of design." To distinguish the different degrees of guilt, felonious homicide is divided into "manslaughter" and "murder."

Manslaughter is defined to be "the unlawful killing of a person without malice." It may be "intentional," as when

---

Give the incident illustrating excusable homicide. Define excusable homicide. Define justifiable homicide. Why is there no wrong done in justifiable homicide? Define felonious homicide. How is felonious homicide divided? How is manslaughter defined? How many kinds of manslaughter?

done in sudden heat and anger, as the result of great provocation; or it may be "unintentional," but in the commission of some unlawful act. A and B were two boys who had a quarrel about some trivial matter. In the course of the dispute A applied to B a very offensive epithet, which B felt should be resented. He thereupon threw a stone at A, which, striking him upon the head, resulted in his death. In this unlawful throwing of a stone there was no intention to kill; no malice, but only an exhibition of ungovernable, dangerous passion, which resulted in death. This is "intentional manslaughter." If the engineer of a locomotive shall run his train at an unusual and unjustifiable speed, contrary to the regulations of the road, and an accident shall occur by which the lives of innocent passengers are lost, he is guilty of "unintentional manslaughter." He is guilty, not because he intended to injure or to kill the passengers, but because of his criminal disregard of the responsibilities of his position.

Murder.—This is the highest crime that is known to the law of the State, and is defined to be "the unlawful killing of a human being, with determined malice, either expressed or implied." Murder is premeditated killing; killing that is thought about, talked of, planned, and prepared for. The crime that is coolly deliberated is already more than half done; the passions will it and the heart assents. "*For out of the heart proceed evil thoughts, murders, adulteries, fornications, thefts, false witness, blasphemies.*" The moral law is violated when the passions are aroused; when the better parts of our nature are overcome by the desire to do wrong; when bitterness and malice take the place of reason and right. The civil law only punishes those who disturb society by the actual commission

---

Define intentional manslaughter; unintentional. Illustrate each. Of what crime is a careless railroad engineer guilty? Why? Define murder. What is essential to the definition? What does the moral law say of a wicked heart? What is the difference between murder and manslaughter?

of crime. A person may be arrested and put under bonds for threatening to commit some act of violence, but the penalties for crime can be suffered only when the crime is committed. In the civil court the murderer must be found guilty before the judge shall pronounce sentence against him. By the moral law, not only is he a murderer who, with revengeful and remorseless hate, stains his hands with the blood of his victim, but he is equally guilty who has the thoughts of murder in his heart.

Punishments.—The distinctions made in the civil law concerning homicide are intended to secure that just degree of punishment to the offender which the nature of the guilt demands. The enormity of the crime determines the severity of the punishment. Not so with the moral law; it prescribes no punishment, in this world, save that which arises from a guilty conscience. This of itself, to most men, is a terrible torture from which there is no escape. No change of scene or circumstances can remove the dreadful consciousness of guilt which accompanies him who has wickedly destroyed human life.

We read, "*The wicked flee when no man pursueth*," and this proverb is often verified in the extreme mental anguish of those who have committed murder and escaped for a time the punishment of the civil law. The common saying that "murder will out," is derived from the fact that its perpetrators are usually discovered, and the circumstances of their guilt pointed out. Years may, and often do elapse, before a criminal is brought to the bar of justice, but the fears, the dread, and the consuming anxiety, arising from an accusing conscience, are often worse than death

---

When is the moral law violated? For what does the civil law punish men? What is the essential difference between the moral and civil laws in this respect? Who is a murderer by the moral law? Why are these distinctions made in the degrees of homicide? In this world what is the terrible punishment of the moral law? What does the proverb, "The wicked flee when no man pursueth," mean? How is it illustrated? What is the meaning of the saying, "murder will out"? What makes the life of a murderer so terrible?

itself. It is written, "*All that a man hath will he give for his life*," and yet many a man gladly dies to escape the horrors of such an existence.

CHAPTER VIII.

"*Whosoever hateth his brother is a murderer.*"

HATRED.

Love and hate are the opposites of each other. The precepts of the moral law are contrary to the natural inclinations of mankind, which are quick to indulge in retaliation for injuries received. Savage tribes cherish hatred and resentment toward their enemies, and transmit them as legacies to their children, but the moral law teaches a very different doctrine. It is written, "*Love your enemies, bless them that curse you, do good to them that hate you, and pray for them which despitefully use you and persecute you.*" There is no doctrine that is taught in the moral code that is so difficult to reduce to practice as the forgiveness of injuries. It is hard to overcome our natural inclination to retaliate, especially when we have received the impression that it is creditable and noble to indulge our resentments.

Manliness.—A young man once received an insult from a companion, and was determined upon revenge. His

---

Why are so many murderers detected? Why do men frequently surrender themselves to justice?

What is the subject of Chapter VIII? What is the text? To what are the precepts of the moral law contrary? What does the moral law say we shall do even to our enemies? Repeat the text. Why is it difficult to forgive an enemy? Give the anecdote.

father tried to soothe his feelings and dissuade him from doing wrong, when he exclaimed, "Why, father, it is unmanly not to resent it." "Ah, my son," the father replied, "it may be manly to resent it, but it would be godlike to forgive it."

Self-control.—If hatred is murder, if the moral quality of the action may be found in the intention, then it is our duty to study the moral character of our intentions before we carry them into practice. If we acquire the habit of coolly reflecting upon the moral qualities of our feelings and desires, our conscience will not disturb us with vain regrets for wrongs, committed, when it is too late to remedy them.

Indications of hatred.—There are certain indications of character, upon which the young should reflect, before they become fixed habits of life. Those who would avoid the feeling, and finally the habits, of hate, should cultivate the language of gentleness and kindness. It is written, "*A soft answer turneth away wrath: but grievous words stir up anger.*" This proverb is confirmed by the experience and observation of every one. It is only necessary to brood over our annoyances and talk about them, until we work ourselves into an ungovernable anger. Oftentimes our intense feeling is manifested by the loud tone and the high key in which we express our thoughts. An angry, passionate man almost always speaks in a noisy, boisterous manner, and the character of his tone serves to increase his excitement.

Under such circumstances, persons have the greatest need to watch themselves, as it is written, "*Whoso keepeth his mouth and his tongue, keepeth his soul from troubles.*"

What did the father mean by saying it would be godlike to forgive? If hatred is murder, what is our duty? What habit should we acquire in this connection? What is one of the indications of hatred? What is the effect of a soft answer? What of grievous words? How do we know these effects? How are the feelings indicated? What does the text say will keep a man from troubles?

If we would learn to control our passions, we must commence with bridling our tongue. It is a "little member," but is capable both of inflaming our own hearts, and stirring up strife in the hearts of our enemies.

Weapons.—Next to the evil influence of an unruly tongue in stimulating murderous designs is the habit of carrying deadly weapons and practicing with them. It is not an uncommon thing for young men and boys to carry knives, pistols, slung-shots, and other death-dealing instruments. What a fearful account must they render who cherish hatred, who encourage strife and coolly deliberate upon the taking of life by practicing for the consummation of the mischief.

It is not strange that a savage, who does not recognize and is not governed by high moral obligations, should continually practice with his weapons, in order to preserve his life and punish his enemy. Nor is it surprising that a soldier, whose trade is to kill, should be so employed; but for a citizen in an enlightened land, under ordinary circumstances, to carry concealed weapons, is a confession of weakness and cowardice of which no truly brave person can be guilty. It leads also to the violation of the civil law, for when a person has prepared himself for a deadly conflict, when his heart is set on it, when the murderous intent is in his words and actions, it is but a short step to the taking of life.

A murderer's testimony.—There is a fearful warning in the following, from the confession of Jeremiah Bailey, who was executed in New Jersey. He said, "To the men,

---

What is an important step toward the control of our passions? What is the meaning of "bridling the tongue?" Name another indication of hatred. What is the difference between a savage and a man in civil society carrying weapons? Why is the carrying of weapons a sign of cowardice? What does the carrying of weapons often result in? Give the experience of Jeremiah Bailey. If a man's life or property is threatened, may he carry arms for his protection?

and particularly the young men and boys, I would say a few farewell words. I am on the scaffold, about to be launched into the other world. What has brought me to this? Let me tell you, and let these words ring forever in your ears. It was whisky and the carrying of fire-arms. Whisky and the bearing of pistols have ruined me. If you do not want them to ruin you, if you do not want to be imprisoned, and in the end brought to the scaffold, do n't drink liquor, do n't carry fire-arms. Boys do n't keep bad company." The moral law says, "*Wisdom is better than weapons of war.*" "*Her ways are ways of pleasantness, and all her paths are peace.*"

The duel.—Several hundred years ago, it was the law in many countries of Europe, that under certain conditions, one of the parties in a controversy should challenge the other to deadly combat, in order to ascertain which was right. It was an age of bigotry and barbarism, when it was supposed that God would give the victory in a battle to the one whose cause He approved. If one of the parties was a woman, a priest, or a cripple, he or she had a right to select a champion who could fill the place.

This appeal to God to defend the cause of innocence and truth was found to be an impious mockery of justice. God does not defend the right in any such way, and good men began to doubt the wisdom of settling controversies in so barbarous a fashion. But it was the custom of the age to carry weapons, and men, heated by passion and stimulated by false ideas of honor, were unwilling to relinquish this method of settling their quarrels, although the church had declared it wrong, and the courts had decided against its permission.

At first, the "Code of Honor," as it was called, required the strictest observance of fairness between the parties to

---

What were the causes that ruined Jeremiah Bailey? What does the moral law teach? What is a duel? Give the brief history of dueling. What is meant by the "Code of Honor"?

the fight, but men soon lost sight of this and became professed duelists, who would give insults without cause, and then, by their superior skill, kill their adversaries without compunction. This misnamed "Code of Honor" is one of the "relics of barbarism" which all wise and good men condemn. It is contrary to the moral law and the laws of our land, and should always be mentioned with abhorrence.

The apology and satisfaction.—But what amends shall we make to our brother, when by accident or design we violate his rights? Do precisely as we would that he should do to us. A story is told of General Washington which illustrates the duty suggested by the above question.

Anecdote.—A company of gentlemen was assembled, among whom were General Washington and Colonel Payne. Some subject arose which caused considerable discussion. The difference of opinion was so decided, that in the warmth of the debate, the General, departing from his usual manner, applied some offensive epithet to Colonel Payne. This so incensed him that he sprang to his feet in an instant, and struck the General so violently as to knock him down. At this, the others interfered and prevented further difficulty. It was the custom at that time among gentlemen, that when an offense was taken, the party offended sent a challenge to the offender to fight a duel. As the General had received a blow, it was supposed by his friends that he would challenge Colonel Payne to meet him with deadly weapons and wipe out the insult in blood.

He disappointed them. Meeting Colonel Payne shortly after, he advanced toward him with extended hand and said, "Colonel Payne, I used language to you that was un-

---

Why did men become professed duelists? Why was this code misnamed? Why should good men condemn dueling? What shall we do when we violate the rights of our neighbor? What is the anecdote of General Washington? Did Colonel Payne do right? In what did he do wrong? In what did Washington do right? In what did he do wrong? Is it manly to make acknowledgments?

becoming a gentleman, and you knocked me down. If you have had satisfaction, now let us be friends." The apology was accepted, and the friendship was restored. General Washington was too good and too brave to insult a man and then to try to kill him in a duel. He had that high moral courage—that real heroism—which enabled him to apologize to a friend when he had done him an injury. If we have wronged any man, in mind, body, or estate, it is our duty to remedy the wrong as far as it is possible. A lady or gentleman never permits a mean pride or a false notion of honor to prevent the making of an apology when it is due.

Prompt apology.—The late Hon. William P. Fessenden once made a remark which was understood as an insult to Mr. Seward. When informed of it, and seeing such a meaning could be given to his words, he instantly went to Mr. Seward and said, "Mr. Seward, I have insulted you; I am sorry for it. I did not mean it." This apology, so prompt, frank, and perfect, so delighted Mr. Seward that, grasping him by the hand, he exclaimed, "God bless you, Fessenden, I wish you would insult me again." Such an exhibition of real manliness may well be cited as worthy of the imitation of the youth of the land.

A nation's apology.—The following incident is worthy of notice, as it illustrates the application of the moral law in the government of nations. During our late civil war, the government of Great Britain performed several acts which produced a feeling of indignation in the minds of the American people. One of these was to permit ships to be furnished in her harbors with arms and men, to prey upon our commerce, contrary to the law of nations. One of the

---

In what did Washington's moral courage consist? What is our duty if we have wronged any one? What is the duty of a lady or gentleman if a person insults them? What is the anecdote of Mr. Fessenden? What did Mr. Seward's reply mean? Give the history of the nation's apology.

most noted of these British ships was the "Alabama," which, sailing under the Confederate flag, destroyed many of the United States' vessels, and brought a great loss to numbers of our merchants.

Such conduct was a violation of our rights, which we, as a great, proud nation were mortified to receive. Many predicted that the British government, equally proud and powerful, would never acknowledge the wrong she had done, nor pay for the damage she had inflicted upon our commerce; and this view was confirmed by that goverment's refusing, in 1865, to make any arrangement or give any satisfaction. In the meantime, some bad men endeavored to provoke the two nations to such anger and hatred that a peaceful settlement would be impossible, but the good sense of the people of both countries demanded a reconciliation upon the principles of the moral law.

After several ineffectual attempts to secure a compromise of the difficulty, a treaty was prepared in 1871, which is known as the "Treaty of Washington," by a "Joint High Commission," composed of eminent statesmen of England and the United States. The most striking section of this remarkable treaty is that in which the British government apologizes for the wrong she had done; thus proving that a great nation may be actuated by the highest moral considerations. The following is the LANGUAGE OF THE NATIONAL APOLOGY:

"Her Britannic Majesty has authorized her High Commissioners and Plenipotentiaries to express, in a friendly spirit, the regrets felt by Her Majesty's government for the escape, under whatever circumstances, of the ALABAMA and other vessels from British ports, and for the depredations committed by those vessels." This is accompanied by the agreement to pay for the losses sustained by American citizens.

Did Great Britain act cowardly in making an apology? What induced her to do it? What was the apology of Great Britain? Why is this treaty worthy of our admiration?

If a grand old nation can lay aside her pride, acknowledge her wrong, express her regret, and pay for the damage done, and all this upon pure principles of right, without force or compulsion, she is worthy of our highest respect and admiration. It is a fondly cherished hope of good and wise men that the example set by these nations will introduce the era of peace, when "*nation shall not lift up sword against nation, neither shall they learn war any more.*"

Forgiveness.—It is written, "*If it be possible, as much as lieth in you, live peaceably with all men.*" Human nature is very weak and liable to err. The moral law says, "*If it be possible;*" but it is not possible, owing to the infirmities of mind, the peculiarities of temper, and the want of proper training, to live peaceably with all men. Misunderstandings will arise, even among good men, even among brothers and sisters. Prejudice and pride, ill-nature and stubbornness, combine to produce hatred and promote strife.

But the question arises, "What shall we do with those who violate our rights?" This question was answered ages ago, as it is written, "*If thy brother trespass against thee, rebuke him; if he repent, forgive him. And if he trespass against thee seven times in a day, and seven times in a day turn again to thee, saying, I repent, thou shalt forgive him.*" "*For if ye forgive men their trespasses, your Heavenly Father will also forgive you; but if ye forgive not men their trespasses, neither will your Father forgive your trespasses.*"

What good is it hoped will result from this treaty? What is our duty regarding forgiveness? Is it possible always to be at peace with all men? Why? Should nations be governed by the moral law? Why? What vices combine to produce hatred and strife? What shall we do with those who violate our rights? What are the texts relating to trespass and forgiveness? Why should a man forgive his neighbor?

CHAPTER IX.

"Blessed are the peacemakers."

COURAGE.

Cowardice.—One of the most trying tests of a young man's virtue arises from an insinuation that he is a coward. Upon this subject most men are very sensitive, disliking to be considered deficient in what they suppose is the very essence of real manhood. But, unfortunately, the test is rarely presented in things that are right; the challenge is not to do deeds that are noble and worthy of praise, but to force the person to do wrong. In this way it becomes an influence for mischief that produces the saddest effect upon character.

If a young man refuses to assist in robbing an orchard, he is stigmatized, by those who have no moral principle or manly feeling, as a coward; if he is unwilling to drink intoxicating liquor, or if he declines to violate the laws of school or society, his refusal is imputed to dishonorable fear. Many a person is driven to do what his judgment and his conscience alike condemn, because he dreads that others will not think him brave. Such fear is the greatest and basest cowardice.

Kinds of courage.—There are two kinds of courage, physical and moral; the former finds its highest type in the

---

What is the subject of chapter IX? What is the text? Why do young men shrink from being considered cowardly? Is the test usually applied to things right or wrong? What is the consequence of a refusal to do wrong? Why are young men charged with cowardice when they refuse to do wrong? What effect do such taunts often have? What is an indication of great cowardice? How many kinds of courage are there? What is a type of each kind?

bull-dog, while the latter is illustrated by those persons who have suffered martyrdom rather than sacrifice their love of right and conscientious convictions of truth.

Physical courage.—An English dog-breeder, who possessed a race of terriers of remarkable ferocity and endurance, offered to bet a large sum of money, that when a certain dog, which he owned, was engaged in fighting, he could cut off three of his legs, and the dog would not give up or relinquish his hold. The bet was taken, and the dogs were set to, when the poor brute actually suffered one leg to be taken off after another, and finally suffered death rather than cease to fight.

It is hard to say which was the greater object of pity, the poor dog, whose savage instincts led him to suffer and die rather than let go his hold, or the brutal, vicious master who could engage in such wicked cruelty and call it sport. We wonder at the ferocious instinct of the bull-terrier and remember that while he possesses physical courage in so remarkable a degree, there is nothing else in him that in any way commends him to our admiration. He is cross, unsociable, untractable, unreliable, and vicious; he is among dogs what the prize-fighter or the professed pugilist is among men—the meanest and most unworthy animal of his kind.

The person who, for money or the love of notoriety, permits himself to engage in an encounter, in which he will receive and inflict serious and sometimes fatal injuries, possesses no quality that raises him in any degree above a brute. In such an exhibition, the bull-dog is his equal and the hyena is his superior. Many a man can even enter a battle, and in the excitement of the conflict, surrounded by his friends and backers, fight ferociously, receive wounds,

---

Give the illustration of physical courage. Which was most to be pitied, the dog or the man? Why? What is the character of the bull-dog? To what may such a dog be compared among men? Why? Do prize-fighters possess high moral courage? Why?

and dare death, who has not a particle of that high moral courage which would lead him to suffer insult and injury and endure them silently for the sake of a principle. It is often a braver thing to be called a coward and not resent it than it would be to fight a battle.

Bad men are not always brave.—During the civil war a regiment was raised in one of the northern cities composed entirely of those men who had become notorious as street bullies, and who were always prominent in drunken brawls and fights. It was supposed that they would make capital soldiers, and great hopes were excited that they would distinguish themselves by their fearlessness and contempt of danger and death.

As might have been reasonably expected, they utterly failed to make any honorable record. How could they? They were not actuated by any principle of honor; they did not enter the army from motives of duty or patriotism, or love for the cause they engaged to defend. The excitement of army life and the hope of bounty and plunder were their only motives. They could kill a man at night in the city and rob him, but as soldiers they were cowardly, unreliable, and worthless. It needs more than rough, coarse, fierce brutality to give a person a character for courage.

Real courage.—True courage is a combination of moral and physical qualities, so united as to secure the noblest character. A pure conscience, a clear, intelligent mind, and a strong body are necessary to the highest form of courageous manhood. A man may have a moral courage which would enable him to dare any consequences to do right, and, at the same time, a physical weakness which would

---

What is one test of real courage? Give the story of the regiment and the result. Why did they not become brave soldiers? Is a dangerous man a courageous man? Why? What constitutes real courage? Is a quarrelsome boy a brave boy? May a weak girl possess true courage? How?

shrink at the slightest pain. Of such a combination martyrs have often been made, but the moral heroism overcame the fear of death and the pangs of torture.

A really brave man never exposes himself needlessly to danger, and if unhappily entrapped in a quarrel, he will always refuse to fight until compelled in self-defense. He will suffer insult and indignity, permit himself to be called hard names and to be misrepresented, rather than allow hatred and murder to enter his heart, or do that which in his calmer moments he would abhor. Forbearance is a divine attribute, and worthy of special cultivation. It is the coward that is driven by his fears of ridicule to do that which he knows is wrong.

A little hero.—A boy in the town of Weser, in Germany, playing one day with his sister, four years of age, was alarmed by the cry of some men who were in pursuit of a mad dog. The boy, suddenly looking round, saw the dog running toward him, but instead of making his escape, he calmly took off his coat, and, wrapping it round his arm, boldly faced the dog. Holding out the arm covered with the coat, the animal attacked it and worried it until the men came up and killed the dog. The men reproachfully asked the boy why he did not run and avoid the dog, which he could so easily have done. "Yes," said the little hero, "I could have run from the dog, but if I had he would have attacked my sister. To protect her, I offered him my coat, that he might tear it."

A similar case of heroism occurred in the city of Evansville, Indiana, in which Emma Carroll, a little girl eleven years old, ran through the flames of burning kerosene and rescued, at the expense of her life, her motherless baby

---

Do brave men expose themselves to danger unnecessarily? Why? What will a good brave man do if insulted? What is a coward? Give the story of the little hero. In what way did he show his coolness and presence of mind? In what his courage? In what his manliness? Give the anecdote of little Emma Carroll. In what did her courage consist?

brotner, of whom she had the care. In the terrible agony of her dying hours, she was consoled with the thought that the baby had escaped unharmed. She had saved him.

The true test of courage.—The celebrated Mary Lyon, one of the noblest and best of women, used the following remarkable words, which were beautifully illustrated by her life: "There is nothing in the universe that I fear, but that I shall not know all my duty, or shall fail to do it." The true test of courage is, in all circumstances, to "DARE TO DO RIGHT!" Dare to do what your conscience will approve, and what will be esteemed right by good society.

CHAPTER X.

"*Blessed are the pure in heart.*" "*Keep thyself pure.*"

CHASTITY.

The heart.—The heart is frequently spoken of as the center of the affections and passions. It is not unusual to hear the expression that a person has a good or a bad heart, according as his conduct is generally good or bad. When we speak of the "pure in heart," we mean those who exhibit chastity of speech and modesty of deportment in their lives as the fruits of purity in their minds. "*A good man,*

What was her consolation? Who was Mary Lyon? What was her fear? What is the grand test of courage always? Why? Why do not all people dare to do right? Are there any trials of this kind at home or in school? What is the subject of Chapter X? Repeat the texts. What allusion is made to the heart? What is meant by a good or bad heart? Illustrate by some examples of your own. What is meant by the pure in heart?

out of the good treasure of his heart bringeth forth that which is good, and an evil man out of the evil treasure of his heart bringeth forth that which is evil: for of the abundance of the heart his mouth speaketh."

The little child is an emblem of purity and innocence. No vulgar thought or impure desire, no lascivious action or vicious suggestion, is manifested in its language or its life: its heart is guileless, and it is written that, unless "*Ye become as little children, ye shall not enter the kingdom of heaven.*"

A large portion of the sorrow and suffering of the world arises directly or indirectly from the want of chastity in thought, speech, and behavior. Characters are ruined, homes made desolate, and fond hearts broken, by the neglect to preserve that purity of heart, of which a little child is the type. How, then, may the young avoid the evils of licentiousness? We have the answer in the moral law: "*Keep thyself pure.*" The law of habit, the subject of the second chapter, finds its illustration here. Right principles lead to right actions, and right actions, constantly performed, make the habitually virtuous man or woman.

Impure imagination.—If we would obey the moral law, we must not permit our minds to dwell upon impure subjects. There are persons with whom we must not associate; there are places where we dare not go; and there are things we should not see or know, if we would preserve our purity and self-respect; and yet our imaginations will carry us to the forbidden places, permit us to mingle with the vulgar crowds, to see and hear improper things, and we can believe there is safety in such an excursion. The fancy may lead us a merry dance in forbidden fields,

---

Repeat the text as to the fruits of a good heart. How do we know the heart? Does the mouth generally reveal the heart? How? What is one of the emblems of innocence? Give the text. What is a chief cause of so much suffering and sorrow? Explain. How shall we avoid the evils of licentiousness? What is meant by impure imagination? Why not indulge the fancy?

and bring us back in safety home—as we suppose; but such is not the teaching of experience. The poet says:

> "Woe to the youth whom fancy gains,
> Winning from reason's hand the reins."

Many a young person indulges his imagination in wandering, where in person, at present he can not follow; in hearing what he dare not tell; in seeing what shame would forbid him to disclose; and in seeking what modesty would blush to reveal. These flights of unbridled fancy can not be indulged in with safety: they are the prolific source of all crime, and sin, and shame, and he who supposes that such humoring of the imagination is not wrong, may, and probably will, live to repent of its gratification. It is written, "*Blessed are the pure in heart:*" "*for out of the heart proceedeth evil thoughts, murders, adulteries, fornications, thefts, false witness, blasphemies.*" The moral law demands that we shall not think wrong; the civil law punishes the thought only when it is expressed in the deed.

Reverie.—The maxim that, "An idle brain is the devil's workshop," reveals a great truth, which all, but particularly the young, should understand. If we would be pure, we must be engaged in subjects of real interest and profit. The mind must not only be kept free from impure imaginings, but it must not be permitted to indulge in useless reverie at all. Reverie is defined to be "a loose or irregular train of thoughts, occurring in musing or meditation." When persons allow themselves to be carried away from present pursuits in the gratification of idle and unprofitable thoughts, they are acquiring habits which will very seriously interfere with their intellectual growth.

Many a pupil passes hours of valuable time in the indul-

Dare we tell all our thoughts to those whom we respect? Why? What is written of the "pure in heart?" What is the product of a wicked heart? What is the difference between the moral and civil law? Why this difference? What is reverie? Why not indulge in reverie?

gence of wandering thoughts which ought to be devoted to real study. Not only is time wasted in this manner, but the mind becomes seriously injured in the exercise of such mental dissipation. Such day-dreaming, castle-building employment is fatal to all real excellence in scholarship, as well as to all real progress in virtue. If we would be pure, we must shun every tendency which leads to the indulgence of improper thoughts.

Unchaste language.—Impure or unchaste language should never pollute our lips. In the fullness of youthful feelings there is a strong temptation to repeat the vulgar story, to recite the lascivious verse, or to tell a smutty joke. Never do it. People may laugh at the *double entendre*, or the witty play upon words, or even at the grosser kinds of vulgar speech, but if they possess any culture they heartily despise the author of their merriment. Such jokes are well named smutty. You can not touch smut without being soiled, so you can not indulge in smutty jokes without a loss of purity. As such a habit must be dangerous, it is written in the moral law for our guidance, "*Put away from thee a froward mouth, and perverse lips put far from thee.*"

Unchaste company.—Avoid the associations of the unchaste, for they are neither good society nor the society of the good. It is written, "*Evil communications corrupt good manners.*" We insensibly imitate the manners, tastes, and language of those by whom we are surrounded, being unaware of the silent influences which are thus shaping our characters. This idea is beautifully expressed in the moral law: "*As in water face answereth to face, so the heart of man to man.*" As surely as the still surface of the

Is profanity meant by the expression unchaste language? Do they generally accompany each other? Why? Why not tell a funny, smutty joke? What does the text say of a froward mouth and perverse lips? Why not associate with the unchaste? Repeat the text. What is meant by good manners? What idea is expressed in the text, "As in water face answereth," etc.?

water mirrors all the features of the face, so surely shall the qualities of those with whom we associate, whether good or bad, be reflected in our hearts and lives. Not only is it unsafe to be in the society of the impure, but it is also perilous to our reputation to be seen in such company, if we aspire, at all, to enter the society of the good.

Unchaste literature.—The prevalence of obscene, immoral, and vulgar publications requires a special notice. Many a youth who has gone to destruction owed his first downward step to the perusal of vicious and demoralizing literature. As physical health is preserved by the use of nutritious, life-giving food, and impaired by the want of it, so the intellectual and moral natures must be supplied with that nourishment which is adapted to their growth and development. We dare not indulge in the reading of immoral books, or the sight of obscene pictures or representations, if we desire to preserve unclouded minds and pure hearts. Such food is moral poison.

Everything that excites the imagination, inflames the passions, stimulates the curiosity, and corrupts the heart by unchaste suggestions, is to be shunned. Impure thoughts, vulgar language, vicious company, obscene books, and lascivious pictures are the bane of good society. No one who is subject, in any degree, to such influences can remain pure.

Why not be seen in the company of the unchaste? Is the wrong found in being in such company or being seen in it? Why? What is meant by unchaste literature? What are given as the bane of good society? Does this include illustrated newspapers?

CHAPTER XI.

"Lying lips are abomination to the Lord, but they that deal truly are his delight."

VERACITY.

Lying.—There is no precept of the moral law that is more frequently and shamefully violated than that which forbids lying, and yet there is nothing about which people generally are so sensitive as a doubt of their veracity.

Liar.—The term liar is one of the most opprobrious epithets which may be applied to a person, and its use has often been the cause of much mischief. This expression is very frequently not only much misunderstood, but badly misused. And just here, it is important to remember that words are the representatives of ideas, and if we use the wrong words to express our thoughts, we are liable to be misapprehended, and thus do ourselves and others injury.

Anecdote.—The following anecdote will illustrate the wrong use of terms. The celebrated John Wesley was on one occasion at table with some friends, when the lady of the house asked him to take another cup of tea. He declined then, but afterward, his appetite improving probably, he said he would be pleased to take another cup; when she, with much surprise, replied that "she did not know before that a minister would tell a lie." He answered that "he did not wish to tell a lie, but he thought that a minister

---

What is the subject of Chapter XI? Repeat the text. What is the meaning of abomination? Why is the epithet liar so offensive? Give the anecdote of John Wesley.

might change his mind." Her difficulty arose from not knowing what was meant by a lie, and, therefore, she was not only led into an act of gross impoliteness, but also of great injustice to an excellent man.

A lie and an untruth.—Few persons make a distinction between a lie and an untruth. That there is a most important difference may easily be perceived. An untruth may be defined as "an assertion that is contrary to the fact," while a lie is the "assertion of an untruth with an intention to deceive." A lie is always an untruth, but an untruth is not always a lie. A man, from ignorance or misunderstanding, may assert what is untrue and not violate the moral law; but if what he says is contrary to the truth, and he knows it, he is guilty of lying.

If my neighbor, for instance, shall say that America was discovered in 1620, he has made a misstatement, for such is not the truth, and it is plain that he has confounded the discovery of America with the landing of the Pilgrims. This he might have done without any intention to deceive: if, therefore, I say to him, "you have stated the fact incorrectly," or "what you have stated is not true," do I charge him with lying? Certainly not. But if I tell him he lies, I mean that the statement he made was false, and that he knew it. It is plain that in making so grave a charge as that a person lies, we must have a clear and unquestionable proof, not only of the untruth, but also of the design to deceive.

Nothing is easier with vulgar people than to use hard names; first, because they are irritating, and such persons have no regard for the feelings of their neighbors; and, secondly, because they have really little regard for truth. A

Why did that woman attribute the lie to him? Why was it not a lie? Give the distinction between a lie and an untruth. Is an untruth always a lie? Why? What may cause a man to tell an untruth? Give the illustration above. What is the difference between telling a person he is mistaken and that he lies? What is the character of people generally who use disgraceful epithets?

truly honorable man is very sensitive in all matters which appear to cast discredit upon his integrity or veracity, and, for this reason, the dishonorable man affects a sensitiveness he really does not feel. The latter may lie, and cheat, and steal, and his distress arises, not from doing these dishonorable acts, but in being discovered and told of it.

Anecdote.—A story is told of a man who had a quarrel with a mathematician, and, after considerable abuse, concluded by calling him a liar. Preserving his temper, the latter calmly replied, "You have called me a liar, which is a very grave charge against one who claims to be a gentleman. Now, if you can prove it, it must be true, and I shall be ashamed of myself; but if you can not prove it, it is you who should be ashamed, because you state what is not true for purposes of mischief. It is you, then, who are the liar."

White lies and black.—As a lie is any intentional violation of the truth, it is plain that to make a lie it is not necessary to use spoken language; it may be uttered in words, or signs, or gestures of the head, or motions of the body. A pupil may cough a lie to deceive his teacher in school—in short, any means taken to create a false impression is a lie. It is no less a lie when told by the old to the young, than by the young to the old; by the parent to the child, than by the child to the parent. When the mother says to her little child, "The bears will catch you if you go into the street," she lies. She knows there are no bears there. Many children are taught to lie in this manner.

A lie may be told by uttering only a part of the truth, and keeping back some facts which are necessary to a complete knowledge of the whole. Again, it may consist in an

---

What is the difference given between the honorable and dishonorable man? Give the anecdote. What was the wisdom of the reply? Is it necessary to speak to make a lie? Are any lies innocent? Give the various ways in which lies may be used.

exaggeration or overstatement of facts. These are the most common forms of deception, and are as base as statements in which there is not a particle of truth. Nor does it matter whether the subject be important or unimportant; a lie told as a joke is no less a lie because it is a joke, and a joking liar can not be a gentleman. There can be no such thing as an innocent lie, or a harmless liar.

Truth as to words spoken.—It is not unusual to hear persons attempt, not only to give the ideas expressed by another, but to state them in the precise language in which they were uttered. While it is very desirable to quote the very words that fall from another's lips, it is also very difficult, and very few persons have the natural ability or the cultivation to do it with entire accuracy.

Anecdote.—To illustrate to his school the necessity of absolute precision in the statement of words, and the difficulty of acquiring it, a gentleman selected from the high school six of his most capable boys, whose average age was, perhaps, seventeen years. He explained the experiment he was about to make, and desired them to give it their close attention, in order, if possible, to repeat the words he was about to give them. The plan was to show Master A a short sentence written on a piece of paper, which he was requested to memorize and whisper to Master B, who, in turn, was to communicate it to Master C, and so on, till the last of the six should receive it, and write it upon the blackboard.

The boys were anxious to prove that they could tell a straight story when they applied their minds to it, especially, since a failure on this trial would show them to be inaccurate, and consequently unreliable in all ordinary state-

---

Is it right to tell a lie as a joke? Is there danger of lying habits? How are they formed? Why is it difficult to give the precise language of others? Is it often attempted? With what results? Give the experiment.

ments, where no unusual efforts were made to report correctly. The following sentence was prepared for the trial. "Maternal affection is an instinct which most animals possess in common with man." After each boy had communicated the sentence to his neighbor, the last one wrote the following, as his version: "Maternal affection is an instinct which all animals possess except man."

A comparison of these two sentences proves that it is a difficult feat of memory to repeat, even under favorable circumstances, any words uttered by another. Since these boys, selected for their smartness, accustomed to give attention as pupils, anxious to show their ability to hear exactly and repeat accurately, failed to make a true report of eleven words, how much more liable must ordinary persons be, under circumstances less favorable, to report incorrectly the precise words in a given conversation. A change of two or three words in the above experimental sentence makes the last boy state the very reverse of the sentiment expressed by the first one. How absurd it is to suppose that persons generally can reproduce the exact language of others, and how exceedingly cautious we should be in giving or receiving statements claiming to be so accurate.

Doubtful Credibility.—There are persons with very remarkable memories, who are able to repeat, not only the sentiments of another in the order in which they are delivered, but also to give the exact language in which they are uttered. Such people are exceedingly rare; so that it may be safely assumed as a rule, that witnesses who unhesitatingly testify to the precise language of another, especially in a long conversation, are of doubtful credibility.

Why did it fail? Repeat each sentence given in the experiment. What is the difference between them? Why was this a favorable test? Why would the boys be anxious to succeed? Would persons generally be more successful than these boys? If there was a failure in a test case like this, is it likely that persons generally can repeat language accurately? Why should we have a care about stating words precisely? Can we always credit those who say they state the precise words of a conversation? Why? What danger is there in attempting to give the precise words?

CHAPTER XII.

"A righteous man hateth lying."

VERACITY. (Continued.)

Gossip.—The following little poem will illustrate the inability of some persons to report words correctly, as spoken of in the preceding chapter:

"Said Gossip One to Gossip Two,
While shopping in the town,
'One Mrs. Pry to me remarked,
Smith bought his goods of Brown.'

"Says Gossip Two to Gossip Three,
Who cast her eyelids down,
'I've heard it said to-day, my friend,
Smith got his goods from Brown.'

"Says Gossip Three to Gossip Four,
With something of a frown,
'I've heard strange news—what do you think?
Smith took his goods from Brown.'

"Says Gossip Four to Gossip Five,
Who blazed it round the town,
'I've heard to-day such shocking news—
Smith stole his goods from Brown.'"

Truth as to things done.—The same principle of evidence holds good with reference to things done as in words spoken. If we are likely to be inaccurate in the report of language, so we may fail to be correct in narrating what

---

What is the subject of Chapter XII? Repeat the text. Give the substance of the little poem. What does the poem teach? Are such exaggerations common? Why?

we see. If, by inattention, we hear erroneously, by the same neglect we may see imperfectly. Several persons may witness an exciting occurrence, and, while they agree as to the general facts, may differ very much in their statement of the separate incidents. One may see what entirely escaped the notice of another who had an equal opportunity for observation.

Now, it is evident that, in giving testimony, they may disagree in many particulars, and yet each may state exactly the impressions made on his mind and be entirely truthful. If they differ, their disagreement is not necessarily an evidence of a want of veracity, but only a confirmation of the truth that two persons are rarely impressed by what they see in precisely the same way.

Promises.—A promise may be defined as "an agreement to do, or not to do, a certain thing." When such an engagement is made, the party or parties are in honor bound to fulfill it in its letter and spirit As no one can look into the future to determine what may happen, the greatest care should be taken not to promise anything that he may not reasonably expect to perform. If a boy promises his teacher, for instance, to prepare a given lesson by to-morrow, and willfully neglects the duty, he lies; for the promise was made with an intention to deceive. If the promise was made in good faith and forgotten, he did not tell the truth, nor did he tell a lie, but his neglect to perform the work was a wrong to himself and his teacher, the repetition of which would result in a habit injurious to his character and reputation.

If the promise was made with the intention of perform-

Do people generally see more accurately than they hear? May two persons state the fact of any occurrence differently and both tell the truth? How? If they disagree does it prove that either is lying? What is a promise? Is a person morally bound to keep his promises? Suppose he is unable, does he lie? Suppose he is able, and does not, does he lie? Is a forgotten promise a lie? Why? Is it an untruth? Why? What is our duty in reference to promises? What must excuse us from performing a promise? Why?

ing it, and in returning home he had fallen and broken his leg, so that it was impossible for him either to study or to return to school, he should not be held responsible, as he is not to blame for the non-performance of his agreement. From these illustrations it will be perceived that we have no right to promise what we are unable or unwilling to perform; but if we make any engagement with the intention of keeping our word, and are prevented by circumstances we did not foresee, and could not control, we do no wrong. Every promise should be understood as depending upon providential circumstances.

Of promises to do wrong.—There are some promises which are made in good faith that ought never to be fulfilled. A boy agreed with his classmates to go to a neighboring orchard to steal apples When the appointed time came, he determined not to go, for his conscience had whispered, "*Thou shalt not steal*," and he concluded to obey it. The boys jeered him for a coward, and claimed that as an honorable boy he should stick to his promise. He reasoned in this way: "Before I made this agreement, I was under obligations to God and man not to steal. I had no right to promise to do wrong. My first duty was to obey God, and while it was wrong to make the promise, it would be a greater wrong to keep it, therefore I shall not go." If this reasoning be correct, it is wrong to promise to do wrong, and therefore such a promise is not morally binding.

If we are under no moral obligation to fulfill a promise made to do a wrong, there can be no dishonor in refusing its performance. Dishonor belongs to those who persist in doing wrong after they have discovered the right.

Is a promise to do wrong binding? Why? Give the illustration and the argument. Is the argument correct? What, then, is our duty in reference to promises to do wrong? Shall we make such promises? Shall we fulfill them?

CHAPTER XIII.

"*Thou shalt not bear false witness against thy neighbor.*"

EVIDENCE.

Oaths.—Among the various classes of men there will always be differences and misunderstandings concerning persons and property. In a state of nature these disputes are settled by a resort to arms, when the stronger and more cunning subdues the weaker, without any reference to principles of right. In enlightened countries, courts are established and judges are appointed to determine, by lawful means, all disputes between citizens. Law-loving and law-abiding people never attempt to enforce their rights except in the way prescribed by law. When an appeal is made to the courts to right the wrongs or settle the controversies of citizens, witnesses are called in to give evidence concerning the facts. As it is written in the moral law, "*Thou shalt not bear false witness against thy neighbor*," every one is under obligation to speak the truth.

Since the giving of testimony in court may concern a neighbor's life or liberty, reputation or property, it is well to impress upon the conscience of the witness the solemn obligation he is under to tell the truth. For this purpose he is expected to take an oath, which is an appeal to Almighty God to witness the truth about to be uttered. Every man is under as much obligation to tell the truth without taking the oath as with it, and every truly good

---

What is the subject of chapter XIII? What is the text? How are disputes settled in a state of nature? How in enlightened countries? What do the courts require? Why is every one under obligation to speak the truth? Repeat the text. What is an oath? Is it our duty to tell the truth at all times?

man's word is as good as his oath, yet there are those who are rendered more careful by this solemn ceremony.

Anecdote.—The virtue of the ancient Athenians is very remarkable, as was exhibited in the case of Euripides. This great poet, though famous for the morality of his plays, had introduced a person, who, being reminded of an oath he had taken, replied, "I swore with my mouth but not with my heart." The impiety of this sentiment set the audience in an uproar; made Socrates (though an intimate friend of the poet) leave the theater with indignation, and gave so great offense that he was publicly accused and brought upon his trial, as one who had suggested an evasion of what they thought the most holy and indissoluble bond of human society. So jealous were these virtuous heathen of the slightest hint that might open the way to the violation of an oath.

The legal oath.—There are two forms in which an oath is administered in our courts, and for the benefit of those who have conscientious scruples against taking an oath, there is provided what is termed "the affirmation." Either of these forms may be used at the request of the witness.

1st. Oath by the uplifted hand.—The witness holds up his right hand to heaven, as if to ask God to hear and help him speak the truth. The officer of the court, who is legally authorized to administer the oath, repeats the following solemn words: "You do swear, in presence of Almighty God, that the evidence you shall give in this case shall be the truth, the whole truth, and nothing but the truth, as you shall answer to God in the great day." The witness bows to the officer, and answers, "I do."

What is the object of the oath? Give the anecdote. Why were the heathen angry at the poet? What is meant by the legal oath? Describe the form of taking the oath by the uplifted hand. Repeat the oath.

2d. Oath on the Bible.—As a peculiar sacredness is attached to the Bible as the word of God, an oath is prepared in which it is used. The witness lays his hand upon it, and the officer administering the oath says: "You do solemnly swear, upon the Holy Evangels, that the evidence you shall give in this case shall be the truth, the whole truth, and nothing but the truth, so help you God." The witness then kisses the Book, to show his willingness to tell the truth as God shall help him.

3d. The affirmation.—The solemn affirmation is used by the Friends, or Quakers, and others who prefer it in preference to the forms of the oath. The officer says to the witness: "You do solemnly, sincerely, and truly affirm that the evidence you shall give in this case shall be the truth to the best of your knowledge and belief, and this you affirm." The witness says, "I do."

Perjury.—The violation of the oath, or affirmation, is not a breach of the moral law only, but also of the civil law, and the crime is denominated perjury. If no dependence could be placed upon the sacred obligation of the oath, there would be an end to human confidence; men would fail to recognize their relation to the moral law whose Author is the very essence of truth, and human society would lose its strongest bond. He who is guilty of perjury is esteemed an enemy of God and the state, and, if convicted by the court, is subject to very severe punishment.

As the best of men are liable, from a great variety of circumstances, to be mistaken, it is quite possible that, even with the best intentions, they may not always speak the truth. All that the laws of God or man require is that the witness shall exercise great care in making his statements,

---

Why do some prefer to take the oath upon the Bible? Describe this method. Is there any difference in sanctity between these methods? Does a good man require the aid of an oath to enable him to tell the truth? Why is the form of affirmation preferred by some? Give that form. Is it less binding than the oath? What is perjury? What is done with a perjurer? Why? What do the laws require?

and that he shall speak the truth "according to the best of his knowledge and belief," and to declare it "without fear, favor, or affection" for the parties concerned.

Involuntary evidence.—The moral law requires that men shall live peaceably with each other, as was discussed in Chapter VIII; but such is the weakness of human nature, that it is not always possible to obey the law. The civil courts must adjust the difficulties that neighbors can not or will not settle. The safety of the individual, and the welfare of the community, depend upon the legal arrangement of all strifes, and all good citizens are bound to afford whatever aid is necessary to effect the object. The moral as well as the civil law requires that we shall give evidence when called upon by the legal authorities.

No man is obliged to be a witness against himself in the courts, but he may be compelled to testify concerning others, even when his feelings and interests would prompt him to keep silent. In case he should refuse to tell what he knows, the court would send him to prison till he should be willing to divulge it. However mortifying to the pride, or distressing to the mind, the evidence may be, it should be given fully and honestly, without any mental reservation or concealment. We are morally bound to tell the truth, and should not yield to any temptation to deviate from this duty.

Voluntary evidence.—The state is composed of individuals who are united to promote their highest welfare in the protection of the rights of life, liberty, and property. Every individual is interested, for every one has some rights that need protection. Any infraction of the law is an injury to the whole community, which every member should,

---

Is it possible to live peaceably with all men? Why? How must differences be settled? What depend upon the prompt settlement of disputes? Should pupils refer their differences to teachers, or continue to quarrel? Is a man obliged to testify against himself? Is he obliged to testify concerning others? What will be done if he refuses to testify? Why should the court compel a man to testify? Is every citizen interested in the enforcement of the law? Why?

if possible, avert. If the incendiary burns a house, it is a loss not only to the owner, but a serious damage to the public; if a horse is stolen, the whole community is disturbed, since every man's horse is liable to be taken; if a man is knocked down and robbed, every man's person and property are insecure if the robber is not detected and punished. The feeling of safety which every good community enjoys is disturbed when outrages of this kind occur.

It is the duty, then, of every good citizen to make his best efforts to discover such perpetrators of crime and bring them to justice. It would be a cowardly wrong for any one to conceal his knowledge of such offenders, and thereby screen them from punishment. While it is an unpleasant duty to become a voluntary informer, yet the welfare of society as a whole, and of every individual, demands that such information be given. A public informer may be a public benefactor.

Opinions in Evidence.—Witnesses are often called to give opinions with reference to things about which they can not speak with certainty. Thus, a physician may be summoned to testify whether, in his opinion, a certain man came to his death by a blow on the head or a stab in the side; a farmer, to give his estimate of the value of a certain horse; a mechanic, to determine the strength and durability of a piece of machinery. These conclusions are matters of judgment, and one man is not to be blamed if his opinion does not agree with that of another.

Opinions are valuable according to the age, experience, intelligence, and general character of the witness. Young people are apt to form judgments too hastily. They often jump at conclusions without carefully weighing all the facts and circumstances, and thus do injury to themselves and

---

Is it the duty of every one to assist in bringing offenders to justice? Why? Why may a voluntary informer be a public benefactor? May a person swear to that which he does not certainly know? Illustrate how one may give an opinion on oath. What is an opinion worth as evidence?

others. If one farmer thinks a horse worth fifty dollars, according "to the best of his knowledge and belief," and another values him at seventy-five, each may speak exactly as he thinks, and thus tell the truth according to his understanding. A jury would be guided in their verdict by the testimony of the man whom they suppose to have the most experience, or the best judgment, and this without any reflection upon the other. We can not be too careful in giving our opinions in evidence when they affect the interests of our neighbor.

Slander.—It is not alone in courts of law that we are commanded not to bear false witness. Comparatively few persons will swear falsely, as the fear of God and man constrains them to tell the truth. It is in the associations of society that the command is most frequently violated. Jealousy, envy, and anger are often exhibited in bitter speeches and slanderous remarks. Slander is defined to be a false report, maliciously put in circulation to injure another's good name. Bad passions are not alone responsible for the circulation of scandal; for the mere desire of telling news leads some persons to bear false witness.

No habit is more dangerous to individuals and society, since neither purity, innocence, nor integrity is proof against the poison of a malicious tongue. It is written in the moral law: "*Thou shalt not go up and down as a tale-bearer among thy people*," for "*The words of a tale-bearer are as wounds.*" It is also declared that "*A good name is rather to be chosen than great riches*," and Shakespeare, a great English poet, thus expresses the same idea:

"Who steals my purse steals trash; . . .
But he that filches from me my good name
Robs me of that which not enriches him,
And makes me poor indeed."

What will govern a jury in a conflict of opinions? Why is it our duty to be careful in expressing opinions? May carelessly expressed opinions do harm? How? Is it in courts alone that we must not bear false witness? What is slander? What are causes of slander? Why is the habit of using slanderous language dangerous? To whom is it dangerous? What is written of the slanderer? What is more valuable than a good name? Repeat the words of the poet.

They say.—It not unfrequently happens that persons invent or circulate an evil story, and, to relieve themselves from the responsibilities of slander, take shelter behind an irresponsible "they say." The following little poem gives some excellent advice concerning this cowardly method of perpetrating and perpetuating mischief:

"THEY SAY."

"'They say'—Ah! well, suppose they do;
But can they prove the story true?
Suspicion may arise from naught
But malice, envy, want of thought.
Why count yourself among the 'they'
Who whisper what they dare not say?

"'They say'—But why the tale rehearse
And help to make the matter worse?
No good can possibly accrue
From telling what may be untrue;
And is it not a nobler plan
To speak of all the best you can?

"'They say'—Well, if it should be so,
Why need you tell the tale of woe?
Will it the bitter wrong redress,
Or make one pang of sorrow less?
Will it the erring one restore,
Henceforth to 'go and sin no more?'

"'They say'—Oh! pause, and look within:
See how your heart inclines to sin.
Watch! lest in dark temptation's hour
You, too, should sink beneath its power.
Pity the frail, weep o'er their fall,
But speak of good, or not at all."

It is not necessary to repeat an injurious story, even if it is true, unless it be done from motives of kindness to the erring one, or to prevent further injury. The mere fact

---

Why do persons quote "they say" when telling a slander? Commit the poem, "They Say." Is it always necessary to repeat what "they say?" Will it do good? Will it prevent harm? If it is true, does that justify spreading it abroad?

that a disreputable rumor is true does not authorize or justify any one in giving it further circulation.

Two parties to a slander.—People sometimes forget that it takes two to make a slander: one to utter it, the other to listen to it. The moral law condemns not only the tale-bearer, the flatterer, and the revealer of secrets, but it equally censures those who have "itching ears," thus: "*A wicked doer giveth heed to false lips, and a liar giveth ear to a naughty tongue.*"

That was a wise reply which a gentleman made to a noted gossip who began telling him how "Everybody was talking about him, and saying terrible things." He listened a moment, and then replied: "Do you talk about me, Mrs. B?" "Why, no!" "Well, then, I do not care what others say."

Two sides to a story.—Since, as has already been shown, some persons do not possess the power of attention necessary to see and hear accurately, nor the command of language which enables them to express the exact truth, nor the proper estimate of the value of a good name, nor an earnest desire to speak justly, we should be exceedingly careful about giving credit to one side of any story affecting life, liberty, reputation, or property, until we have heard the other. It is a rule of our courts, based upon justice, that no one shall be found guilty of any charge until he has had a chance for a hearing and a defense. So it should be in private affairs. There are always two sides to a question, and he is only half informed who hears but one.

"Stop and weigh it."—One morning an enraged countryman came to Mr. M's store with very angry looks. He left his team in the street, and had a good stick in his hand.

How many does it take to make a slander? What does the moral law condemn? Repeat what is written of a wicked doer and a liar. What was the reply of the gentleman to Mrs. B? Why was it wise? Can we learn the truth by hearing one side? What is the rule of the courts? How much can we learn by hearing one side of a story?

"Mr. M," said the angry countryman, "I bought a paper of nutmegs here in your store, and when I got home they were more than half walnuts; and that's the young villain that I bought 'em of," pointing to John.

"John," said Mr. M, "did you sell this man walnuts for nutmegs?"

"No, sir!" was the ready answer.

"You lie, you little villain!" said the countryman, still more enraged at his assurance.

"Now, look here," said John; "if you had taken the trouble to weigh your nutmegs, you would have found that I put in the walnuts *gratis*."

"Oh, you gave them to me, did you?"

"Yes, sir; I threw in a handful for the children to crack," said John, laughing at the same time.

"Well, now, if that ain't a young scamp!" said the countryman, his features relaxing into a smile as he saw through the matter.

Much hard talk and bad blood would be saved if people would *stop to weigh* before they blame others.

The following little verse is suggestive of our duty, and is worthy of being committed to memory:

"It's a very good rule in all things of life,
When judging a friend or a brother,
Not to look at the question alone on one side,
But always to turn to the other.

"We are apt to be selfish in all our views,
In the jostling, headlong race,
And so, to be right, ere you censure a man,
Just 'put yourself in his place.'"

Mistakes.—Mistakes in the statement of facts are likely to occur even with the most careful and reliable persons; and, although sometimes very mortifying and annoying,

---

Repeat the poem, "Put Yourself in His Place." Can we know the whole truth by hearing one side of it? What is our duty?

they should always be rectified kindly and in a charitable spirit. The following anecdote will show how errors should be corrected:

"Once, during the temporary absence of Dr. Hall from the city of Washington, his clerk made out some bills, and, among others, sent one to Gen. Jackson. On his return the doctor found a note from the president, inclosing a check for the amount, deducting an old charge which had been called for and settled, and for which he held a receipt. The fact that a bill had been sent was not less a mortification to Dr. Hall than the error in the account itself. But on looking at the president's check, he found that the signature had been omitted. He therefore returned it, with the expression of his regret that the bill had been sent, and pointed out the general's omission. The check was duly signed and sent back, inclosed in a note with this remark:

"*Dear Doctor:* The best of men are liable to mistakes.

"ANDREW JACKSON."

Flattery.—Flattery is defined as "false praise bestowed to accomplish some purpose." Self-love is so blind as to receive commendation where none is really deserved. The flatterer, perceiving this weakness, takes advantage of it to promote his own plans. Lying and flattery go hand in hand, as it is written: "*A lying tongue hateth those that are afflicted by it; and a flattering mouth worketh ruin.*" It is mean and cowardly to take advantage of weakness and credulity in order to promote our own schemes, as it is written: "*A man that flattereth his neighbor spreadeth a net for his feet.*"

"No flattery, boy! an honest man can't live by 't:
It is a little, sneaking art, which knaves
Use to cajole and soften fools withal.
If thou hast flatt'ry in thy nature, out with 't!"

What was the incident of General Jackson? What does it prove? Define flattery. What is the object of the flatterer? Repeat the texts concerning liars and flatterers. Repeat the poetry.

As it is base to exercise the arts of a flatterer by spreading a net for an unwary victim, so it is weak and silly to be so overcome by false praise as to lose all proper estimate of our real worth. Approbation is certainly more agreeable than censure, but false praise is more dangerous than unjust reproof. It is sometimes trying to the feelings to accept advice, even when we know it is prompted by kindness; but it is harder to receive rebuke patiently, even when it is deserved. The young and inexperienced are more likely to be enticed from the path of duty by the lying arts of the flatterer, than to be governed by the less agreeable advice of those who love them. It is written, and is worthy of our remembrance, that "*Faithful are the wounds of a friend; but the kisses of an enemy are deceitful.*"

Habits of untruthfulness.—There is no habit which so easily and insensibly grows upon the young as that of speaking thoughtlessly. They often fail to see and hear attentively, to use exact language; they censure—they disguise—they utter opinions as facts; and thus, like the Athenians who "*spent their time in nothing else, but either to tell or to hear some new thing*," they fall into habits of untruthfulness—bearing false witness. Thus, when a lady talks of a dreadful glove, a horrid ribbon, an awful-looking bonnet, a lovely fan, a perfectly splendid calico dress, or an exquisitely delicious cup of coffee, she shows but little knowledge of suitable language to express thought, and her friends should be anxious for her reputation. In the use of language, as in other things, we should endeavor to "*abstain from all appearance of evil.*"

If the flatterer is dangerous, what shall be said of the victim? Why is it easier to accept flattery than kind reproof? Whether is it better to receive flattery or reproof? Why? Which is the more agreeable? What is meant by the faithful wounds of a friend? Why is it that so many acquire bad habits of expression? What are some of the common exaggerations? Is such the language of truthful people? How shall we correct such habits?

CHAPTER XIV.

"*Wine is a mocker, strong drink is raging: and whosoever is deceived thereby is not wise.*"

TEMPERANCE.

The experience of the world for three thousand years confirms the truth of the text that "*wine is a mocker.*" Of those who read this book, there is not one who expects to be a drunkard; not one who thinks it possible that his strength shall fail, his senses become impaired, his character ruined, and his life rendered wretched by the use of strong drink. Of those who have been lost to health, happiness, home, and heaven, through the terrible temptations of a diseased appetite, not one ever supposed, in the flush of youth, that he should fill a drunkard's grave. And yet the fact that so many are going to destruction proves how sadly and surely men are deceived when they do not listen to the voice of reason, and give heed to the lessons of experience.

The drunkards of to-day were innocent school-children a few years ago, and the drunkards of a few years hence will be of those who are boys to-day. "Wine is a mocker." It deceives the boy with false ideas of manliness; it disappoints the man by giving him the weakness without the innocence of boyhood; to the cold it offers warmth; to the overheated it promises coolness; the weak it tantalizes with

---

What is the subject of Chapter XIV? What is the text? Do you expect to be a drunkard? Why? Do people when young ever expect to become drunkards? Why do so many drunkards exist? Is it impossible that you will be a drunkard? Why? Who were the drunkards of to-day? Who will be drunkards a few years hence? In how many ways is it proved that wine is a mocker?

anticipated strength; the sick it cheers with false hopes of health; it deludes the coward with expectations of courage, and makes the really brave reckless and fool-hardy; it ridicules the wise by giving them the tongues of fools; it offers pleasure, but derides the seeker by only giving mortification and pain; it makes the very ground mock the step staggering with unsteady motion, and at the bitter end of protracted dissipation it sums up an accumulation of horrors in dreadful "delirium tremens," when the sufferer is taunted by fiends who seem to laugh and jeer and revel with satanic satisfaction about the wreck of their unfortunate victim.

The description of the fearful effects of intemperance, written thousands of years ago, is the best representation that can be given of them to-day: "*Who hath woe? Who hath sorrow? Who hath contentions? Who hath babbling? Who hath wounds without cause? Who hath redness of eyes? They that tarry long at the wine.*"

If these are the probable inheritance of him who uses strong drink; if drunkards' graves are recruited from the ranks of the young; if hearts are broken and homes are destroyed; if the best and the bravest in the land, through the mockery of a feeling of security, fall victims to this terrible destroyer, what must we do to escape a calamity so awful?

An old and experienced physician of Illinois remarked: "I would not drink one glass of intoxicating liquor each day in a year for the state of Illinois; if I did, I should become a miserable, degraded drunkard." That man had studied the terrible effects of alcohol upon the human system; he had also observed the operations of the law of habit, discussed in Chapter II, and, knowing that he was neither stronger nor better than many who had been ruined, he could not feel safe to put himself in any degree of temptation. He had seen enough to confirm the truth that

---

Repeat the text, "Who hath woe?" Why does the tarrying at the wine produce these results? Will we escape these distresses? How? Give the old physician's observation.

"*wine is a mocker, strong drink is raging: and whoever is deceived thereby is not wise.*"

"Wild oats."—People sometimes console themselves with the remark that, "Young folks will be gay;" "You must not expect to see old heads on young shoulders;" "Boys must sow their wild oats," etc. Such suggestions indicate a total lack of reflection and observation. It is written: "*They that plow iniquity and sow wickedness reap the same,*" and "*He that soweth iniquity shall reap vanity.*" We may search the pages of the moral law, but we find no promise that they who violate its precepts shall be exempt from its punishments. It is written that "*A prudent man foreseeth the evil and hideth himself; but the simple pass on and are punished.*" He is simple indeed who supposes that he will be an exception to those rules which operate on mankind generally. Such a delusion has been fatal to many a poor soul, who has discovered when too late how corroding are the links of the terrible chain which fetter and gall him.

Temptation.—The prayer of every wise man who knows the force of bad habits, and the weakness of human nature to resist them, is, "*Lead us not into temptation, but deliver us from evil.*" If it is the part of wisdom to shun the allurements of vice, it is no less the part of prudence and love to avoid placing temptations in the way of our neighbor which may possibly entice him to ruin. There are certain customs of society whose tendency is to lead the innocent and unwary into evil habits, and to confirm those who have already acquired a taste for strong drink, thus destroying the hope of their reformation. When Christmas festivities, New Year's calls, and social parties are made

What is meant by wild oats? Repeat the texts about sowing and reaping. What should prudent people do? How do simple persons act? To which class do you belong? What is the prayer of every wise person? May we pray, "deliver us from temptation," and then seek the temptation? Why? Name some of the wrong customs of society that lead to temptation.

the occasions of wine drinking, they are to be shunned by those who have either respect for themselves or love for their neighbor. The society of the good requires no such aids as wine and strong drink to add to the amusement or sociability of its members.

When people must be stimulated, sometimes even to intoxication, in order to enjoy the pleasures of social intercourse, it is evident that the moral and intellectual qualities of the company must be of a very low order. It is written: "*Woe unto them that rise up early in the morning, that they may follow strong drink; that continue until night, till wine inflame them. And the harp, and the viol, the tabret, and pipe, and wine, are in their feasts.*" Some of the saddest histories that have been written record the temptation and fall of those who have struggled to gain a mastery over their appetites, but who, in an unlucky moment, amidst a party of revelers, were presented with the fatal cup, and drank and were lost. And not the least sorrowful part of the story is the fact that many a man has been enticed to ruin by the fascinating glass presented by the hands of a thoughtless woman.

"Put it out of sight."—Bishop Asbury was a guest of a family who were profuse in their hospitalities. Brandy was placed on the table, and he was invited to partake; but he declined. The lady blushed and said:

"Bishop, I believe that brandy is good in its place."

"So do I," said the bishop; "if you have no objection, I will put it in its place." So he put it in the old-fashioned cupboard in the corner of the room, saying, with emphasis:

"That is the place, and there let it stay, never to be brought on the table again."

Is it necessary to our amusement to drink wine or strong drink? What must be the quality of the company that needs such stimulus? What is written on this subject in the moral law? Do women ever tempt men to drink? How? Why? Shall you ever tempt a person to such ruin? What was Bishop Asbury's advice?

"Touch not, taste not, handle not."—There is only one absolutely certain method of avoiding the miseries of drunkenness, and that is given in the moral law for our guidance. It is written: "*Look not thou upon the wine when it is red, when it giveth his color in the cup, when it moveth itself aright. At the last it biteth like a serpent, and stingeth like an adder.*" If every youth in the land would solemnly determine to conform to the spirit of that law, and shun every thing which intoxicates, there would be no more drunkards.

Moral courage.—Charley P was engaged as a clerk and errand boy in the store of Mr. L, who was accustomed to treat such of his customers as desired it with intoxicating liquor. One day the bottle was empty, and Charley was requested by his employer to go to the drug store and have it replenished. He very kindly, but very decidedly, declined to obey the command, which caused the proprietor no little confusion and annoyance. When evening came, Charley was asked if he had refused to go for the liquor as a matter of principle, or simply from pride. He replied that he could not do it because he did not think it right. The answer was satisfactory, and the boy kept his situation.

Charley was simply obeying the moral law, as it is written, "*Woe unto him that giveth his neighbor drink, that putteth the bottle to him, and maketh him drunken also.*" Did every youth in the land have the moral courage to do right according to his conviction of duty, we would be a better and a happier people. The only safety for ourselves and those we love is to set our faces resolutely against the sale and the use of any thing that intoxicates, and in doing this we fulfill our highest obligations to God and our neighbor.

What is the only safe rule on this subject? Repeat what the moral law says. What shall we do to avoid being bitten? Is it a self-denial not to use strong drink? Why use it then? Give the anecdote of Charley P. Did he do right? Why? Repeat the text. What is the duty of every one in this respect? What can you do to prevent drunkenness?

CHAPTER XV.

"The hand of the diligent maketh rich."

RIGHT OF PROPERTY.

The right to get and hold property is universally recognized. Every man is entitled to employ his talents of body and mind in procuring the pecuniary means that will add to his comfort and happiness, and when it is obtained no one has a right to take it away or use it without the owner's consent. This is a truth of which every one is conscious—it needs no demonstration.

Ownership by possession.—There are various methods by which the right to property is acquired. One of the first and most natural of these is ownership by possession. Some kinds of property can be said to be owned only when they are subject to our control. A man may catch a fish, snare a rabbit, or shoot a deer, and it becomes his only when secured, on account of the labor and skill employed in getting it. These are wild animals and are the prize of any who may capture them. They only become property when reduced to possession. A man has no right to snare his neighbor's chickens, or to shoot his sheep, as by so doing he interferes with that to whose possession he can lay no just claim, a prior right having already been established by the owner in rearing them.

What is the subject of Chapter XV? Repeat the text. What is meant by the text? Has every man a right to earn and possess property? Has any one a right to interfere with the property of another? What is one of the first methods of ownership? When do wild animals become our property? If we capture a bird, and it escapes, and another person captures it, whose property is it? Would the same rule apply to a chicken? Why? May a person justly snare our doves? Why?

Ownership by labor.—It is a wise provision of Providence that man should labor in order to live, it being necessary to his physical, mental, and moral well-being that he engage in some kind of work. The occupations best suited to his growth and development are those which employ his muscles, interest his mind, and at the same time give full exercise to his moral faculties. No one can be said, in any proper sense, to be independent; and yet that person is least dependent who has the best use of all his powers. Some kinds of labor are preferable to others, and they receive a higher remuneration because a greater degree of talent and skill is required in their performance; but all work honestly and faithfully done is worthy of respect, as it adds to the comfort, convenience, and prosperity of society.

The farmer, the mechanic, the tradesman, the artist, and every operative, adds to the wealth of the community by just as much as he produces above what he consumes. A man has no right to enjoy life who is not willing to do his part in the production of something which adds to the general happiness or wealth of the community. The Chinese have a proverb that, "The hog is the greatest gentleman, since he can live without work;" but the sentiment of good society is that all work is worthy of respect, and that a man may be a gentleman even if he be a groom, and a woman may be a lady though she be obliged to earn her living by washing clothes.

Ownership by inheritance or will.—Property may be acquired by the operation of the law; as when a blood relation dies without making a will or giving direction to whom his property shall be given, the civil law determines to whom it shall go and in what proportion it shall be divided.

Is work necessary? Why? Who is most independent? Why do some kinds of labor receive better pay than others? Is this right? Is all work worthy of respect? Why? What is the Chinese proverb? Is it true? Is it the duty of every one to work with head or hand? May a groom be a gentleman, or a washerwoman be a lady? Why? Is it the business in which he engages that makes one a gentleman? What is meant by inheriting property?

But if a person makes a will and dies, his property will be distributed as the will prescribes, since after a life of toil and economy it would be unjust and prejudicial to the best interests of society, if a man could not direct in what manner his accumulations should be employed.

It is a singular fact, which shows the importance of labor in the development of character, that large fortunes rarely descend through three generations. The intelligence, thrift, economy, and work necessary to make a fortune is also necessary to keep it; and these virtues rarely descend to the grandchildren of those who have accumulated great wealth. It is not unfrequently the case that even the expectation of an inheritance takes away the noblest and best incentives to manly enterprise and honorable ambition.

Ownership by exchange.—When a man kills a deer, catches a fish, or raises a crop of corn, he may exchange the products of his skill and labor with the men who make his shoes, his powder, and his plow. This exchange of labor for labor and product for product is called commerce. Rules are required for the regulation of commerce which are founded in justice between man and man. If the strong and the cunning were permitted to despoil the weak and ignorant, a condition of savage selfishness would follow, and the right of property be found in him who has the possession and is able to defend it.

The moral law prescribes the principles by which neighbors shall be governed in their commercial intercourse. It is written: "*Thou shalt not defraud thy neighbor, neither rob him;*" "*Ye shall not steal, neither deal falsely, neither lie one to another;*" "*Ye shall do no unrighteousness in judgment, in meteyard, in weight, or in measure. Just balances, just weights, shall ye have.*" Nothing can

---

Do large fortunes generally descend to grandchildren? Why? Why does the expectation of riches injure many persons? Is it safe generally to obtain wealth except by working for it? What is the exchange of products called? Why are commercial rules necessary? What is written in the moral law?

be added to give force to these plain, simple commands, except the one already quoted: "*Whatsoever ye would that men should do unto you, do ye even so to them.*"

The business contract.—A contract may be defined as "an agreement between two or more persons for a legal consideration or price to do, or not to do, a certain thing." The parties to such agreement must act without any compulsion, and be of such equal conditions that no advantage may be taken by either. They must be both able and willing to contract.

Thus, a large boy can not rightfully force a bargain with a little child, for the little one may not be able to understand his own interests. Nor can a strong boy justly compel a weak one to make a contract—he might as well rob him. A contract to do an illegal act is no more morally binding than a promise to do wrong, as we learned in Chapter XII. Every contract should be carefully made, clearly understood, and then scrupulously fulfilled. When an engagement is made upon the general statement that, "We'll fix the pay at another time," or, "We'll make it all right," it is altogether probable that when the settlement is attempted, one or both the parties will be dissatisfied. The safe way to do business is to agree in all particulars, in the first place, and then there is little danger of fraud or misunderstanding.

As it requires two or more individuals to make a contract, neither party can dissolve it, morally or legally, without the consent of the other. Each is in honor bound to carry out the agreement, even if it works to his own disadvantage. To illustrate this principle, suppose that A is employed in

---

What is added to these rules of justice? Why shall we not give short weight and measure? What is the golden rule? Why is it called the golden rule? What is a contract? When one man is compelled to contract with another, can he be compelled to perform it? Why? Why may not a big boy bargain with a little one? Is a promise to do wrong binding? Is a contract to do wrong binding? If a man has been paid to do wrong, shall he do it? What care should be used in making a contract? Is it right to settle the terms of a contract at the time it is made, or defer it? What is the better way? Can either party dissolve a contract at pleasure? Should a man carry out the contract if he loses by it? Why?

the purchase of wool, and that he contracts with Farmer B, from whom he engages the produce of his flock at a given price. The wool is to be delivered at a certain time after the usual sheep-shearing season.

The price of wool is not always the same, but rises or falls as the demand for it increases or diminishes. These changes in price are not governed by invariable rules whose operations can be clearly and accurately foretold, therefore each buyer and seller must judge for himself concerning the probabilities of a rise or a decline. Contracts of this kind must be made in advance, so that a large amount shall be kept constantly at the mills; for, if the supply ceases, they must stop, thus injuring the manufacturer and the operators, whose families must suffer when they cease to have employment. Suppose, from any cause, the price of wool rises suddenly, and the farmer finds that, if he had not contracted for forty cents a pound, he might have realized forty-five, which would pay him better for the keeping of his flock. Still, he is in honor bound to deliver the wool and fulfill the terms of his agreement. In this case, A gains and B loses. But suppose the conditions changed, and that the wool crop is greater than was supposed, and the price falls five cents a pound. If B was the loser before, and had been unwilling to carry out his agreement, he could not conscientiously claim the benefit of his bargain; but, having borne his loss before, he is not unwilling now to claim his advantage to make it good.

Public interest in business integrity.—The interests of society are so interwoven that whatever benefits one member is an advantage, directly or indirectly, to all; and that which works an injury to one is a loss to the whole. Thus, A and B make a contract by which, for a proper con-

---

Give the illustration. Do people always know the results of their contracts? Why? What, then, is necessary to make a contract? Is it right to make a contract by which you know your neighbor must lose? Why is an injury to one in society an indirect injury to all?

sideration, A shall, at a given time, receive one hundred dollars. Upon the strength of this agreement, A makes other contracts with C, D, and E, expecting to pay them money when B pays him. If B is prompt, A will receive his hundred dollars, and be enabled to make good his promises to these parties; and thus this sum, when passed from hand to hand, may pay, perhaps, a thousand dollars' indebtedness in the community. If B fails, then A fails also, causing confusion, trouble, and perhaps suffering, as the result, to many individuals.

Small contracts.—There is a class of small traders and working people, whose business and labor are necessary to the convenience and comfort of every community, and for which there is often too little consideration. These people are almost always humble and poor. Earning comparatively small wages, and having but little economy or thrift, they can not lay by a store for future necessity. They are engaged in occupations which require more strength than skill, and frequently have to depend upon odd jobs rather than permanent, steady work. Of these are the wood-sawyer, the white-washer, the coal-carrier, the washer-woman, the paper-carrier, etc. They make their living by their daily labor, and have a right to expect prompt payment when the work is done. It is cruel carelessness to expect or require a washer-woman to call for her wages and to be told to call again. She has neither time nor strength to waste in running after her money, which should have been paid, as she expected, when her labor was over. There is an implied obligation in all such contracts for labor to pay promptly, and this for the reasons that such laborers need their money when it is due, and are unable to keep ac-

Give the illustration. What may be the effect on others if we do not fulfill our agreements? What on ourselves? Why is it necessary to be particularly careful in small contracts to pay promptly? Who are those who generally make small contracts? What effect may it have to disappoint them? Have we a right to injure the poor? What kind of payment do small dealers expect? Why? What implied obligation is in all such contracts?

counts. It is written in the moral law, "*Blessed is he that considereth the poor;*" "*He that despiseth his neighbor sinneth; but he that hath mercy on the poor, happy is he.*"

CHAPTER XVI.

"*The laborer is worthy of his hire.*"

RIGHT OF PROPERTY. (Continued)

The value of labor, like that of wheat, corn, and articles of commerce, is subject to the same laws, rising or falling, according to the amount of work to be done and the number of hands to perform it. The two relations which we sustain with reference to labor are either those of employers or workers. As employers we may endeavor to secure the best services for ourselves, and at the same time do no injustice to those whom we employ, by requiring of them unusual hours of labor, or work exceeding their strength or ability, or by paying less than a reasonable rate of remuneration. Nor have we the right to take advantage of the necessities of laborers to force them to work for less than their services are really worth, and thus "*Grind the faces of the poor.*" Such conduct is not in accordance with the law of love. Nor, on the other hand, has the laborer any right to give less than a full day's honest work

What is written in the moral law? Why is a man happy that hath mercy on the poor?

What is the subject of Chapter XVI? Repeat the text. What is the law affecting labor? What are the two relations that we sustain to labor? What is right for us as employers? If the laborer is worthy of his hire, should the hire be worthy of the laborer? Why? Is it our duty to get all the work we can for the least pay? Is it the duty of the laborer to get all the pay he can for the least work? May the employer take advantage of the laborer?

for a fair day's pay; nor is it proper for him to take advantage of the necessities of the employer to compel him unjustly to pay more than the services are really worth. The moral law says, "*Thou shalt not defraud thy neighbor, neither rob him*," and the command applies alike to the master and the servant, the employer and the laborer. Nor does this law apply alone to those who engage in the humbler kinds of toil. Every laborer, whether public officer, minister, lawyer, teacher, or doctor, is bound in honor to render his best and fullest service to those who employ him, without any reservation, except that which was distinctly understood when the engagement was made. The same rules of right apply to all kinds of service, whether it be performed with the head or the hands. The law of love requires perfect justice in respect to labor and its rewards.

Renting or hiring.—A limited or temporary right of property may be acquired by renting or hiring. A wealthy man can not live in all his houses, or employ all his horses; so, if he would make them profitable, he must rent or hire them, to be used by others for a given time, at a proper price. When a house is rented, or a horse is let out to service, it is done under an implied condition that the user shall take the same care of the property that he would under similar circumstances if it were his own. If the house be injured, or the horse abused, the careless party is morally and legally accountable to the owner for the damage. Inhuman people sometimes misuse a hired horse, under the impression that because he is hired they have a right to overtax his strength or speed. Such conduct is a wrong to the owner and an outrage against an innocent, uncomplaining animal.

May the laborer take advantage of the employer to raise his pay? What does the moral law say? Do these rules apply alone to those who work with their hands? Why? What kind of a right may we acquire by renting or hiring? What is the implied condition of the transfer when we rent or hire property? How shall we take care of rented or hired property? Is it right to abuse a horse because we have hired him? Why?

Borrowed property.—Persons are sometimes placed under circumstances in which they can not buy or hire property, and are obliged to borrow. When it is thus obtained, if there be no agreement in words, there is an implied obligation, which every honorable person will be careful to observe, that the borrowed article shall be promptly returned in as good condition, quality, or measure as it was received, and at such a time as was agreed upon, or at such time as would cause the least inconvenience to the lender. If loss or damage occur to the property when in the possession of the borrower, he should make it good to the lender.

Thus, if a boy should borrow another's penknife and break it, he is in duty bound to return as good a knife to the owner, or render satisfaction for his loss. If he borrow a defective knife, and it breaks in his hands, he is not responsible for the injury or loss if he used it with proper care. Many conditions of a practical character might be discussed concerning this subject, but sufficient has been detailed to indicate the principle of kindness and fair dealing upon which they may be settled.

There is no class of persons who suffer so much annoyance from borrowers as those who lend books. It is often a kindness and a compliment to receive the loan of a book, and the least acknowledgment of the favor that can be made by the borrower is to return it promptly, unsoiled and unabused, to the owner. In order to preserve friendships and prevent misunderstandings, it is better never to borrow if it can be avoided. This is a good rule to observe even among friends, for, though it is very kind to lend, it is sometimes very unkind to borrow.

Borrowed money.—Money may be loaned upon the same principle that other property is rented or hired. If a man may hire his horse for profit, he may also loan his money

---

If we borrow an article, what are the implied obligations of time, weight, measure, care, etc.? Give the illustration. What care should be taken of borrowed books? Is it wise to borrow? Why? Why may it be unkind to borrow?

for gain. When it is thus loaned it is said to be at interest. Sometimes money is more plenty than at others, owing to the demand for it in business. When it is plenty the interest is low, but when it is in great demand men will pay a higher rate for its use. When a man borrows money he gives his note, which is a written promise to pay the lender at a certain time the amount loaned, with interest. The borrower procures the signatures of one or more persons to the note, who promise to pay it when due if he fails. These persons are said to be the sureties.

When the note is due, it is presented to the borrower, who will pay it if he is able; but, if he can not meet it, the surety will be obliged to do so for him. It is a very common business transaction to secure money in this manner, but it sometimes happens that men's plans of business miscarry, and they are not able to raise the funds to meet their engagements. When such accidents happen, their sureties have to pay. Several principles are to be observed in transactions of this kind:

First. The money lender has no right to take advantage of the real or supposed necessities of the borrower, and to charge an extravagant rate of interest for the money loaned. It is written, "*A good man showeth favor and lendeth*," and, "*He that oppresseth the poor reproacheth his Maker, but he that honoreth Him hath mercy on the poor.*"

Second. No one has a right to borrow money unless he has a reasonable prospect of paying it according to promise at the appointed time. Many a thoughtless speculator, desirous of acquiring wealth suddenly, has ruined himself and his sureties by investing borrowed capital in some uncertain business which failed to make the expected return, and has

---

When money is loaned, as a general rule, what is expected of the borrower? Is it right to loan money for gain? Why? What is the increase called? Why do the rates of interest vary at different times? When a man borrows money, what does he give the lender? What is a note? What is a surety? Why do men have sureties for their notes? What is the first principle to be observed in transactions of this kind? What is written of him that oppresseth? What is the second principle? What is written of the borrower? What does that text mean?

found to his sorrow the truth of the saying, "*The borrower is servant to the lender.*"

Third. No man has a right to become surety for another unless he is able and willing to pay the debt in case the principal fails. It is written, "*Be not thou one of them that strike hands, or of them that are sureties for debts. If thou hast nothing to pay, why should he take away thy bed from under thee?*" Many a man has lost his all, and become penniless, because he became surety for money he never expected to be called on to pay. It is very kind for a man to become surety for his neighbor, but if the kindness be performed at the risk of his own business, it is of questionable propriety. It is written, "*The wicked borroweth and payeth not again.*"

Collection of Debts.—The business relations of society are so various and complicated, that in many cases it is impossible to prevent the contracting of debts. As far as it is possible this should be avoided. It is written in the moral law, "*Render therefore to all their dues: tribute to whom tribute is due; custom to whom custom; fear to whom fear; honor to whom honor. Owe no man anything but to love one another.*" The habit of permitting small debts to accumulate is very injurious to the interests of the trader, as well as to the individuals who secure the credit. The trader is damaged on account of the unproductive capital lying idle in the hands of his customers; by the time and labor necessary to make his collections; by the losses that occur from giving credit to dishonest people, and by the annoyances arising from disputed bills. These are serious inconveniences, and add materially to the expenses of business.

What is the third principle? What is written of him who becomes surety for another? Under what circumstances may a man become surety? When should he refuse to go surety? What is said of the wicked borrowing? May debts always be avoided? Should debts be avoided when possible? Why? What is written about rendering to all their dues? Why are small debts to be avoided? What are some of the injuries arising to the trader?

The buyer is often injured by getting a credit for goods he does not really need, and would not purchase if they were to be paid for at the time; by the habit of running accounts without knowing their extent; by insensibly becoming more and more involved until he is astonished and almost, if not entirely, overwhelmed by the discovery of his indebtedness; by the loss of credit, and possibly of character. One of the best methods of preserving our credit is to use it sparingly. He who pays as he goes is never harassed by debt and always knows the extent of his means.

There are several rules of business life which it is especially desirable that the young should learn and practice:

First. Never buy what you do not need because it is cheap.

Second. Never purchase on credit if you can pay the money down.

Third. Do not buy on credit unless the goods are indispensable.

Fourth. Never get goods on credit without knowing their precise cost and fixing the time at which you will cancel the debt.

Fifth. Never lose your temper or exhibit annoyance at the presentation of an unpaid account.

There are many occasions when, from sickness, misfortune, want of work, or failure to receive expected money, a person is unable to pay his debts at the appointed time. Under such circumstances, one may be vexed that he is not ready to meet his engagements, and should make such apology or explanation as the facts will justify; but if he exhibit anger, it is very strong presumptive evidence that he is not honest, and should never have been trusted. The least that a gentleman can do is to state his condition

---

What are those arising to the buyer? How shall we best preserve our credit? Why, if possible, should we pay as we go? What is the first rule? The second rule? The third rule? The fourth rule? The fifth rule? Sometimes debts can not be paid; what must be done? Should a man ever show anger on the presentation of an unpaid bill? Why?

kindly and frankly, and to make the best efforts in his power to pay the debt. "*Owe no man anything but to love one another.*"

CHAPTER XVII.

"*Thou shalt not steal.*"

RIGHT OF PROPERTY. (Continued.)

Theft.—Stealing is defined to be "the taking and carrying away of the goods of another without his knowledge and consent." It will be seen that there is no mention of value in this law. The command is not that we shall not steal gold, jewels, or horses, but its evident meaning is, thou shalt not steal anything. In this the moral law is different from the civil law, which makes it a greater crime to steal a large amount of property than a small one. The reason of this difference is that the former is given by God to guide the conscience of each individual, while the latter is made by man for the protection of the rights of the citizen in society. Greater punishments are prescribed for great thefts than for small ones, since the community is disturbed more by the loss of much property than of a little.

Sometimes young persons fancy that they may take apples, melons, nuts, etc., without serious blame. It is true that such things as these are not of great value, but we are

---

What must a gentleman or lady do? What should be our rule in life?

What is the subject of Chapter XVII? Repeat the text. Define stealing. How much or how little shall we steal without wrong? What is the difference between the moral and the civil law? What is the object of the moral law? Of the civil law? Why does the civil law prescribe great punishments for great thefts? Is there a moral wrong in stealing fruit? Why does not the civil law punish such theft?

discussing a question of right and not one of value. The moral law makes no distinction as to the value, as by it we are not authorized or permitted to steal at all. Habits of theft must have a beginning, and that beginning is usually the taking of little things. Scrupulous honesty, even in the smallest things, is what the law requires, in order to prevent the formation of habits so dangerous. Sometimes the excuse is made for a petty theft that, "the owner would not care." The only safe way to know that fact is to ask him. To some it may seem a joke to rob a dinner basket, a melon patch, an orchard, or a hen roost, but, were we to reverse the ownership, possibly the fun would be less apparent. "*Whatsoever ye would that men should do unto you, do ye even so to them.*"

Plagiarism, or literary theft.—A person has a right to the products of his brain as well as those of his hands. It requires great study and preparation to fit a man to compose a piece of music or to write a book. When such a work is completed, it is a property having a pecuniary value. To secure the profits of his labor, the government grants to the author a "copyright," or exclusive permission to print or publish it for a certain number of years, or to sell the right to others. The design of the government in thus protecting the works of authors is to encourage literary and artistic labor by securing to them its profits. To use an author's works, and to derive a benefit from them without his consent, is grossly dishonest. Such theft is called plagiarism, and is as dishonorable as the stealing of a pocket-book.

Young folks sometimes find it more convenient to copy the compositions of others, and to attempt to pass them off as their own, than to prepare original essays. This is wrong; it is an effort to get credit for work never performed—to

---

How are habits of stealing formed? What is the golden rule? What is plagiarism? Is there property in brain work? Why? What has government done to protect such property? Why? What is meant by a copyright? Why is it dishonest to plagiarize? Did you ever know it to be done in school?

secure commendation that is entirely undeserved. Such persons should receive no more countenance from the good society of the school than any other thief. The public, as well as private, sentiment of the pupils should condemn all such dishonesty.

Quotations.—It is often convenient and appropriate to use the sentiments of an author by way of quotation. If the name of the writer is known, it is courteous to mention it; if not known, the least acknowledgment that can be made is to indicate the sentiment selected by quotation marks, thus: "Honesty is the best policy."

Property lost and found.—When property is found without an apparent owner, the finder has no right of ownership, though he have it in possession. The loser does not cease to have the right to the property because he does not know where it is. If a man shall discover a horse astray, he may take him up as lost, and take care of him for the owner. It is the finder's duty to employ all the usual and reasonable means to find the master, and restore the animal, charging a fair price for the time, labor, and expense incurred in keeping and returning him. The finder has no right to demand an additional reward for his honesty. If the owner choose to give an extra sum as a compensation, aside from the necessary costs of keeping and advertising, he may do so; but he wrongs no one if he omits the gratuity.

So, if a person find a sum of money, and the finding costs him neither trouble, care, nor expense, he has no right to demand that the owner shall pay any thing for its return. It is the duty of the finder to restore lost property, and he has no claim to remuneration for the simple performance

---

In what esteem should such a person be held? How are quotations made? What right has the finder in lost property? What shall be done when we find lost property? What shall be demanded for the return of lost property? Has the finder a right to demand any thing extra for his honesty? Is the owner under any obligation to pay more than the necessary expenses? Would the owner do wrong to offer a gratuity? Would the finder do wrong to receive a gratuity above his expenses?

of his obligation. There would be no impropriety in the owner's offering the finder a gift in token of his thankfulness, but he is not under any moral obligation to do so. When every proper means is taken to discover the owner of lost property without success, it belongs to the finder, since no one can show a better right to its possession.

Destruction of property.—Because property is apparently neglected by the owner, it does not follow that it is right for anybody to destroy it. We have no right to injure our neighbor, either by stealing or abusing his property. The disposition wantonly to destroy indicates a depraved and vicious character which entirely disregards all the obligations of both public and private duty. Such vandalism is often seen among certain classes of youth in the breaking of windows in unoccupied houses, in cutting and breaking shade trees, in taking off gates and defacing fences, in daubing painted and whitewashed walls, and in tearing down handbills. This conduct is sometimes called fun, but it must be a depraved mind that can derive enjoyment from such wantonness. No excuse can be offered for behavior which sets at defiance all the obligations of good citizenship, and he who acts thus should be considered a public enemy, for there is no more reason why a boy should break a window for fun than that he should set a house on fire.

The whittler.—There is a great propensity in some to cut and deface even painted and polished surfaces, such as those of chairs, tables, door and window frames, and the habit is so inveterate that nothing seems secure from their destructive hands. A story which illustrates this disposition to destroy is told of a whittling fellow, and the method taken to rebuke and punish him. He entered a store with

When the owner can not be found, whose shall the property be? Why? Have persons a right to destroy property not in use? How is this spirit shown? Is it fun to destroy property? Have we any right to destroy property for fun? Do you know of any property destroyed willfully? Give the anecdote of the whittler. Is the habit of cutting and defacing common?

his wife to make some purchases, and, while she was busy examining the goods, he amused himself by cutting a chip with his penknife from the edge of the nicely polished walnut counter. A clerk, observing the outrage, quietly walked around where he was sitting, and, before the whittler was aware of his intention, cut off one of his coat-tails with his scissors. The astonishment of the gentleman (?) with the knife was very great when he discovered his loss, and he demanded the reason for such conduct. The clerk pointed to the defaced counter as an explanation. The counter was much more valuable than the coat, but the whittler failed to see that there was any joke in the retaliation. We leave it as a question whether the cutting of the counter or the coat was the greater outrage.

A public shame.—It is a shame that no public building in our country is safe from injury and abuse without the intervention of the police or some similar officer. Court-houses, public halls, hotels, and even churches and cemeteries, are thus despoiled. Buildings admirably adapted for the amusement, instruction, comfort, and convenience of the public, beautifully constructed ornaments to city or town, are defaced and deformed by the hands of citizens. The finest monuments in wood, metal, and stone are often mutilated without any feelings of shame or compunctions of conscience. For the credit of our people this practice should be changed, and public property rendered as secure and safe from abuse as any other. These practices have their origin in the schools, and it is there that the reformation must commence. When our school-houses are kept, year after year, as models of neatness and good taste, then may we expect that the public taste will be reformed.

Who was most to blame—the man who injured the counter, or the clerk? Why is it that such a spirit of vandalism prevails? Why is it a public shame? How shall such outrages on good taste be prevented? Can the young be educated to respect the rights of others? Why should there be a change in these habits? Where do these things have their origin? Is your school-house neat, clean, and tasteful? Is it free from marks, stains, and abuse? If not, can it be reformed and purified?

CHAPTER XVIII.

"*Thou shalt not covet thy neighbor's house, thou shalt not covet thy neighbor's wife, nor his manservant, nor his maidservant, nor his ox, nor his ass, nor any thing that is thy neighbor's.*"

COVETOUSNESS.

An intense desire to perform any particular action, or possess any special object, is the incentive to extraordinary efforts for its accomplishment. This craving may be right or wrong, according as the objects sought are good or bad. If the mind be filled with anxiety to acquire knowledge, no effort will be spared, and no study remitted, to secure the object; if, however, the desire be toward the performance of some unworthy action, the operation of the mind is not changed—the wish prompts the effort.

But unlawful cravings are more likely to affect the mind, and engage the fancy, than those that are right; and thus we are enticed into unlawful actions. Therefore, the moral law declares, "*Thou shalt not covet thy neighbor's house, . . . nor any thing that is thy neighbor's.*" In this sense covetousness is a wrong, for it leads to the transgression of the rights of our neighbor. Theft, robbery, and even murder are not unfrequently the effects that date their origin from covetousness. We may wish for wealth, be-

---

What is the subject of Chapter XVIII? Repeat the text. What is the cause of covetousness? Whether are we more likely to have good or evil desires? When such desires arise, what efforts do we make to accomplish them? Why may we not covet our neighbor's house? Is it lawful to buy my neighbor's ox? What is the difference between desiring to buy the ox, and coveting it? What are the fruits of covetousness? Explain how theft is produced by covetousness.

cause it may enable us to do good; we may desire friends to minister to our comfort; we may crave position, as it adds to our influence; and in hoping to gain these things we need not necessarily do wrong, unless the desire is so extreme as to endanger our sense of right and duty by leading us to use improper means to secure our ends. The inordinate ambition of many a man has caused his ruin. The intense desire manifested by some young people to attract attention, their undue love for dress and ornament, is a violation of this law which has often resulted in shame and sorrow and crime.

Covetousness a virtue.—There is a sense in which covetousness is spoken of in the moral law as a virtue, since there are mental and moral attainments which are worthy of our most ardent aspirations. We are not likely to overestimate their value, or to make undue efforts to obtain them. We may very properly covet "*Love, joy, peace, long-suffering, gentleness, goodness, faith, meekness, temperance,*" as the adornments peculiar to the lady and gentleman. These are the "fruits" of the highest and noblest education, and in endeavoring to secure them we only obey the moral law, which enjoins us to "*covet earnestly the best gifts.*"

Gambling.—One of the worst manifestations of covetousness is seen in the effort to secure wealth suddenly and without the intervention of labor. There are various means resorted to, to escape the necessity of working for a living; of these, one of the principal is gambling, which may be defined as the playing of some game for money or other valuables. A gambler may be described as one who is unwilling to engage in honest employment, is fond of social excitement, and secures his living without any visible means

---

Does the desire for good things always cause us to do wrong? How does an intense desire for dress and show cause some to sin? Is covetousness ever a virtue? What may properly be coveted? Is it likely we shall do wrong in intensely desiring these virtues? Why may gambling be included under covetousness? Why do persons gamble? Define gambling.

of support. Idleness is the source of infinite mischief, because idlers must live, and if they will not live honestly by their work, they must contrive to secure, by dishonest means, a livelihood by their wits.

The first step in the direction of gambling is in the learning of the games of chance and skill in which the "fraternity" indulge. These, in the beginning, seem simple and harmless; but when a passion for playing them is once created, it is exceedingly difficult to overcome. Many a young man, led on by evil associates, and surrounded by influences he can not resist, becomes a victim, bound by the cords of habit, which he can not sever, and is brought at last to ruin.

The devices for winning money are various, ingenious, and bewitching, and he who permits himself to enter a gaming establishment, even as a spectator, or to associate with those who gamble, serves to illustrate the fable of the spider and the fly. The majority of young men engaged as clerks and cashiers who lose their places by dishonesty, owe their misfortunes to the associations and temptations of the gambling hell.

The habit of betting on cards, dice, horse-races, and elections, is highly prejudicial to good morals; for he who bets is naturally anxious to win, and has the strongest temptation to use dishonest means to secure his wager.

J. M. was a promising young man, of good connections and fair education. Like many another, he was remarkably confident of his own strength of mind and power of self-control. Leaving home at an early age to engage in business, he was thrown into the society of the gay and dissipated. At first he learned to play cards for fun; but when the excitement of simple amusement failed, he began to bet,

---

Why is gambling wrong? Describe a gambler. What is the first step in the gambler's life? What evil habits are encouraged by the gambler? In what ways is gambling performed? Why should we not even enter a gambling hell? How are many young men ruined? What is said of betting? Why does it lead to evil ways.

as he said, "only for a dime a game, to add interest to the play." When asked to drink, he drank, but "only for the sociability."

Between his companions, the gaming, and the drink, he became bewildered, and night after night found him at home, in his own little parlor, gradually nearing the brink of a precipice over which he was soon to tumble to ruin. When friends—true friends—remonstrated, he scouted the idea that he could become a gambler or a drunkard. After a time he prided himself upon his ability to play well, and also upon his discrimination of the flavor of fine wine. By the combined influence of his vanity and his vice he became a doomed man. He lost his business, he alienated his friends, he broke up his once happy home, and, leaving his wife and little one, started to the far West, where he hoped to retrieve his errors. On the way he fell into the company of gamblers, was overcome by the temptation to play, was drugged, robbed, and beaten, and finally died of remorse by his own hand.

If it is wrong to play for dollars, it is wrong to gamble for dimes; and if it is dangerous to play for dimes, we leave it to the boys to determine the propriety of gaming for marbles and pins.

The lottery.—In the earlier days of our history, it was not uncommon for the legislatures of the colonies and states to grant authority to establish lotteries, the profits of which were for the purpose of endowing schools, building churches, etc. The lottery is a game of chance which is determined by the casting or drawing of lots. The design in legalizing these establishments was not to encourage the people to acts of benevolence, and to teach them liberality from a sense of duty, but to appeal to their covetousness,

---

Give the story of J. M. Are you sure you are wiser, better, or stronger than J. M.? How do you know that you will escape his misfortunes? Is it wrong to play for dimes? For dollars? What is the moral distinction between dimes, dollars, cents, marbles, or pins? May gambling habits commence with covetousness for winning marbles? Why? What is said of the lottery? Why is it fascinating?

and lead them to invest their money in the hope that, by a lucky turn of the wheel, they would be the fortunate possessors of valuable prizes, which cost but a trifle, and thus be saved the necessity for work. It was found by observation that, whatever good might have accrued from the churches and schools thus erected, the evil effects upon the community were greater. People who purchased tickets became excited with expectations of sudden wealth; they ceased to work steadily, and became idle and dissipated.

Although their money was in most instances expended in that which yielded them no return, for the prizes were very few compared with the blanks, so infatuated did men become, that they would try and try again, in the hope of a future success, and thus waste their entire means. Young men were peculiarly liable to be affected by this desire for gain, and were tempted to steal from their employers in the vain hope that they would be so fortunate as to restore the stolen funds. Such was the extent of the mischief produced, that almost all the states abolished lotteries as prejudicial to the public welfare and injurious to individual prosperity and happiness. All such institutions foster the spirit of covetousness, which makes men discontented, idle, and vicious.

Religious lotteries.—If the experience of our own and many foreign countries is such as to compel them to abolish state lotteries, and pass severe laws against the sale of tickets, as prejudicial to the interests of the people, the question arises, are not all schemes of this character liable to the same objection? There is a great diversity in the methods that are used to stimulate people's cupidity, and yet the principle involved is the same in all, however ingenious or plausible they appear. On the one hand, the plan is to extort money, for which little or no equivalent is rendered, by

What was the experience of the states? Do lotteries foster covetousness? How? What effects do lotteries have on people? Does the size of the prizes affect the principle which is involved in lotteries?

inflaming the avarice under a plea of charity, benevolence, and duty. On the other hand, there is the desire to get more than is given, cloaked under the flimsy and transparent excuse of liberality.

If covetousness is wrong, then no one can be justified in enticing his neighbor to its commission. It is written, "*Blessed is the man that endureth temptation*," and, we may add, that does not attempt to impose upon his own conscience by the argument that benevolence prompts him to invest in a raffle for a silver pitcher. Such liberality is a delusion and a snare, and is a violation of the command, "*Thou shalt not covet thy neighbor's house, . . nor any thing that is thy neighbor's.*"

CHAPTER XIX.

"*My son, keep thy father's commandment, and forsake not the law of thy mother.*"

FILIAL OBEDIENCE.

The helplessness of childhood.—Most animals soon arrive at maturity, and are able to leave their parents to seek food and shelter, but not so the child. Long years must elapse before it can procure its own food and clothing. The young robin needs the shelter and protection of the mater-

---

What shall be said of raffles, grab-bags, etc.? In a lottery at a church festival, is it the church's welfare, or the hope of a prize, that induces people generally to purchase tickets? Is it covetousness? Is it right for a church to stimulate the covetousness of any person? Is it right for persons to permit themselves to be so tempted? Is it liberality that prompts the greater number of people to buy chances in a lottery, or the hope of great gain? Is it right? Repeat the text.

What is the subject of Chapter XIX? What is the text? What difference is there between the young of animals and of man?

nal nest only until its wings are fully fledged and strengthened for flight. Then it can take care of itself, for it possesses that faculty called instinct, which enables it to procure food, build its nest, and rear other broods. To man God has given a very limited instinct, but He has imparted mind and conscience instead that can be developed only by long discipline.

Childhood is a protracted pupilage, and its education must come largely from the father's commandment and the mother's law. Patience, gentleness, kindness, watchfulness, days of care and nights of anxiety, are spent in ministering to the comfort and supplying the wants of the infant. Parental love spares neither labor of body nor weariness of mind in securing the happiness of the child. What, then, is due from the child to the parent? It is written, "*Honor thy father and thy mother, that it may be well with thee, and thou mayest live long on the earth.*" This is God's command and the promise attending it.

"Honor thy father and mother."—The direction to honor implies that we shall respect, reverence, love, and obey our parents in all lawful requests. Children are under an obligation of gratitude, aside from that of authority, to render these returns for all the years of care devoted to them. This honor must be exhibited by kindness of manner, gentleness of behavior, a pleasant voice, an agreeable countenance, and a cheerful and willing yielding of the will of the child to the desire of the parent.

Filial obedience.—There are certain rules of action prescribed by parents for the government of every well-ordered home. Children are under a moral and legal obligation to

---

What enables the animal to take care of itself very soon? Has man instinct? What has he that animals have not? Why does mankind need so long a childhood? What are necessary to the support and education of the child? What is due from the child to the parent? Why? What is the promise of the moral law? What is meant by honor? How is this honor to be made manifest? Should the parent yield to the child, or the child to the parent? Must every home have its laws? Why?

observe these rules as long as they remain inmates of the family, or until they arrive at the legal age of manhood. Their will should conform to the matured reason and experience of the parents, for it is a fair presumption that parents are wiser than children, and better able to judge of what is right. Submission to their authority, and compliance with household and other duties, should be rendered cheerfully and promptly. When children will not yield kindly and gracefully to the rules of action prescribed by the parents; when gentleness, reason, and persuasion fail to secure obedience; when love loses its power to secure compliance with parental entreaty, a resort must be had to some penalties to enforce the law.

A compulsory acknowledgment of parental authority, enforced by harshness and severity, is base and slavish; and yet the moral law prescribes extreme punishments to overcome the perverseness and stubbornness of a willful child. It is written, "*A whip for the horse, a bridle for the ass, and a rod for the fool's back.*" "*The way of a fool is right in his own eyes: but he that hearkeneth unto counsel is wise.*" "*Foolishness is bound in the heart of a child; but the rod of correction shall drive it far from him.*" "*He that spareth his rod hateth his son; but he that loveth him chasteneth him betimes.*"

Happy is the child that is early impressed with the necessity of conformity to law, even if it be done by the use of the rod; but happier he who learns to obey from motives of right and duty. Parents have no right to ask their children to do any thing in violation of God's law. If they do, the child is not morally bound to render obedience, for "*We ought to obey God rather than man.*" A child

---

Who shall prescribe the laws of home? Why? What is the duty of children? Why? When children do not yield to gentle and persuasive influences, what is necessary to secure obedience? Have children a right to disobey? Ought home laws to be enforced? Why? How? What is written in the moral law concerning stubborn children? Repeat the texts. What is meant in the text by the fool? Have parents a right to require any thing of their children contrary to the moral law? What says the moral law?

may be compelled to do wrong, but it should protest against every act which will cause a violation of the right.

Assistance to parents.—As parents provide for the wants of their children during their years of weakness and helplessness, it is but a fair return for this kindness that the children, when they arrive at a suitable age, should afford their parents such assistance as may be necessary. Should accident or infirmity render the parents incapable of further labor, it is the duty of the children to preserve them from want, to alleviate their sufferings, and to add, in every possible manner, to their comfort and happiness.

"Home, sweet home."—A beautiful poem has been written by Mrs. V. S. French, entitled, "Mother, Home, and Heaven." The delightful idea it conveys is, that the mother is the ministering angel of home, and the home—as it should be—is the nearest earthly resemblance to heaven. It is sad that all homes are not happy, but the reason they are not is often seen in the restlessness, impatience, irritability, and uncharitableness of its members. Children are frequently negligent in duty, careless of obligations, and unreliable in promises. Is it a wonder that homes in which perpetual discord occurs are unhappy? Every well-ordered family must have its rules of government, which should be observed by each of its members, or troubles surely follow.

How important, then, that the young should learn that easy acquiescence which renders them able and willing, habitually, to prefer the wishes and comforts of their parents and the happiness of their homes, to their own convenience and selfishness. Many children are in constant opposition

---

Are children under obligation to assist their parents? Why? How long? Why are homes so often unhappy? What may children do to make their homes pleasant? Are they in duty bound to do all in their power to make home happy? Do negligence and carelessness add to the pleasure of home? Tell some other causes that make home trouble. How should they be avoided? Is this subject important? Why?

to parental influence and government, thereby making themselves unhappy and the family miserable. They are not always responsible for the wretchedness of their homes, and yet they may do much by the exercise of care and kindness, prudence and forbearance, love and charity, to make them better. It is worth the effort of any one to attempt such a reformation where it is needed.

Step-parents.—It sometimes happens that the father or mother is removed by death, and that for various reasons a step-father or step-mother is brought in to take the place of the one that is lost. In a special manner is it true in such peculiar and trying circumstances that, "*A wise son maketh a glad father, but a foolish son is the heaviness of his mother.*" Obedience and honor to the living parent require that the child shall give a kind welcome to the new member of the family.

The sacrifice in such a case may be very great on both sides, but mutual forbearance, sympathy, and charity should be exercised to their fullest extent. Selfishness would induce a wise child to cling to its home in such circumstances, but love and honor would prompt it still more in the same course. The moral law requires the frequent sacrifice of our personal feelings for the good of others, and there is no way in which greater good may sometimes be accomplished than in thus preserving the peace, comfort, and happiness of a family.

Who are step-parents? Why does unhappiness often occur when step-parents come into the family? Can it be prevented? How? What is the text? What is due the living parent under such circumstances? Is it well to break up the happiness of a home because we can not be suited? What is our duty? How do tale-bearers and flatterers interfere under such circumstances? Do such people give advice that tends to preserve peace and promote patience and charity?

CHAPTER XX.

"*The thoughts of the diligent tend only to plenteousness, but of every one that is hasty, only to want.*"

BUSINESS.

The moral law enjoins upon every one to put his faculties to some profitable use, which shall be helpful to himself or to his neighbor. This use must depend upon the peculiarities of the individual and the circumstances which surround him. There is a work for every man and woman who is desirous of contributing to the aggregate of the world's comfort and happiness. This work requires a special preparation, more or less difficult as it demands more or less skill or experience in its prosecution. It is often a question among young people, what they shall aim to be or to do when they enter upon the stage of active life. The subject is a serious one, and demands no little consideration.

Labor conquers.—The first grand requisite to success in any business is a willingness to work. It is written, "*The soul of the sluggard desireth, and hath nothing; but the soul of the diligent shall be made fat.*" It is not seldom that persons engage in building grand air-castles, desiring great successes, and dreaming of their accomplishment, who lack the energy, the determination, the courage, or the training, to insure their prosperous issue. Men may plan, and contrive, and speculate upon great achievements, but

---

What is the subject of Chapter XX? Repeat the text. Who are meant by the diligent? Explain the meaning of the text. What does the moral law enjoin? What kind of work should each one perform? What is necessary to make a good workman? What is the first requisite of success in business? What is written of the sluggard?

unless they are willing to put forth all their energies, and work for results, their schemes will amount to nothing. For the instruction of such it is written, "*Go to the ant, thou sluggard; consider her ways and be wise: which having no guide, overseer, or ruler, provideth her meat in the summer, and gathereth her food in the harvest.*"

Instinct guides the ant, but reason and moral responsibility must govern the man. There is a saying that, "It is easy for a dead fish to float down stream, but it requires a live fish to swim up." The dead fish of society float listlessly and uselessly upon the current of life, but it requires strong, active, thinking, working men and women to achieve the world's conquests.

Preparation for business.—When the shepherd David asked permission to fight the champion of Philistea, "*Saul armed David with his armor, and he put a helmet of brass upon his head; also he armed him with a coat of mail. And David girded his sword upon his armor and he essayed to go; for he had not proved it. And David said unto Saul, I can not go with these; for I have not proved them. And David put them off him. And he took his staff in his hand, and chose him five smooth stones out of the brook, and put them in a shepherd's bag which he had, even in a scrip; and his sling was in his hand.*"

It is stated that between eighty and ninety per cent of those who engage in mercantile pursuits are not successful. If this be true, or even an approximation to the truth, there must be a cause for such wide-spread failure. It is safe to say that one prominent reason for this shortcoming in business, is that so many young men vainly imagine that they can go into the battle of life clad in armor like Saul's, which

---

What lesson does the ant teach? What idea does the saying concerning the "dead fish" convey? Who are the live fish in society? Give the story of David in connection with the quotation. What idea is conveyed by the allusion to David? What per cent of merchants fail? What is one probable reason of such failure?

is not fitted to them, and which they have not proved; in other words, they expect to do business without having learned thoroughly how it is done, and the consequence is loss of property, loss of character, and oftentimes mortification and shame. There is a great tendency to leave the farm and the workshop to enter the counting-house and the store, because of an erroneous idea that merchandising does not involve hard work. All successful enterprise, in any department of business, demands a thorough understanding of its requirements, and unremitting labor in its prosecution.

"Stephen Girard and his clerk."—By learning a trade, a boy has one safeguard against vicious habits. Besides this, it offers an honorable support should the more ambitious schemes of life fail. Old Stephen Girard had a long head, and he well knew the rugged paths that make rugged men, as the following shows: He had a favorite clerk, and he always said he "intended to do well by Ben Lippincott." So, when Ben got to be twenty-one, he expected to hear Mr. Girard say something of his future prospects, and, perhaps, lend a helping hand in starting him in the world. But the shrewd old man carefully avoided the subject. Ben mustered courage:

"I suppose I now am free, sir," said he, "and I thought I would say something to you as to my course. What do you think I had better do?"

"Yes, I know you are," said the millionaire, "and my advice is that you go and learn the cooper's trade."

The young man was astonished, but recovering himself, he said that, "If Mr. Girard was in earnest, he would do so."

"I am in earnest." And Ben forthwith sought the best cooper in Spring Garden, became an apprentice, and in due time could make as good a barrel as the best.

He announced to Old Stephen that he had graduated, and was ready to set up in business. The old man seemed grati-

---

What is the result of such failure? What two things are necessary to success in any business? Give the story of Girard and his clerk.

fied, and forthwith ordered three of the best barrels he could turn out. Ben did his best, and wheeled them up to his counting-room. Mr. Girard pronounced them good, and demanded the price.

"One dollar," said Ben, "is as cheap as I can afford them."

"Cheap enough. Make out your bill."

The bill was made out, and Old Stephen settled it with a check for twenty thousand dollars, which he accompanied with this little moral to the story: "There, take that, and invest it in the best possible manner. If you are unfortunate, and lose it, you have a good trade to fall back upon, which will afford you a good living." Stephen Girard well knew the risks attending mercantile life, and wisely advised a trade, in which there is no failure.

Attention.—Another of the chief causes of failure in business of all kinds is the want of attention to its details. Habits of close observation are absolutely indispensable to any intelligent success in life. If a man pursue his daily work in a formal manner, without apparent interest or concern; if he go through his duties as a mere machine, or like a horse in a tread-mill, without using his faculties for improvement, he will always remain a drudge. A man must not only be willing to work to insure success, but he must work with all his might, and heart, and strength. He must observe closely, must think wisely, and reason carefully.

Charles Dickens.—In an address delivered at Birmingham, England, Mr. Charles Dickens, the eminent author, announced what he considered the secret of his great success in a single word: ATTENTION! With him it became

Why did the old man desire the boy to learn a trade? Why is it safer to have a trade than to be a merchant? What is another reason of failure in business? Why is attention necessary to success in any business? How may attention be acquired? May it become a habit? Does success in school require attention? Why? How must a man work to insure success? Who was Charles Dickens? To what did he attribute his success?

an intellectual habit. He declared it to be, "The one serviceable, safe, certain, remunerative, attainable quality in every study and every pursuit." "My own invention or imagination, such as it is, I can most truthfully assure you, would never have served me as it has, but for the habit of commonplace, humble, patient, daily, toiling, drudging attention." Such evidence is certainly very valuable, as it records the experience of one whom the world has esteemed as a genius of a very high order. Carelessness, indifference, and neglect are vices for which the most brilliant talents can offer no compensation.

"Stoop as you go through."—Benjamin Franklin, the son of a tallow-chandler, the printer's apprentice, the printer, the philosopher, and the patriot, wrote the following incident of his visit, when a young man, to the celebrated Cotton Mather, a clergyman of New England. The letter was written to Cotton Mather's son:

"The last time I saw your father was in the beginning of 1724, when I visited him after my first trip to Pennsylvania. He received me in the library, and, on my taking leave, showed me a shorter way out of the house through a narrow passage, which was crossed by a beam overhead. We were still talking as I withdrew, he accompanying me behind, and I turning partly toward him, when he said, hastily, 'STOOP! STOOP!' I did not understand him till I felt my head hit against the beam. He was a man that never missed any occasion of giving instruction, and upon this he said: 'You are young, and have the world before you. STOOP as you go through it, and you will miss many hard thumps.' This advice, thus beat into my head, has frequently been of use to me; and I often think of it when I see pride mortified and misfortunes brought upon people by carrying their heads too high."

What is meant by a genius? Who was Ben Franklin? State the incident he relates. What is the moral of the incident? Shall we stoop to dishonorable actions? Why? How was this advice valuable to Franklin?

False pride.—When Ben Franklin was a young man, no false pride, or fear of work, or care for ridicule, stood in the way of his success. "He not only was industrious, but took care to let his neighbors see that he was so. He dressed plainly, attended no places of public diversion, never went fishing or shooting, and, to show that he was not above his business, sometimes brought home through the streets, in a wheelbarrow, the paper he had purchased for his printing office. His credit constantly improved, and his business constantly increased."

Franklin never lost his dignity or self-respect, even when trundling a wheelbarrow; but in him there was a literal fulfillment of the proverb, "*Seest thou a man diligent in his business, he shall stand before kings—he shall not stand before mean men.*" If the first part of the proverb is rarely true to Americans, the latter part may be verified by every day's experience.

William Cobbett was an eminent Englishman, who exerted a great influence in his country and our own. His early life was distinguished by poverty and hardship, and his success was due to a laudable ambition, supported by good sense and a will to work. Speaking of the difficulties under which he labored, he says: "I learned grammar when I was a private soldier on the pay of sixpence a day. The edge of my berth, or that of my guard bed, was my seat to study in; my knapsack was my book-case, and a bit of board lying in my lap was my writing-table. I had no money to purchase candles or oil; in winter time it was rarely that I could get any light but that of the fire, and only my turn even at that. To buy a pen, or a sheet of paper, I was compelled to forego some portion of food, though in a state of half-starvation.

What is meant by false pride? State what Franklin's habits were as given above? What was the result of this attention and self-denial? Did he stand before kings? What is the meaning of the proverb? What is said of William Cobbett? Give his experience as a student.

"I had no moment that I could call my own, and I had to read and write amid the talking, laughing, singing, whistling, and bawling of at least half a score of the most thoughtless of men; and that, too, in hours of freedom from all control. And I say, if I, under circumstances like these, could encounter and overcome the task, can there be, in the whole world, a youth who can find an excuse for the non-performance?"

It is said of him that, "Early rising, temperate living, concentrated industry, and health preserved by much out-door exercise, enabled him to get through a larger quantity of brain work than any other author of his day, not excepting Walter Scott."

CHAPTER XXI.

"*Exhort servants to be obedient unto their own masters, and to please them well in all things, not answering again; not purloining, but showing all good fidelity.*"

FIDELITY

Independence.—The most independent condition of man is exhibited by the savage, who, having no artificial wants, and needing only the necessaries of life, can for the most part supply them by his own strength and skill. There is no such thing as being independent of our neighbors among

---

If Cobbett was a successful student under these circumstances, what may any plucky boy do? What was the effect of such study? Who was Walter Scott? What enabled Cobbett to do so much work?

What is the text to Chapter XXI? Why is the savage the least dependent of men?

civilized men. As men increase in civilization their wants increase, and these must be supplied by a division of labor. Few men are masters of more than one trade, and if they were they could not supply their wants, unless they did it by an interchange of products. The shoe-maker can supply himself and the community with shoes, but he is dependent upon the tanner and many others besides for the materials to prosecute his trade. He must have tools, twine, wax, paste, and pegs; and, in addition to these, he must be furnished with food, clothing, house, and home comforts. In fact, as his wants increase he becomes dependent upon the labor and skill of others.

Nor is the man of great wealth independent of society. His money may secure him many gratifications of which others are deprived, and yet the mere care of wealth requires the assistance of others. The possession of large means does not relieve the possessor of labor or anxiety. Besides, there is a danger of loss, as it is written, "*For riches certainly make themselves wings; they fly away as an eagle toward heaven.*" Injudicious investments, fire, storm, and the waste of war, have destroyed many a grand fortune, and left its former possessor in abject, helpless, pitiful want, without the knowledge, ability, or skill to do any thing to relieve his necessities.

Nothing is so distressing to an honorable mind as the idea of utter and hopeless dependence. To avoid the danger of such a pitiable condition, every youth should discuss the question with himself and his friends, as to what calling he is best adapted. It is a matter of great importance how the talents of each one shall be most suitably employed to secure an elevated position in the society of the good, and to render the best service to himself and others. Having selected a business, trade, or profession, the next inquiry is,

Why does civilization render men dependent? How are the various wants of civilized men supplied? For what is the shoe-maker dependent upon others? Why? In what sense may men of wealth be said to be independent? Are they really so? What is written about the uncertainty of riches? What causes may destroy wealth? What reliance ought every one to possess?

what shall be done as a proper preparation for the business that has been chosen?

Apprenticeship.—Any trade, business, or profession that does not require time and patience, labor and skill, in its acquisition, is not worth the learning. There is no royal road to knowledge. He who would be independent, as far as a safe and profitable occupation will secure independence, must set himself to work resolutely to learn his trade. He must expect difficulties, hindrances, annoyances, and learn to overcome them. In a great majority of occupations an apprenticeship is desirable. Such a relation is one of mutual interest and dependence, securing the best attention and kindest care from the master, and the greatest opportunity for improvement by the apprentice. But there seems to be a great aversion to this method of learning the mysteries of any business, and it arises from several causes.

Wrong impressions.—One reason why young men do not desire apprenticeship is the erroneous idea that by engaging to serve a master for a term of years, in order to learn a trade, there is an unmanly surrender of personal freedom. This feeling comes from an indisposition to submit to any restraint—from instability of character, which opposes the requirements of regular, systematic daily work. It indicates a desire to escape the routine of labor prescribed by a master, and to indulge at will in gayety, frivolity, and company, without supervision or control. The text at the head of this chapter prescribes the way in which the servant should be obedient to his master—endeavoring to please in all things, not idle and impertinent, not indifferent and careless, not wasting nor purloining, but showing all good fidelity.

Having selected an occupation, what is the next step? What is the next topic? What is meant by no royal road? How may one secure a comparative independence? What must every one expect in learning a business? Why is apprenticeship desirable? Why is there an aversion to becoming an apprentice? Is there any loss of manliness in this relation? What other causes lead young persons to dislike apprenticeship? How should the apprentice serve his master?

The moral law requires corresponding duties on the part of masters, as it is written, "*Masters, give unto your servants that which is just and equal.*" This freedom and equality does not mean a freedom that permits the apprentice to determine the time and manner of his service. Young people are apt to be jealous, suspicious, and fault-finding, and for such it is written, "*Servants, be subject to your masters with all fear; not only to the good and gentle, but also to the froward.*" Even if the master does not make himself agreeable and pleasant, it is the duty of the servant to obey promptly, kindly, gently, patiently, and charitably. The moral law requires the exercise of all these virtues.

Obeying orders.—An English farmer was one day at work in his fields, when he saw a party of huntsmen riding about his farm. He had one field that he was specially anxious they should not ride over, as the crop was in a condition to be badly injured by the tramp of the dogs. So he dispatched one of his hands to this field, telling him to shut the gate, and then to keep watch over it, and on no account to suffer it to be opened.

The boy went as he was bidden, but was scarcely at his post before the huntsmen came up, peremptorily ordering the gate to be opened. This the boy declined to do, stating the orders he had received, and his determination not to disobey them. Threats and bribes were offered alike in vain. One after another came forward as spokesman, but all with the same result; the boy remained immovable in his determination not to open the gate. After awhile, one of noble presence advanced, and said, in commanding tones:

"My boy, you do not know me. I am the Duke of Wellington, one not accustomed to be disobeyed, and I command you to open that gate, that I and my friends may pass through."

What is required of masters? What is the meaning of just and equal? What is written concerning service to disagreeable masters? What virtues does the moral law require in every one? Narrate the anecdote, "Obeying Orders."

The boy lifted his cap, and stood uncovered before the man whom all England delighted to honor, then answered, firmly:

"I am sure the Duke of Wellington would not wish me to disobey orders. I must keep this gate shut, nor suffer any one to pass but with my master's express permission."

Greatly pleased, the sturdy old warrior lifted his own hat, and said: "I honor the man or boy who can neither be bribed nor frightened into doing wrong. With an army of such soldiers I could conquer, not only the French, but the world." And, handing the boy a glittering sovereign, the old duke put spurs to his horse and galloped away, while the boy ran off to his work, shouting, at the top of his voice, "Hurrah! Hurrah! I've done what Napoleon could not do—I've kept out the Duke of Wellington!"

Unskilled labor.—Another reason why there are comparatively so few apprentices at the present time, is because the demand for help in the various departments of unskilled labor is so great that young persons can get employment without special preparation. No young man can afford to waste his time, except in a most pressing emergency, in doing any work or business in which he is not learning something for future use. A laudable ambition should spur every one to prepare himself for a life of usefulness and honor. If one is an errand boy in a store to help his mother make a living, or to earn money to enable himself to go to school, he acts wisely; but if he does such work in preference to that which is more instructive, he makes a great mistake. There is only one boyhood in a man's life,

---

What is worthy of imitation in this boy? Why should the boy not obey the duke? Why did he lift his cap? Who was the Duke of Wellington? Why did all England honor him? Why did the boy expect that the duke would not wish him to disobey orders? Why was the duke greatly pleased? What did he mean by his reply to the boy? Why did he give him the coin? Why had the boy a right to be pleased? What is the next topic? What is the reason assigned for few apprentices at the present time? State the argument. What kind of business should a boy endeavor to get?

and if the life is a success, it will be largely because the boyhood is spent in a wise and diligent preparation for life's duties.

Haste makes waste.—A third reason why there are so few apprentices, is that there are so many who desire to go into the battle of life without properly fitting and proving their armor. It is said that skilled workmen are becoming very scarce in some departments of labor in the United States, and that the best artisans are now imported from other countries to take charge of our shops. The reason assigned is that our young men become impatient to practice their trades, and secure their profits, before they have become skillful craftsmen. In every trade and profession men may be counted by the hundreds who are not, and never will be, proficient. Had they patiently learned the mysteries of their craft by years of discipline, under competent masters, their success would have been certain.

Franklin's indentures.—The following is the indenture by which Ben Franklin was apprenticed to his brother. It will be seen that it enjoins nothing more than faithfulness, kindness, and attention to duty, the very traits that have been discussed in this book as the distinguishing characteristics of a young gentleman:

"This INDENTURE witnesseth, that Benjamin Franklin, son of Josiah Franklin, and Abiah, his wife, of Boston, in the colony of Massachusetts Bay, with the consent of his parents, doth put himself apprentice to his brother, James Franklin, printer, to learn his art, and with him, after the manner of an apprentice, to serve from the — day of ——, in the year of our Lord, 1718, until he shall have fully completed the twenty-first year of his age. During which term the said apprentice his master faithfully shall or will serve, his secrets keep, his lawful commandments everywhere gladly do. He

---

What is the third reason? Why are skilled workmen becoming scarce? Is a boy wise who only half learns his business? What is necessary to success in life? To whom was Ben Franklin apprenticed? What are the virtues enjoined by the indenture? Is this more than a good boy should do to his father or master?

shall do no damage to his said master, nor see it to be done of others; but to his power shall let, or forthwith give notice to his said master of the same.

"The goods of his said master he shall not waste, nor the same without license of him to any give or lend. Hurt to his master he shall not do, cause, nor procure to be done. He shall neither buy nor sell without his master's license. Taverns, inns, or ale-houses, he shall not haunt. At cards, dice, tables, or any other unlawful game, he shall not play. Matrimony he shall not contract. Nor from the service of his said master day nor night absent himself; but in all things as an honest and faithful apprentice shall and will demean and behave himself toward his said master and all his during the said term.

"And the said James Franklin, the master, for and in consideration of the sum of ten pounds of lawful British money, to him in hand paid by the said Josiah Franklin, the father, the receipt of which is hereby acknowledged, the said apprentice in the art of a printer, which he now useth, shall teach and instruct, or cause to be taught and instructed, the best way and manner that he can, finding and allowing unto the said apprentice meat, drink, washing, lodging, and all other necessaries during the said term. And for the true performance of all and every the covenants and agreements aforesaid, either of the said parties bindeth himself unto the other firmly by these presents.

"In witness whereof, the parties aforesaid to these indentures interchangeably have set their hands and seals, this — day of ——, in the fifth year of our sovereign lord, George the First, by the grace of God of Great Britain, France, and Ireland king, defender of the faith, and in the year of our Lord 1718."

Illustrious American apprentices.—The following are a few of a long list of names that might be given of eminent Americans who commenced life as apprentice boys:

Roger Sherman, of revolutionary memory, was bound to a shoe-maker, served out his term, and worked on the bench till he was twenty-two years of age.

Stephen A. Douglas, United States senator from Illinois, was apprenticed to a cabinet maker, and served diligently,

---

State the requirements made of the apprentice. Are these requirements right or wrong? State the requirements made of the master. Is there any advantage in such a contract? What are the disadvantages, if any? Tell all you can of Roger Sherman. Stephen A. Douglas.

till, upon his health failing, he was released from his engagement.

Nathaniel Bowditch was bred to his father's trade, as a cooper, and was afterward bound to a ship-chandler. He became eminent as a mathematician and astronomer.

Amos Lawrence was apprenticed to a merchant, and by his diligence, faithfulness, and integrity acquired an immense fortune. He was one of the best, as well as the wealthiest, men of New England.

Andrew Johnson was indentured at ten years of age to the tailor's trade, and served his term of seven years. During his apprenticeship, he learned to read, and, after he was married, his wife taught him to write and cipher. He became President of the United States.

Elihu Burritt, the eminent scholar and friend of peace, is known as the "Learned Blacksmith."

Governor Jewell, of Connecticut, was a tanner; Governor Claflin, of Massachusetts, was a shoe-maker; Vice-President Wilson, of Massachusetts, was a shoe-maker; President Grant was a tanner; and Vice-President Colfax was a printer.

He is truly the independent man who has a trade, and is neither ashamed nor unwilling to follow it. All honest work is honorable.

The student would do well to read the lives of these and other eminent men, who learned to work when young. Tell what you have learned of Nathaniel Bowditch; Amos Lawrence; Andrew Johnson; Elihu Burritt; Governor Jewell; Governor Claflin; Senator Wilson; General Grant; Schuyler Colfax. Who comes the nearest being an independent man? Why?

CHAPTER XXII.

"*Rejoice, O young man, in thy youth; and let thy heart cheer thee in the days of thy youth, and walk in the ways of thine heart, and in the sight of thine eyes: but know thou, that for all these things God will bring thee into judgment.*"

AMUSEMENTS.

What are the amusements in which the young may properly indulge? This is a question involving much discussion among those who wish to advance the interests and pleasures of youth, as well as among the young people themselves. Assuming, without any argument, that some amusements are necessary and proper, the only question is to determine the kinds which may be enjoyed without the danger of moral or physical injury to the young, or of interference with the rights and feelings of the old. Were we inclined to discuss the merits or demerits of all the games, plays, and methods of diversion in which youth are accustomed to indulge, it would far exceed the limits proposed for this book, The most, and probably the best, that can be done, is to ascertain some general principles, which will apply to every case of amusement, determining its propriety or impropriety, or whether its exercise be right or wrong. When these principles are clearly understood, their

---

What is the subject of Chapter XXII? Repeat the text. Does the moral law prohibit amusements? Why do amusements require caution? What judgment is expected of those who do wrong? Are the ways of the heart always right? Why are not all the games and plays discussed? What is proposed?

application will become a conscientious duty, as every one is morally bound to do what he believes to be right.

PRINCIPLES RELATING TO AMUSEMENTS.

Good or bad amusements.—In determining the propriety of indulging in any kind of amusement, the first question which should occupy the mind is, is this right or wrong in itself? In some cases, the answer can be easily and promptly given, and there can be no doubt of its correctness. If conscience says it is wrong, there should be no hesitation in refusing the indulgence, however fascinating it may seem. We can not afford to violate the dictates of conscience for the sake of any momentary pleasure.

Amusements of doubtful propriety.—Our observation and experience may not enable us to determine whether a certain recreation is injurious, and if we have a doubt, it will be safe to learn the estimation in which it is held by good people, in whose judgment we have confidence. If its history, its associations, and its influences are approved by those who have had the opportunity to know whether it be right or wrong, it will certainly be a strong argument in its favor. We can not afford to disregard the advice of those who are wiser and more experienced than ourselves, nor can we run the risk of losing their respect for the sake of any paltry gratification. We have no right to offend our friends by doing what they consider wrong, and their judgment should lead us to have great doubts as to the correctness of our own views. A decent respect for the opinions of those who love us, demands that we conform to their conscientious views in questions of this character.

Is it the duty of every one to be guided by principle or feeling? Why? If one knows what is right, what is his duty? What is the first principle that should claim our attention? If conscience says a certain pleasure is wrong, what shall we do? If we have a doubt, what shall we do? Who have the best opportunity of judging of such matters, the young or the old? Why? Should we respect the judgment of our elders in selecting our amusements?

Anecdote.—A party of gentlemen were traveling from Pittsburgh to Wheeling, by the Ohio river. In order to relieve the tiresome monotony of the trip, it was proposed that they should indulge in a game of cards. One of the party politely declined to engage in that kind of sport. On being asked the reason for his unwillingness to participate in the play, he replied: "I have always endeavored to preserve an unblemished reputation, and I can not afford to be classed in the mind of any person as directly or indirectly associated with gamblers or gaming. There are many good people, whose esteem I should regret to lose, who would hear with much pain that I had engaged in playing cards on a steamboat; therefore, you will excuse me for not running the risk of doing myself and others a moral injury."

The relations of amusement to business.—Every youth has, or ought to have, some employment, whether of study or business, which will help to fit him for a life of usefulness and honor. When any particular kind of amusement becomes so engrossing as to interfere with the duties belonging to the school, the family, or the employer, it should cease at once. If the love of pleasure is so absorbing as to interfere with the demands and obligations of business, it is time to stop for a little reflection. When recreation is pursued as a vocation; when mere fun is followed as an occupation, to the exclusion of everything else, nothing but sorrow and mortification can be the result. It is written in the moral law, "*He that loveth pleasure shall be a poor man.*" When the desire for diversion is so controlling that duties are neglected, business is forgotten, and the mind is led from the consideration of serious affairs, the remedy can only be found in the complete and conscientious renunciation of the fascinating folly.

Why should every youth have some employment or business? Can the mind be intensely occupied by business and pleasure at the same time? Which is likely to suffer? What is written of him who has an intense love of pleasure? When amusement and business clash, which should yield? Why?

The illustration of this absorbing attachment to play was witnessed in every city and town in the land where the game of base-ball was introduced. Young men, in many instances, seem to be infatuated to such an extent as to unfit them entirely for every useful employment. Such devotion is surely worthy of some better cause. When amusement ceases to be a recreation, and becomes a business, it should be abandoned.

Amusement as it affects habits.—In the selection of any method of enjoyment, it would also be well to inquire whether it may not lead to the acquisition of injurious habits. It is not safe for us to follow the road that has led others to ruin. If persons have been injured by such an indulgence, what reasons have we to suppose that we shall be exempt from the same danger? Are we stronger, wiser, or better than they? Self-love may induce us to set a very high estimate upon our powers of self-control; but a superior wisdom has said, "*Lead us not into temptation.*" We have no right to put ourselves in danger of acquiring injurious habits, for the gratification of our love of pleasure.

The amusements of bad company.—It is a matter of the first importance to inquire whether the enjoyment of any particular form of recreation will lead us into disreputable company. Is its exercise confined to the society of the good, or may we be thrown by its pursuit among those of questionable character? No one can afford to sacrifice his self-respect by associating with the vicious or vulgar for the sake of any temporary gratification.

Amusement in improper places.—Does the proposed

What is your observation of those who are intensely absorbed in pleasure? What prospect have they in life, if they continue so? Why? Is it wise for us to go in the way of temptation? Is the pleasure worth the risk? Are we likely to escape the snares into which others have fallen? Why? What is good society? What is our duty in reference to our company? Why? Dare we go into any improper place for amusement.

pleasure lead us into any place of questionable propriety, in which we would not be willing to be seen by those whose good opinion we value? If so, we should abstain from the amusement by shunning such resorts.

The influence of our amusement.—Our methods of enjoyment may be altogether harmless to us, but our neighbor, who has not much self-control, may be in danger of serious injury from following our example. Ought we not to be solicitous for his welfare, and have we a right to do anything which may serve as a pattern to lead him to ruin? Is it not our duty to abstain from any gratification, if we discover that our conduct is the means of tempting a weaker brother to do wrong? Have we a right to persist in following a course of conduct which induces him to violate the commands of parents, guardians, and teachers? The gratification of our own selfish purposes can not afford us a sufficient compensation for the injury that our brother may receive from making us his model.

The expense of amusements.—Some kinds of amusement are expensive, involving a considerable outlay of time and money. If the indulgence of our taste requires the expenditure of money, it may be a serious question whether we can afford it. When injury, inconvenience, or annoyance shall arise to ourselves or our friends, on account of our wasteful pleasures, we are committing a serious injury by persisting in such a course.

Sometimes young people have not the moral courage to say, frankly, "I can not afford such indulgence;" and will permit themselves to be drawn into expenses which they are really not able to bear. When we consent to run in debt

---

Should we lead others into temptation? Suppose certain pleasures do not hurt us, but do hurt our friends. what should we do? Can we take the responsibility of leading our neighbor astray? What is our duty in regard to expensive pleasures? Is there any test of moral courage in this? What should every young man do in reference to this subject? Is there any disgrace in being poor? Why not say so and avoid trouble?

for anything that is unnecessary, from a foolish fear that we shall be considered mean or parsimonious, we are preparing the way for much future annoyance and discomfort. It would be better to say, with manly independence, "I have no money, and can not incur a debt for amusements," and thus save the mortification which always follows the unavailing attempt to conceal our poverty.

Amusements contrary to law.—We have no right to indulge in anv pleasure that injures, endangers, or incommodes the person or property of our neighbors. The civil, as well as the moral law prescribes to us rules of conduct in reference to amusements, that are often very thoughtlessly and sometimes intentionally violated. Thus, there are some plays and pastimes particularly unsuited to certain times and places, because they are liable to cause serious injuries. The rolling of the hoop on the crowded sidewalk; the explosion of fire-crackers or flying of kites in the streets of a town or city; the shooting with the bow and arrow among the children in a school-house yard; or the racing of horses in a crowded thoroughfare, are illustrations of dangerous fun. Such amusements are not wrong, provided they are enjoyed at proper times and under suitable circumstances; but when they are persisted in at the risk of great damage to persons and property, they indicate an inexcusable selfishness.

The debatable ground.—From the above principles, we may determine whether the pleasures in which we indulge, or wish to indulge, are beneficial or injurious. Duty to ourselves, and regard for our neighbors, demand that we shall examine critically whether the course of amusement is really the best adapted to our happiness. If there is the least possible doubt as to its propriety, we should not con-

---

Name some dangerous amusements. Why are they so? What is our duty in reference to such? Have we a right to endanger the rights of others? Why? When and where should such amusements as have been named be enjoyed? If there is a doubt in our mind as to the propriety of any game, play, or recreation, what should we do?

test the point with our conscience, but immediately obey its dictates. There are, and often will be, honest differences of opinion in regard to kinds and places of amusement; but it is our duty to side with those whose character demands our admiration, and whose opinions, matured by observation and experience, are worthy of our respect and confidence. A few brief questions should determine whether we may engage in any specified game, play, or exercise for amusement. These, briefly stated, are as follows:

1. Is it right?
2. Do good people generally approve of it?
3. Will it interfere with school or business?
4. May it be productive of bad habits?
5. Will its enjoyment lead into doubtful company?
6. Will it lead into places of questionable propriety?
7. Will my example influence others injuriously?
8. Can I afford the cost in time and money?
9. Will my pleasure affect the rights of any one in person or property?

If, upon reflection, we conclude to indulge in the proposed pastime, let it be with an unquestioning conscience, based upon a clear conviction that the action is right. If, on the other hand, we think the indulgence may be wrong, let the doubt control us, and let us deny ourselves the gratification.

Honest reasons for refusal.—When questioned as to our motives for declining a proposed amusement, there should be no evasion or quibbling, but a resolute, courageous answer, the expression of the truth. He who endeavors to secure friendship and admiration by appearing to agree with every body, will soon lose the respect of those whose good

Name these principles in the order given. If these tests are correct, what should be done with any amusement to which they are applied? Should our feelings or our conscience rule us in this indulgence? If questioned about our refusal to play or perform, what should be our answer? What is meant by moral courage? Who is the really brave person? If we shirk or quibble, do we command respect? Can you afford to be laughed at? If you are laughed at, what is the character of those who do it?

opinion is worth having. Be manly, honest, and truthful. When convictions of duty are forced upon us, let us acknowledge their influence; let us stand up for what we think is right. Such courage will command the admiration of the good, because it is based upon a sense of duty.

CHAPTER XXIII.

"*He that hath pity upon the poor lendeth unto the Lord, and that which he hath given, will He pay him again.*"

THE POOR.

Pity is a divine attribute, which is manifested among men by sympathizing with the sorrows, lessening the burdens, and alleviating the distresses of the poor, the needy, and the unfortunate. The exhibitions of this virtue are as various as the wants and conditions of human society. There are objects of beneficence everywhere, as it is written, "*For ye have the poor with you always, and whensoever ye will, ye may do them good.*" We can not fail to recognize the obligation to do good, but there are questions of great practical importance, concerning the methods by which we shall best accomplish the desired end.

Classes of the poor.—Who are the poor that have a claim on our pity? They are those whom misfortune has made

---

How will good society consider any conscientious act? Do you desire the praise of the good or bad?

What is the subject of Chapter XXIII? Repeat the text. How is pity exhibited? Where shall our pity find the objects for its exercise. What is said of the poor? Why shall we pity the poor? Who is our neighbor? What obligation are we under to him? Who are the poor that have a claim upon our pity?

miserable in many ways. They may be classed as the PROFESSIONAL, IDLE POOR, the CRIMINAL POOR, and the INNOCENT POOR.

All these are our brethren, and, if possible, we must do them good; not in the same way, or by the same means, but in that manner which will conduce most to their individual welfare, and the best interests of society. Society itself is largely responsible for the number and character of its poor. To prove this, it is only necessary to refer to the class of people called Friends or Quakers. As a people, they are frugal, industrious, and temperate. They live, generally, in large communities, and there are neither paupers nor criminals among them. They recognize the necessity and dignity of labor; it is an essential part of their education. They are not ashamed or unwilling to work; but it would be exceedingly mortifying for any of them to beg. When sickness or misfortune overtake any of their number, they feel that all must bear a part of the burden, and afford, as far as is possible, the necessary relief. It is written in the moral law, "*Bear ye one another's burdens;*" and these people endeavor to fulfill that command by assisting each other.

So with the class of people known as Jews. They are, as a class, diligent in business, frugal, and temperate. It is their boast that they are quiet, peaceable, law-abiding citizens; that they rarely have representatives in prison or poor-house. This is something to be proud of; and one reason of the fact is, they educate their youth to obey their parents and to work. In this, they make excellent citizens. If society at large would take the means to educate all its youth properly, much of the poverty and suffering that now exists might be prevented. But until preventive measures are

---

How are the poor classified? What benefits shall we endeavor to confer upon all these classes? How is society responsible for the existence of many of its poor? What is said of the Friends? What is written about bearing burdens? Why is it the rarest occurrence to find a Jew in prison? Why are they never found in the "poor-house?" How shall society prevent poverty? Can it be entirely prevented?

put in operation, the question remains—what shall be done for the poor?

Charity.—We have already learned that the moral quality of an action lies in the motive or intention with which it is performed. It is possible for us to do good actions from mean and selfish motives. Pride, self-esteem, and the desire for praise, may induce persons to give liberally, and to work vigorously for a good cause; but such benevolence brings with it no blessing to the giver. Charity is an operation of the mind and heart, and is the product of love. "*Charity suffereth long, and is kind; charity envieth not; charity vaunteth not itself, is not puffed up, doth not behave itself unseemly, seeketh not her own, is not easily provoked, thinketh no evil, rejoiceth not in iniquity, but rejoiceth in the truth, beareth all things, believeth all things, hopeth all things, endureth all things.*"

It is that gentle spirit of kindness that endeavors to do and to make the best of every thing; that views every human being as a brother, and every needy one as a special object of consideration and care. It has no sympathy for crime, but only endeavors to benefit the criminal; it has no indulgence for wrong, but has no unjust censure even for the wrong-doer. It is merciful, kind, and just. Without such feelings, no one can be truly benevolent, as it is written in the moral law, "*Though I bestow all my goods to feed the poor, and have not charity, it profiteth me nothing.*" The mere giving of alms, unaccompanied by the true feeling of brotherhood, is not a charity that is commended. That alone is worthy of admiration, which is prompted by a desire to make one poor, needy, fallen brother a wiser, better, and more helpful man.

In what does the moral quality of an action lie? May men do good from bad motives? What is written in the moral law of charity? Repeat the text. How many ways does charity exhibit herself? Illustrate the idea that charity suffereth long; is kind; envieth not, etc. Has charity sympathy for crime? Does the giving of alms illustrate charity? Repeat the text. What is worthy of admiration?

Personal benevolence.—Every person has it in his power to do something to alleviate suffering and to relieve distress. The charitable heart will find no difficulty in discovering those who need assistance. A kind, approving smile, a gentle, encouraging word, a cup of cool water, a friendly visit or a timely pecuniary help, are little things in themselves, and yet are invaluable.

Personal benevolence should be manifested in such a delicate manner as not to wound the feelings of the recipient. If the giver bestows his gifts in such a way as to make the receiver painfully conscious of the kindness, it is not a charity. Neither is it true benevolence to offer our kindnesses so that we shall expect or receive the public approbation. It is written, "*Take heed that ye do not your alms before men, to be seen of them; otherwise, ye have no reward of your Father which is in heaven. Therefore, when thou doest thine alms, do not sound a trumpet before thee, as the hypocrites do in the synagogues and in the streets, that they may have glory of men; but when thou doest alms, let not thy left hand know what thy right hand doeth; that thine alms may be in secret, and thy Father, which seeth in secret, himself shall reward thee openly.*"

Benevolent discretion.—An indiscriminate giving of alms to every applicant is not a wise benevolence; it may be a positive wrong. There are persons who are too indolent to work, and yet expect to receive from kind, inconsiderate persons a supply for their necessities, without any exercise of mental or physical exertion. It is not a kindness to give a man money to squander for strong drink or in gambling, but it would be a great blessing to give him an

---

May every one find opportunities for benevolence? When? How? What are evidences of a loving spirit? How should persons exercise benevolence? What is written of those who display their benevolence? How shall we not do alms? How shall we do alms? Why? Is the giving to every claimant true benevolence? How may we injure a man by giving him alms?

opportunity to work, and thereby earn his living, and possibly be set on the road to reformation.

It is written, that "*An idle soul shall suffer hunger;*" and it is not unkind to say that an idle soul, who is able, but not willing to work, should be permitted to suffer hunger. It is our duty to relieve the destitute, in such a manner as will enable them to help themselves in whole or in part. Helpless children must be fed, clothed, and educated, but must not be permitted to grow up to a life of idleness and crime. The widow and the fatherless must be provided for, and suitable work must be furnished them; for when people can do any thing for their own support, and are permitted to live without exertion, they become discontented and unhappy, and learn to receive kindness without gratitude, and to expect favors as rights.

Professional paupers are the most thankless and, at the same time, the most rapacious of mankind; and the only method of conferring upon them and society a permanent good, is to give them employment, and pay them for their work. Such persons as are incapacitated by sickness, deformity, or disease to do any thing for themselves, must be supported; and every thing possible should be done to make their lives tolerable and happy.

> "Think not the good,
> The gentle deeds of mercy thou hast done,
> Shall die forgotten all: the poor, the pris'ner,
> The fatherless, the friendless, and the widow,
> Who daily own the bounty of thy hand,
> Shall cry to heaven, and pull a blessing on thee."

John Howard.—There are many noble examples of women and men, who have devoted their lives to philanthropic labors, in Europe and in our own land, whom it

What shall be done for the idle soul? How shall we relieve the destitute? What must be done for the helpless? What should be required of every one who can work? Why? How shall professional paupers be treated? What shall be done for those who can not work? What is the sentiment of the poetry? Give what is said of John Howard. Why is his memory revered?

would be pleasing to mention. It will be sufficient, as an illustration of heroic devotion to duty, to allude to John Howard. He was an Englishman by birth. At the age of twenty-eight, he set sail for Lisbon, in order to carry relief to the surviving sufferers of the terrible earthquake that devastated that city in 1755. England and France being at war at that time, the ship in which he sailed was captured by the French and carried into the port of Brest. Being made prisoner with the officers and crew, he was put into prison and treated with the utmost cruelty.

This was his first experience of prison life. Upon his release he returned to England. Being a man of considerable wealth, which was left him by his father, he spent much time and money in schemes of benevolence. Assisted by his noble wife, "they built improved cottages, established schools, administered to the sick, and relieved the necessitous." In 1773, he was elected sheriff of Bedford. He thus became officially acquainted with the condition of the prisons of his county. He found them dark, damp, and deathly, badly ventilated, and cruelly managed. Instead of being places where bad men might be made better, he found them horribly vicious, wretched, and indecent. From his own county, he proceeded through England, inspecting the jails, and he found them, invariably, dens of mental, moral, and physical corruption.

The observation of such misery, and the hope that he could be instrumental in relieving it, determined his course for life. The inspection and reformation of prisons now became his business. From England, he traveled over the whole of Europe, seeking admission into the most dismal, loathsome, and dangerous dungeons, that he might report their condition and have them reformed. Vice, cruelty,

---

Why did Howard become enlisted in prison reformation? Was it wise to spend his money and his life for prisoners? What is the golden rule? How far may every man attempt to benefit his neighbor? In what estimation do the wise and the good hold John Howard? Are there any other fields of benevolence waiting for a reform and a reformer?

disease, and every earthly abomination, he found immured in those terrible dens. The prisoners were confined together, without reference to age, sex, or condition.

Into such places, and among such associates, this good man ventured, that he might be the means of relieving the sick, releasing the innocent, and benefiting the bad. His life was the forfeit of his benevolence. He died at Cherson, in the south of Russia, in 1790, from a disease contracted in visiting a prison. The publication of his work on prisons stirred up a spirit of philanthropy, which is operating to this day in making the prisons of our land less places of vindictive retribution than of humane reformation.

Public benevolence.—There are certain classes of the innocent and unfortunate poor, that can only be taken care of properly in places specially provided for their reception. The means of private individuals are generally insufficient to furnish suitable accommodations for large numbers, so that the state must make provision for their wants. Of these, are the idiots, the insane, the deaf and dumb, the blind, the orphan poor, the aged poor, the homeless sick, etc. The same principle should be observed, when it is practicable in institutions for these classes, of furnishing the inmates with occupations suited to their conditions, mentally and physically.

What effect had the labors of Howard? What classes of the poor should be provided for by the state? Why? To what extent should labor be required of any of these classes? Why?

CHAPTER XXIV.

"A righteous man regardeth the life of his beast."

HUMANITY.

The world was created, in the exercise of Infinite Wisdom, as the abode of man. It was given him, with all that it contains, to admire, to use, and to enjoy. The products of earth, air, and sea were furnished to assist in his labors, to minister to his pleasures, and to satisfy his wants. The animal creation was to afford him food, clothing, and companionship. The earliest records of the race are not old enough to give the account of the subjugation of the domestic animals. The care of these has always been one of the chief employments of a large portion of mankind.

Without the assistance afforded by the domestic animals, mankind would be very helpless. The horse, the sheep, the ox, the ass, the camel, the elephant, the llama, the dog, and the reindeer are fitted peculiarly for the regions in which they are found, and each is indispensable to the comfort or safety of man. Some of these are no longer found in their wild condition, and are so completely domesticated as to have lost much of their natural instinct of self-defense and preservation. Many of these animals possess a sagacity that is wonderful. They have perception, memory, recollection, and often seem endowed with powers of reason and

---

What is the subject of Chapter XXIV? Repeat the text. What is a righteous man? Is it lawful for man to use all the animals for his own welfare? Why? How have a portion of mankind been employed from the earliest history? How is man dependent upon the domestic animals? To what purposes can the ox be put? Name the principal domestic animals of the world, and the regions they inhabit. What surprising faculties do many of these exhibit?

judgment. Some possess ardent affection for their masters, and a fidelity that nothing can disturb.

That man should treat such faithful servants with any thing save the greatest kindness seems to be unreasonable; and yet, alas! for man's weakness and passion, it is often true. It would seem that self-interest alone, without any higher or nobler motive, would prompt every man to take great care of the poor brutes, upon which he is so dependent; but even his own property is often made the sport of his baser nature. Still, it is true, as it is written, "*A righteous man regardeth the life of his beast.*"

Cruelty to animals.—In some parts of our country, humane laws have been enacted for the prevention of cruelty to animals, that are a credit to our civilization. Societies have also been formed by humane people, having in view the protection of the rights of God's poor creatures, which are abused by thoughtless or cruel men.

Animals that afford us pleasure or profit should be treated with humanity, and every attention paid to their wants. If the innocent and helpless brutes, that are ill-fed, overworked, unsheltered, and injured by all manner of cruelty, could make an appeal to our sense of justice and humanity, how eloquent and how touching it would be. Neglect and abuse not only injure the pecuniary value of the animal, but what is of infinitely more importance, the moral constitution of the man; for he who has no feelings of kindness and consideration for the poor dumb animal that labors for him, would probably have as little feeling for one of his own kind in circumstances of distress.

Animals that furnish us food should not be overdriven and abused simply because they are destined soon to be

---

Does self-interest always save these animals from injury and abuse? Why? What laws have been enacted referring to this subject? How should domestic animals be treated? How do some animals show kindness? How do they act when abused? Should we permit an animal to suffer if we can prevent it? Repeat the text. What might we expect if put in the power of a man who abuses a harmless animal?

killed. Men are accustomed to see many forms of cruelty, and think nothing of it, because it is so common. It seems to make no impression, that chickens are brought to market tied together in bunches, and suspended by the legs from the back of a hard-trotting horse. Such cruelty is indefensible. If it is necessary to bring them alive, they should be brought in coops. Poor, innocent calves and pigs are often securely tied by the legs, in such a way as to destroy the circulation of the blood, and cause the parts to become intensely painful. In this manner, they are often carried long distances, and exposed to the extremes of heat and cold.

If any one has a doubt as to the humanity of this method of transportation, let him tie a string tightly around the base of his forefinger and let it remain half an hour. The ligature alone, without the jolting ride, will soon convince him that there might be more gentle methods of treatment. Such usage is not only a cruelty, but a serious injury to the flesh of the animal when prepared for market. It is said that the Hollanders always kill their fish when they take them from the water, because, when left to die by degrees in the air, the flesh is injured. Might we not add the argument of humanity as an additional reason why they should be quickly killed when taken from their own element. A book might be written upon this subject, but enough is here given to direct the attention and enlist the sympathies of the gentle and the humane.

Killing of animals.—When animals are to be killed for food, they should not be tortured or hurt. Not one pang of needless distress should be inflicted, but they should be dispatched in the speediest manner, and with the least pain. There is an element of barbarity in the torturing of any

---

Why may we have so little sympathy for suffering animals? Give the instances that you have seen of cruelty. What experiment is spoken of? What effect does abuse have upon the flesh of animals? How do the Hollanders treat fish? Why? When animals are to be used for food, how should they be treated? Is it right to take revenge on a dumb brute? Should you whip the cat for killing the canary?

living thing, that is abhorrent to every kind and noble sentiment in our nature. Animals that are injurious to ourselves and our property may be destroyed, but it need never be done in a cruel or vindictive manner. They simply act in accordance with their nature, and although they may do us great injury, it is not because they have any sense of right or wrong; it is the operation of their instinct. To retaliate on a dumb and unreasoning brute, even a snake, by unnecessary cruelty in killing it, is inhuman and savage.

Hunting.—As all animals were made for the benefit of man, directly or indirectly, there is no wrong in hunting and killing such as are either useful for food and clothing, or are injurious to the crops or to other animals in his employ. While it is entirely proper to kill those that are either useful for food or injurious, it is wrong to deprive any of life merely for sport. It is cruel to kill any thing that breathes merely for the love of killing, and there can be no excuse or apology for it. It is pitiable to witness the spirit of wantonness frequently manifested by men and boys in the destruction of little singing birds, so pretty, so innocent, and, at the same time, so valuable to the farmer and to the fruit-grower.

If such birds could be used for food, or if their feathers were valuable, or if any purpose were served that is economical, the outrage against nature would be pardonable. It is sometimes urged that such birds are injurious to vegetation, and that it is a matter of economy to destroy them. "Were it not for the birds that frequent our gardens, and insects, which prey upon each other, the number of destructive insects produced would be such as soon to overpower the industry of man, and put an end to his miserable existence. The ingenious Dr. Bradley has computed that a

---

Is it right to hunt wild animals? What for? Is it right to hunt and kill buffaloes for sport, and then to let them lie on the plains and rot? Is it wise or kind to kill little birds. Why not kill singing birds? What is said of the value of birds?

pair of sparrows carried to their young in one week not less than three thousand three hundred caterpillars." "Of fifty-four little victims whose crops were examined from the 18th of April to the 24th of May, forty-seven had eaten insects alone, and seven had their crops filled with grain and seeds. Of forty-six old sparrows that were dissected at the same time, only three proved to be grain-eaters, while all the rest had been feasting on beetles and caterpillars."

These facts are not only in favor of the sparrows, but as much may be said for all kinds of these beautiful creatures. The little harm they do in taking fruit and grain is more than paid for by their incessant labors in ridding the fields and forests of injurious insects. But self-protection is not the motive that prompts their destruction; it is simply the satisfaction of trying to shoot them. If skill in using fire-arms is only achieved at such a sacrifice, it is not worth what it costs. In this connection, a plea may also be urged in behalf of the little birds' nests. As no profit can be derived from their destruction, it is a cruel invasion of the rights of the birds to disturb them. Every argument is in favor of the encouragement and protection of the birds; they are pretty, gentle, innocent, and valuable.

Cruel sport.—The savage instincts of man are most strikingly displayed in those enjoyments which are derived from the shedding of the blood of beasts or men. It is not strange that animals, exhibiting their natural ferocity, should fight and destroy each other; nor is it strange that ignorant, uncultivated, and brutal men should find a special delight in such encounters. It is one of the relics of our barbarism.

In the days of ancient Rome, it was the custom to celebrate a great victory, or to commemorate the death of an eminent man, by the exhibition of gladiatorial shows, in

What investigations prove their value? What is the true reason why these birds are killed? Is it right? Is it right to rob birds' nests? Why? How is the savage nature of man shown? What kind of men delight in cruel sports? What is said of Roman festivals?

which slaves fought with each other or with wild beasts, for the amusement of the people. These shows were announced to the public like the plays in our theaters. The gladiators were trained and sworn to fight to the death. If they showed cowardice, they were killed with tortures. At the time of the dedication of the famous amphitheater called the Colosseum, Titus gave an exhibition which lasted a hundred days, in which five thousand wild beasts were slain. At another time, the Emperor Trajan gave a show of one hundred and twenty-three days' duration, in which two thousand men fought with and killed each other, or fought with wild beasts, for the amusement of the seventy thousand Romans who were assembled to witness the terrible tragedy.

The progress of civilization may be traced from that date to the present in the decline of such blood-thirsty and barbarous exhibitions. The lowest and most degraded of our people exhibit these ferocious inclinations as the patrons of the prize-ring, where brutal men engage in combats for money, or in the dog-pit, or cock-pit. The moral law condemns cruelty both to man and to beast. No persons of delicate sensibility can derive any pleasure from witnessing such degrading contests.

An eye that can see poor brutes worry and mangle each other without pity; an ear that can hear their cries of rage and distress without a pang; a heart that can endure the idea of such unnecessary suffering without any emotion save of satisfaction, can never belong to that society whose claims we advocate. It seems as if the innate cruelty of some natures finds vent in trying to injure or alarm every living thing they dare attack—dogs, cats, pigs, doves, chickens, little birds—every thing that has nerves to suffer, seems to be the object of their aversion.

How may the progress of civilization be traced? What class of people among us compare with the Romans? What must be said of the man who enjoys the agony of a suffering brute? What shall we expect of those who delight to torture animals? Can we expect refinement and gentleness from one who is cruel to animals? What must we expect of boys who are cruel, who delight in injuring animals? Why should we hurt any thing that lives?

As before stated, there can be no objection to the taking of wild game birds by the gun; but when poor, little domestic doves, the emblems of innocence and love, are sprung from a trap into the air in order to be shot for sport, there can be no excuse or palliation for the deed. Such sport is only worthy of unrefined, uncultivated, semi-civilized men.

CHAPTER XXV.

"*Happy is that man that findeth wisdom, and the man that getteth understanding. Length of days are in her right hand, and in her left riches and honor. Her ways are ways of pleasantness, and all her paths are peace.*"

WISDOM.

We have endeavored to point out in the preceding chapters some of the obligations we are under to God, to our neighbor, and to ourselves, as members of that society which an honorable ambition should impel all to enter—the society of the good. There are many topics to which we have barely alluded, and many that are important, of which no mention has been made. Enough has been written, however, to prove the desirableness of habits based upon the principles described in the moral law. In concluding the chapters upon this branch of the subject, we can not do

---

Is pigeon shooting a manly employment? Why? Can not skill with the gun be acquired without cruel and unnecessary injury to harmless birds?

What is the subject of Chapter XXV? Repeat the text. What is meant by wisdom? Why is length of days promised? Why are her ways pleasantness? Why are her paths peaceful?

better than give the following brief but striking summary of this wonderful code. It is written: "*These six things doth the Lord hate; yea, seven are an abomination unto Him: a proud look, a lying tongue, and hands that shed innocent blood, a heart that deviseth wicked imaginations, feet that be swift in running to mischief, a false witness that speaketh lies, and he that soweth discord among brethren.*"

The society of the good demands that we abstain from these "abominations," and, that as true men and women, we shall strive to acquire "*The wisdom that is from above, that is first pure, then peaceable, gentle, and easy to be entreated, full of mercy and good fruits, without partiality and without hypocrisy*"

Conclusion.—"*Let us hear the conclusion of the whole matter: Fear God and keep his commandments, for this is the whole duty of man.*"

What seven things are an abomination to the Lord? Repeat the text. What is that wisdom that is from above? What is the conclusion? Repeat the text. What is the whole duty of man? What is the "first and great commandment"? The second is like unto it. What is it?

PART II.

MUNICIPAL LAW.

CHAPTER XXVI.

"Great God! we thank Thee for this home,
This bounteous birth-land of the free;
Where wanderers from afar may come,
And breathe the air of liberty!
Still may her flowers untrampled spring,
Her harvests wave, her cities rise;
And yet, till Time shall fold his wing,
Remain earth's loveliest paradise."

PATRIOTISM.

Patriotism is defined to be the love of one's country. Why should American youth love their country? There are many reasons why her glory should be their pride; her history should enlist their admiration; her interests should be their care; and the principles upon which her government are founded should be the subject of their ardent devotion. Never had children a more valuable inheritance than that which they have received, and never were greater obligations imposed than that they should protect and preserve this land, and transmit it, full of the grandest achievements and most glorious recollections, to their posterity. Men may love their homes for the same reason that a wild animal loves its lair, and they may defend them as a wolf

Of what does Part I treat? Of what does Part II treat? What is the subject of Chapter XXVI? Define patriotism. Why should American youth be patriotic? What is an inheritance? Why does a wolf love its den?

might defend its den from unwarranted intrusion; but the love which it is desirable that American youth shall cherish for their land and its institutions is not a mere instinct; it is a principle which is derived from a knowledge of her history, her constitution, and her laws.

It is the object of these pages to impart briefly some of the reasons why young Americans should love their country with a devotion unequaled by the people of any other land. It is not alone because our territory is unsurpassed in extent; in the diversity of its productions; in the fertility of its soil; in the richness of its mineral resources; in the extent of its forests; in the commercial facilities of its great rivers and lakes; in the variety of its climate; or in the general intelligence and enterprise of its citizens, compared with any other country, that we may feel a just pride in our own. These are important advantages, but they are not equal in value to the possession and enjoyment of our political rights.

Political rights.—The United States government is founded on the principle of the equality of natural rights among men. From the moral law, we have already learned (see Chapter VI) that mankind is a brotherhood, of one Father and of one blood. This principle is reaffirmed and proclaimed as one of the fundamental doctrines in the famous Declaration of Independence, which was adopted by the fathers of the republic, on the 4th of July, 1776, the nation's birthday. It says:

"We hold these truths to be self-evident: that all men are created equal; that they are endowed by their Creator with certain inalienable rights; that among these are life,

---

What is instinct? What should our patriotism be based on? What is said of the extent of our territory? What is meant by diversity of productions? How do we judge of fertility of soil? Name some of our mineral productions, and where they are found. What advantages do our forests afford? What advantages do our rivers and lakes afford? What variety of climate does the country possess? What is more important than all these advantages? Why is mankind a brotherhood? Why is the 4th of July called the nation's birthday? What are the inalienable rights alluded to?

liberty, and the pursuit of happiness; that to secure these rights, governments are instituted among men, deriving their just powers from the consent of the governed; and that when any form of government becomes destructive of these ends, it is the right of the people to alter or abolish it, and to institute a new government, laying its foundation on such principles, and organizing its powers in such form, as to them shall seem most likely to effect their safety and happiness."

Self-evident truths.—A self-evident truth is one that does not need to be proven, since no one doubts it. To state it, is to know its truth. No person need prove that "the sum of the parts of a unit is equal to the whole." It is so plain as to be incapable of proof: it is self-evident.

Natural equality of men.—It is self-evident that all men, without reference to country, color, creed, or condition, are equal in natural rights; and also, that no man or set of men has a natural right to exercise authority over others in opposition to their wishes. No sane man will willingly surrender his life, his liberty, or his chances for happiness; these are God's gifts, and are inalienable. They can be justly taken away from a man, only when he violates the laws and becomes a dangerous member of society.

The duty of government.—It is self-evident that the design of government should be the protection of the people in the just exercise of their rights; to secure to every man his life, liberty, reputation, and property, by the enactment and execution of good laws. Governments ought not to be established for the glory and pride of kings, but for the welfare of the people. Ours was instituted by the people for the people. They alone have the right to determine what

---

What is the object of government? What is a self-evident truth? What is a self-evident truth in reference to natural rights? What are inalienable rights? What should be the design of government? Who have the right to determine the form of government?

kind of a system to adopt, and when they are not suited, they may, in an orderly and legal manner, change it, and select some other form that is better adapted to promote their safety and happiness.

This is not a mere theory, for such a change was actually made in our own history. The first national government established in this country, three years after the Declaration of Independence, was a confederacy of thirteen colonies. After a trial of eight years, it was found not to answer the purpose, when a new government, upon a different and better plan, was legally and peacefully substituted for the former. Our present system is called a constitutional republic, under which the nation has lived, enjoying unexampled prosperity, for a period of more than eighty years.

The constitution of the United States.—The constitution of the United States is an article of agreement or contract entered into by the people of this nation, in order to secure a government adapted to their necessities. The preamble or introduction to this grand document explains the object of its preparation, and is as follows: "We, the people of the United States, in order to form a more perfect union, establish justice, insure domestic tranquillity, provide for the common defense, promote the general welfare, and secure the blessings of liberty to ourselves and our posterity, do ordain and establish this constitution for the United States of America." It is the fundamental law of the land, and any statute which is made in any degree contrary to it is void, or of no legal effect. All the departments of the government are subject to its provisions, and all the legislators, judges, and executive officers take a solemn oath to obey its requirements. As may be learned from the pre-

---

How may the form of government be changed? What change was made in our national system? What is our government called? What is meant by the constitution of the United States? Who were the parties that established the constitution? What was its object? What is the meaning of a fundamental law? What effect have laws made contrary to the constitution? What oath do all officers of government take? Why?

amble above cited, it is the guaranty of the personal rights of every citizen.

Personal rights.—We have already alluded to certain rights belonging to every man, and they have been termed inalienable. Growing out of these, there are others no less important, among which are the right to worship God, the right of free speech, of a free press, and of trial by jury.

The right of worship.—Our obligations to God have already been briefly discussed in Chapters IV and V. As every individual is responsible to God, and to God alone, for the use of his talents, the state has no right to prescribe "what man is to believe concerning God. or what duty God requires of man." The only obligation devolving on the state is to enforce obedience to those precepts of the moral law which directly and immediately affect the welfare of the community. The government may very properly enforce the law which says, "*Thou shalt not kill*," and "*Thou shalt not steal*," for the violation of these precepts creates disturbance in society, endangering the rights of its citizens; but it can not properly enforce the law which says, "*Thou shalt love the Lord thy God*," for it has no right to interfere in matters that are only spiritual. When the moral law is violated, it is not the duty of the state to punish the offender, unless the wrong is of such a nature as to work open and serious injury to society, and is at the same time a violation of the civil law. God is able to vindicate his own precepts, as it is written, "*Vengeance is mine, I will repay, saith the Lord.*"

There are also differences of belief among men; one conscientiously worships God in one way, and another in a differ-

What personal rights are mentioned? Has the state a right to determine our forms of worship? Why? What is the duty of the state in reference to religion? Why shall the government punish murder? Why shall it not punish unbelief in God? How far should the state vindicate the moral law?

ent way. Each may truly believe he is right, but who shall be umpire to decide. Matters of conscience can not be determined by majorities; and if the state prescribes the mode of worship, then the rights of all who do not agree with the government are violated. When men obey the moral law, in such a manner as not to interfere with the rights of others, the state has no right to meddle with their religious opinions or modes of worship. Nothing is more tyrannical than a system of government, which, under any pretense, attempts to force men to acts of worship which are contrary to their conscientious convictions of duty.

According to the American view of personal liberty, the Chinese who is an idolater, may build his temple, and erect his idols in this land; may adore his ancestors, and worship the creatures of his imagination, and no one has a right to interfere: provided, that in the enjoyment of his religion he does not disturb the rights of others. If he violates no law, but performs all his obligations, pays his taxes, and deports himself as a good citizen, the state has no authority to restrict him in matters of religious belief or practice. If an idolater, however, should claim the right to offer his infant child as a sacrifice, the law would restrain him, and no claim of conscientious obligation would be allowed. Nor do our laws permit the indulgence of polygamy or plurality of wives; not alone because it is a violation of the moral law, but because it is a custom at variance with the best interests of enlightened civil society. The history of all nations, as well as the moral law, condemns it.

Free speech.—In most of the governments of the world the people are not permitted to assemble for the purpose of

---

Why is it wrong for the state to establish some form of religion? Should men be forced to worship God? May the Chinese worship his idols in this land? Should it be permitted? Shall the heathen mother sacrifice her child to her god? Why? Is polygamy right? If it is a part of any religious belief, should it be tolerated? Should any religious practice be exercised to the injury of society at large? If a man believes in polygamy, should he be punished if he does not practice it? Why do some governments prevent free discussion?

discussing freely the political, social, and religious questions in which they are interested. The government thinks and acts for the people. In our land, it is considered not only the right, but also the duty of the citizen to gain all the knowledge that can be obtained upon every subject of public interest, and for this purpose religious, political, commercial, and educational conventions are frequently held to discuss topics affecting the welfare of society. Our government gives every man the right to speak, if he can secure an audience, and every audience the right to listen to such discussion as it may wish to hear.

It has been said that, "Error is not to be feared, if truth is free to combat it." No man is sure of the truth until he has heard it fairly discussed. As was stated in Chapter XIII, there are always two sides to a story, and he is only half informed who has listened but to one side. For this reason, our government grants the fullest liberty of discussion, that every man may become completely acquainted with any subject that may engage his attention. Free speech is one of a freeman's rights.

Free press.—Tyrants are always afraid of the freedom of speech and of the press; they dread discussion, as they can not bear that the truth shall be known. But the same reasons that entitle men to speak freely, entitle them also to print their opinions and scatter them abroad. There have been occasions in the history of our country when attempts were made to stifle free discussion, and suppress the publication of unpopular doctrines. Meetings have been broken up, speakers have been abused, and printing presses destroyed. But "might does not give right," and the exercise of mob law and violence, though it may temporarily suc-

---

How does our government encourage free discussion? What subjects interest our people? What is the maxim concerning error and truth? When is a man sure he is right? Why is it a duty to learn? Why should we hear both sides? Why are tyrants afraid of a free press? Have efforts been made in this country to suppress freedom of speech and the press? What has been the result?

ceed, is never a match for truth. The cause of right and justice, however it may be hindered, is sure to prevail.

There is no more certain evidence of the weakness of any cause than the fact that its friends are afraid of its free discussion by an untrammeled press. As Americans, we can not be too jealous of any attempt, by any person or party, to violate this right of every citizen; for, if we permit the rights of one, however obscure or humble, to be trampled on to-day, upon the same wrong principle we may suffer in the loss of our rights to-morrow.

Qualified rights.—Upon the subjects of religion and politics there is no restriction of the freedom of the citizen. Men may speak and publish any thing they desire concerning the public policy of the country, or concerning matters of faith and worship. There is no limitation upon these topics, because they are only matters of individual opinion. Every man has a right to the expression of his views, since no individual is bound to accept them as true. But if, in the exercise of the liberty of speech and of the press, any thing is uttered which is calculated to pollute the morals of the people, the person so offending may be called to account for the abuse of his privilege.

No man has a right to print and publish indecent and obscene language or illustrations, since it is by such things that the public taste becomes depraved, and the public manners corrupted. No people can remain pure where such mental and moral poison is freely disseminated, and consequently the civil law expressly forbids this abuse of the liberty of the press. So, also, is every man responsible for

---

What is a good evidence of a bad cause? What may we expect if we prevent the exercise of free expression in others? Why should there be no restriction put upon the free expression of political or religious views? Why may vile language and lascivious pictures not be published? May we speak or print injurious reports of our neighbor, if they are untrue? May we if they are true? Have editors the right to defame or ridicule private persons? Or public officers? Under what circumstances is it right to expose the improprieties of any one?

the injury he may inflict upon his neighbor's reputation or business by the public exposure of his private affairs.

Trial by jury.—Another reason why Americans should be proud of their government, is that they can not be deprived of life, liberty, or property, except by due course of law. Every person who is arrested has a right to a hearing, to determine whether he shall be detained as a prisoner. If he is charged with the commission of crime, he has the right to a trial in open court; to secure counsel to assist in his defense; to procure witnesses, and to be tried by a jury of twelve unprejudiced men, who will patiently hear the case, and determine his guilt or innocence.

These are a few of the more important reasons why American youth should be proud of their country and its government.

CHAPTER XXVII.

"Here, beneath a virtuous sway,
May we cheerfully obey;
Never feel oppression's rod—
Ever own and worship God."

DUTIES OF CITIZENSHIP.

"**Municipal law** is a rule of action prescribed by the supreme power in a state, commanding what is right, and prohibiting what is wrong."

What is the next right of the citizen? When a man is arrested for crime, what are his rights? What is meant by a jury? Why has a man a right to trial in open court? Review some of the reasons why American youth should love their country and its government.

Define municipal law.

The terms "rule of action" and "prescribed" have been already defined in Chapter III. To understand this definition of municipal law, it is necessary to understand what is meant by "the supreme power in a state." In the great variety of national governments this power is very differently vested. In some, the supreme power is lodged in the hands of the sovereign; in others, in the hands of the nobility or aristocracy. Ours is called a republican form of government, which is defined as "one in which the exercise of the supreme power is lodged in representatives elected by the people." As has already been stated, this is a government *of* the people *by* the people. They elect their representatives to make their laws, and the laws thus made by the will of the majority are the rules of action for the government of all.

Departments of government.—Our government is divided into three departments: the LEGISLATIVE, or law making; the JUDICIAL, or law defining; and the EXECUTIVE, or law enforcing departments. The legislative branch of the government makes the laws, and prescribes the punishments that may be inflicted when they are disobeyed. The courts determine by legal forms and evidence whether the laws have been violated, and the executive officers carry out or enforce the decisions of legislation and the sentences of the courts. All the officers of the government, whether legislative, judicial, or executive, must act in conformity with the constitution, and are themselves, as much as other citizens, the subjects of law.

As our grand constitutional government affords the citizen protection in life, liberty, reputation, and property; as under it he may worship God according to his sense of duty; may

---

What is meant by a rule of action? By prescribed? What is the supreme power in many countries? What is our government called? Define it. Who make the laws? May laws be changed? How? How many, and what are the departments of our government? Define the legislative department. The judicial. The executive. To what must the officers of these departments conform? Why?

speak as he wishes; print and publish what he pleases, and vote for whom he prefers as public officers, the question arises what shall he do for the government in return for all these, and many other inestimable privileges?

Duties of citizenship.—Rights, as was stated in the discussion of the principles of the moral law, are always accompanied by corresponding duties. If we insist upon our rights as citizens, we ought willingly to perform all the duties that citizenship imposes. What, then, shall we do to become good citizens?

Intelligence.—The good citizen should be intelligent; should be well acquainted with the history of his government, and the principles upon which it is founded. Our beautiful flag is the emblem of freedom all over the world: the oppressed look upon it with loving eyes, while tyrants hold it in utter detestation. It is the representative of free institutions, which recognize the inalienable rights of man, and is therefore odious to those rulers who have no sympathies with the masses of the people whom they govern.

As we can not understand the value of a delightful, health-giving breeze, and a pure draught of refreshing water, until we have been burned with the sun's fierce glare and tortured with feverish thirst, so we may not fully appreciate the blessings of our constitutional republic until they are contrasted with the customs and laws of those governments which do not recognize the principles of human rights. They who have suffered in their persons and property from the tyranny of despotic governments, can best understand the value of the freedom they possess in this. It is the duty, therefore, of every American to study the Declaration

---

Review the advantages enjoyed under our government. What duties shall the good citizen return for all these advantages? To what do rights always correspond? Why? Why should the American citizen be intelligent? How is our beautiful flag esteemed? How do foreigners know the advantages of our land? What should be studied to understand our government? Why should we study the Declaration of Independence?

of Independence, the Constitution of the United States, and Washington's Farewell Address, and from these grand documents learn the views of the fathers of the republic, by whose wisdom and courage the government was founded.

Political parties.—There were great differences of opinion among the founders of the government upon many questions of public policy; and as the years rolled on, new questions arose on many subjects to divide the sentiments of the people. These differences of opinion are the origin of political parties. No person should blindly accept the policy of any party without thoroughly understanding its principles. Every intelligent man will think for himself, and not be controlled by mere party names.

To enable him to form a correct judgment of public affairs, he should seek to learn the views of statesmen of all parties. A decent respect for the opinions of our opponents requires that we give them a hearing, and while we desire due credit for honesty and patriotism, we should not fail to accord the same to them. No man should vote who has not a clear understanding of the prominent questions which divide the public attention.

National morality.—It is written in the moral law that, "*Righteousness exalteth a nation: but sin is a reproach to any people.*" As the nation is composed of individuals, the moral condition of these individuals will determine the character of the nation. There are often moral questions involved in the actions of nations, upon the decision of which their character for righteousness or unrighteousness depends. "Our country, right or wrong," is a motto often used by bad men to hide their evil designs, under a pretense of

---

Why the Constitution? Why the Farewell Address? What is the origin of political parties? Before joining a party, what should a man do? How shall he know the truth? Are there honest, truthful men in all parties? Why, then, do men differ? What should men do before they vote? What exalts a nation? Repeat the text.

patriotism. No such miserable doctrine can be tolerated by good men. Rather let it be, "Our country, always right." The citizen who loves justice, mercy, and truth will never consent that his voice and vote shall sanction a public wrong.

Every community will be agitated by discussions of moral questions, which must be settled by the moral sense of the people. The standard of right should be as high when the people act collectively as when they act as individuals. No man can be trusted as a public officer who is dishonest or untrue in private life; so no one should be considered trustworthy in private life who has proved himself politically dishonest. Integrity is not a virtue to be put on and off like a coat at the convenience of the wearer. A good man will advocate what he thinks is right, in public or private affairs, whether it concerns his party or his purse. "Honesty is the best policy" for nations as for individuals.

A moral hero and patriot.—It is pleasant to reflect upon the integrity of a man like General Joseph Reed, of Pennsylvania, who was prominent in the war for independence. He was an influential citizen, and intensely devoted to the interests of his country. It was very desirable that the agents of George III should bribe him to be a traitor to the cause of liberty, so Governor Johnston, one of the three commissioners of the king, secretly offered him £10,000, or $50,000, and a public office, if he would engage to promote the British interests. To this impudent offer he nobly replied: "I am not worth purchasing; but such as I am, the king of Great Britain is not rich enough to buy me." What a contrast there is between this man of strict integrity and true patriotism, who is always remembered with pride and

---

On which side of moral questions should good men be found? Is the motto a good one? Why? What should always be the motto? Has a man a right to vote to support a wrong? Why? Name some moral questions upon which the people are called on to vote. Can a bad man be trusted as a public officer? Why is "honesty the best policy?" Repeat the story of General Reed. What made him worthy of admiration?

admiration, and that other general, Benedict Arnold, who was despised as a traitor, even among those by whom he was bribed.

Bribery.—There are many ways of bribing and of being bribed. He is not less a traitor who sells his vote for a reward than he who surrenders an army to gain some personal advantage. All good men detest the person who offers a bribe as well as him who receives one. The purity of the ballot should be preserved, if we wish our country's laws to be just and our public officers to be good.

The freeman's vote.—The exercise of the right to vote is a grand privilege to a freeman who has intelligence to know and honesty to do what he thinks is right. True patriotism makes it not only a right but a duty to vote, and to use all proper means of persuasion to secure a wise and honest public policy. Not only should the vote be cast for good measures, but the greatest care should be taken to elect good men as public officers. It is sad to think that in some cases drunkards, gamblers, and dishonest men have been elected to the highest positions of honor and trust in our country, thus bringing shame and disgrace upon us as a people. Two questions should always be asked concerning a candidate for office. These are, "Is he honest?" and "Is he capable?" If these can be satisfactorily answered, he may be worthy of election, but not otherwise.

Who was Benedict Arnold? In what estimation is he held everywhere? Why? Whether would it be preferable to be poor General Reed or rich General Arnold? Why is it a great privilege for a freeman to vote? Is it a duty? Why? What should we vote for? Why is it a disgrace to elect unworthy men to office? What two questions should be asked of every candidate? What should be the answer to them?

CHAPTER XXVIII.

"He who maintains his country's laws,
Alone is great; or he who dies in the good cause."

DUTIES OF CITIZENSHIP. (Continued.)

It is the duty of every good citizen to obey the law, for disobedience is a breach of fidelity to the state. It is fair to suppose that the supreme power, composed of representatives elected by the people, will enact wise statutes, but whether we think they are the best that could be made, or otherwise, it is our duty to comply with their requirements. It is not for any individual to be the judge of the wrongfulness of a law, and refuse submission and compliance because it does not meet his approval; for, if it were left to each person's convenience or judgment to determine his obedience, good citizens alone would obey, while the evil disposed would neglect or refuse to do their duty. If the good do right, the bad will have less excuse for disobedience. When a law proves to be unwise, inexpedient, or unjust, there is a legal and proper way to change it, for ours is a government of the people, and when they are convinced that a change is desirable, it will be legally effected.

Conscientious opposition to certain laws.—If the law-making power shall enact a statute which is clearly contrary to the moral law, it is the duty of the citizen to protest strongly against its execution, or refuse obedience, for it is

---

Why should every citizen obey the law? Are representatives bound to obey the laws they make? Are the laws likely to be unwise? Is it our duty to obey all laws? Why? Can it be left to every man's choice whether he will obey the laws? Why? When a law proves to be unwise or unjust, how may it be changed? If a law should be made clearly contrary to the moral law, what is our duty?

written, "*We ought to obey God rather than man.*" Before coming to the conclusion that a refusal is preferable to obedience, it would be wise to deliberate very coolly upon the question of right, in order to be satisfied of the justice of our opposition. But the same conscience that leads us to violate the law should enable us to suffer the penalty for conscience, sake.

A notable instance of conscientious opposition has been witnessed in the Friends, who, believing it to be wrong to engage in war, have willingly suffered personal injury and pecuniary loss rather than enter the army as soldiers. No one can fail to admire that courage, and respect that devotion, which lead a man to suffer injury rather than violate his conscience. It requires a strong exercise of moral power to enable us to do what we think is right, when we know we shall suffer evil consequences as the result of our action. Such conduct is heroic.

The power of the government.—There are thousands of citizens in this land, who have grown to advanced age without seeing a single company of United States soldiers. One may travel thousands of miles and never see any evidence of the power of our government to enforce its laws. The true strength of the republic is discovered in the general willingness of the people to render obedience to authority. The people are the power, and the prosperity and safety of every community depend upon their willingness to execute the law. Popular sentiment is the lever that moves the whole political machinery, and every good citizen is interested not only in obeying the statutes himself, but also in compelling the obedience of others.

Repeat the text. Should we be careful about opposing the execution of the law? Why? Name an instance of conscientious opposition to law. How should we view a man who is willing to suffer, rather than do what he thinks is wrong? Why does our government have so few soldiers? What enables the officers to execute the laws so easily? In what does the strength of our government consist? Upon what does the safety of every citizen depend?

Punishment for violated law. —The very idea of law, as has already been stated, implies a power to enforce its commands. The safety of every citizen in life, liberty, and property depends upon the prompt and impartial administration of justice and the execution of all legal requirements. There is a sentiment of disgrace attached to punishment, that ought rather to belong to the commission of crime: the shame is in the perpetration of the offense, and not in the penalty. It is not the severity of punishment that deters men from the violation of law, but the certainty that the penalty will be exacted.

No good citizen can connive at the escape of any criminal, or be indifferent to the administration of justice, or sympathize with those who commit crime, for the wrongs that he tolerates to-day may be the same that he will suffer to-morrow. The safety of society depends upon the speedy administration of the courts; for, when people, from indifference or injudicious tenderness, permit their sympathies to shield the criminal, they injure the community whose laws are defied; they wrong the culprit, for whose crime they apologize, and they outrage the innocent victims of injustice, by preventing the execution of the law that was made for their protection.

The American Union.—Our country has an immense extent of territory, which is capable of sustaining a vast population. The people, spread over so great a surface, engaged in so many kinds of business, will often find their interests conflicting. The great variety of climate, soil, and situation, the woods, waters, and mines afford infinite diversity of productions, which add to the wealth of the country and the comfort of its citizens. This diversity will

---

Should the laws be executed impartially? Why? Is the disgrace in the violation of law, or in its punishment—the stealing or the going to jail? Is it severity that makes obedient citizens? May a good citizen assist a criminal to escape? Why? Why is it likely that opposition and rivalry will cause disaffection among different sections of our country?

create rivalry and opposition in trade, that will tend to estrange one portion of the people from another, unless a sense of common security and a patriotic pride shall prevent the alienation.

When the constitution of the United States was adopted, it was intended to prevent jealousy and bitterness from arising between the different sections of the country. The former government, called the Confederation, only lasted eight years; it did not secure a perfect union, establish justice, or secure the blessings for which the new constitution was instituted. The constitution was intended to unite the whole people from Maine to Texas, from Oregon to Florida, in a great, grand government, whose mission is to secure and "*Proclaim liberty throughout all the land unto all the inhabitants thereof.*" For convenience in the administration of justice, and for the better execution of the laws, the nation is divided into states; these are subdivided into counties; these again into townships; and these, for various reasons, are sometimes cut up into smaller districts.

The interests of the different communities are best promoted by these separations, but it does not follow that because a person lives in a certain school district that he should feel no concern for the education of the other children of the township; nor is it wise that because he lives in one township, he shall advocate its interests to the neglect of the rest of the county; neither is it liberal, because he lives in a certain county, that he shall seek to gain for it a special advantage, to the injury of other parts of the state; nor is it patriotic that, happening to be born in a certain state, he shall love it in preference to the republic of which it is only a fraction. Let it be the proud boast of every American boy and girl, "I, TOO, AM AN AMERICAN."

What was the constitution adopted for? How long did the confederation last? Why was tne form of government changed? Repeat the text. How is our nation divided? A state? A county? A township? What are these subdivisions for? Should patriotism or selfishness govern the citizens of each state, county, township, and school district? Why? What should be the motto of every citizen?

The counsel of the beloved Washington, in his Farewell Address, is worthy of a perpetual remembrance. He urged the people to beware of sectional strifes, and besought them, as they valued the principles of liberty and the success of constitutional government, not to consider themselves the citizens of the north or the south, the east or the west, but to unite, and by sympathy, kindness, charity, and brotherly love, to secure the welfare of their common country—the United States of America. Let the youth of the land now "rally round the flag," cultivate fraternal feelings with all sections, and promote the interests of every state, and thus, in the language of Mr. Webster, make practical the "sentiment dear to every American heart—LIBERTY and UNION; NOW and FOREVER—ONE and INSEPARABLE."

CHAPTER XXIX.

"He who loves not his country can love nothing."

EDUCATION.

The School is a miniature state: a little commonwealth. The object of the government is the preservation and protection of the people; the object of the school is to prepare the people properly for living in the government. The state has laws "commanding what is right, and prohibiting what is wrong;" the school must have laws for the same

---

What did Washington advise? How should we be united—by force or by love? What was Mr. Webster's sentiment? Why should it be dear?

To what is a school compared? Why? What is the object of the government? What of the school? For what are the laws of the state made? What the laws of school?

purpose. The state has officers appointed to execute its laws; the school must have the same. The moral law makes it a duty to obey the laws of the state, and therefore it is right that habits of respect and obedience be learned in school. A bad state government is better than confusion and anarchy; so even an inferior government in school is better than none. As our republican system of government depends on the self-control of the citizens, so the excellence of the school will to a very great extent depend upon the dispositions of the pupils to do right. Morality, intelligence, obedience to law, and politeness are the distinguishing marks of good society; so, also, will these virtues characterize those pupils who are preparing to enter good society.

School laws.—The law of the school may be defined as "a rule of action prescribed by the supreme power in a school, commanding what is right and prohibiting what is wrong."

The teacher.—The exercise of the supreme power in a school is generally vested in the teacher, subject to the supervision of those from whom he receives his appointment. We have already learned that in our system of civil government there are three departments—the legislative, judicial, and executive. These in the school are usually united in the person of the teacher, making his duties sometimes trying, and always responsible. He frames the rules of action for the pupils while they are intrusted to his care; he is master to direct, friend to advise, teacher to instruct, and executive to enforce his rules. It is his duty to look after the health, secure the comfort, protect the rights, and preserve the morals of his pupils.

As he assumes to be a teacher, there are those who expect

Upon what does the excellence of the government, as well as the school, depend? Define school law. How does it differ from the definition of municipal law? In whom is supreme power in schools generally vested? Why? What are the teacher's duties? Is it an easy position? Why? What attributes is the teacher sometimes expected to possess?

him to be learned, wise, careful, prudent, amiable, gentle, sociable, forbearing, long suffering, impartial, charitable, diligent, attentive, studious, energetic, polite, commanding, healthy, omniscient, and omnipresent. Such expectations are never realized, and consequently it will not be surprising that he does not give full satisfaction to all his pupils and their parents. Still, it may safely be asserted that, as a class, teachers do possess at least the desire to do right.

Teachers' rights.—The teacher has rights which are due to his position, his age, and his superior acquirements. He also has feelings as tender, sensibilities as delicate, pride as sensitive, and self-love as strong as any of his pupils, and no pupil has a right to impose upon him in violation of the golden rule. It is not to be expected that he shall be overcome by passion, prejudice, or pride, unless under very strong provocations, but what moral right has any one to exercise his patience by provocation? Teacher and pupils are under the same obligations to each other to be kind, patient, charitable, and forgiving. It may safely be said, however, that whenever the pupils of a school endeavor to do right, no fear need be entertained that any teacher will attempt to provoke them to act differently.

"Why they went to war."—Most of the troubles in school arise primarily from the same reasons that led the two kings to make war on each other.

"A certain king, it is said, sent to another king, saying: 'Send me a blue pig with a black tail, or else ——.' The other, in high dudgeon at the presumed insult, replied: 'I have not got one, and if I had ——.' On this weighty cause they went to war for many years.

Do parents have the same? Why do all teachers fail to give satisfaction to some? Are people generally more reasonable than teachers are? Has the teacher rights? Name them. Is the golden rule binding equally on teacher and pupils? When pupils do right, do teachers generally find fault with them? What is the character of the pupils, generally, who complain of the teacher? Give the anecdote of the two kings who went to war.

"After a satiety of glory and misery, they finally bethought them that as their armies and resources were exhausted, and their kingdoms mutually laid waste, it might be well to consult about the preliminaries of peace; but before this could be concluded, a diplomatic explanation was first needed of the insulting language which caused the quarrel. 'What could you mean,' asked the second king of the first, 'by saying send me a blue pig with a black tail, or else ——?' 'Why,' said the other, 'I meant a blue pig with a black tail, or else some other color.' 'But,' retorted he, 'what could you mean by saying I have not got one, and if I had ——?' 'Why, of course, if I had, I should have sent it.' The explanation was entirely satisfactory, and peace was concluded accordingly."

When difficulty arises in school from misunderstanding, it is the duty of both teacher and pupil not to emulate the folly of the two kings, but to have a fair, frank, and common-sense settlement.

Teachers' partiality.—It is the interest of the teacher to make every reasonable exertion to secure the friendship of his pupils. Those who meet him in a spirit of friendliness, and show a disposition to please him, will, of course, be more esteemed than those who are indifferent to his feelings and comfort. The teacher will necessarily be more attracted to those who are kind, polite, and attentive, and who manifest a disposition to make themselves agreeable. To do otherwise would be unnatural. His favorites are those to whom his sympathies are drawn by acts of kindness and respect. But while he may admire and love some pupils for their agreeable qualities, it does not follow that he shall dislike or hate those who have not tried to win his favor.

Did quarrels ever originate in your school from so unreasonable a cause? When misunderstanding arises, what is the duty of pupil and teacher? How does the golden rule apply to such cases? Is it the interest of the teacher to secure the friendship of his pupils? Why? What is the duty of the pupil? Who are esteemed most, those who please or displease us? Why? Who should be the teacher's favorites? Who are your favorites, those who please or those who displease you?

He may be kind, attentive, and faithful to every one in school, and yet he may and must be partial to such as try to do their duty.

The term partiality is often used to indicate a want of fairness on the part of the teacher. If investigated thoroughly, the charge will frequently be found to originate with such pupils as are conscious of their own neglect of duty, and their indisposition to make an effort to merit the teacher's friendship. The teacher is in honor bound to do justice to all his pupils; but that he should be expected to possess an equal regard for all is absurd. Jealousy and ill-nature are generally the causes that originate the charge of unfair partiality in school.

Common sense forbids the idea that any teacher should exercise injustice toward a pupil without a cause, and in opposition to self-interest; and yet, when the impression of partiality takes hold of some minds, it is almost impossible by any reasoning to remove it. It is so mingled with passion, prejudice, and pride that its correction seems an almost hopeless task. The sooner such a habit of mind is overcome by the exercise of reason and charity, the happier will all parties be in school.

School habits.—A good education is but little more than the formation of good habits. To insure a systematic training in all that is necessary to fit a young man or woman for good society, time, patience, and industry are required. Good habits must be formed. There are certain rules which experience has demonstrated to be necessary in management of every good school. These are not merely arbitrary regulations; they are founded in reason, and can not be

---

Who are those, generally, that complain of the teacher's partiality? May the teacher do justice to all, and yet love some more than others? How may every pupil secure the kind attention of the teacher? How may the pupil make the teacher dislike him? Whose fault is it if some pupils are disliked? How may it be corrected? How may a good education be defined? What are necessary to fit a youth for good society? Are school rules generally arbitrary and tyrannical?

dispensed with, if the school shall be made to accomplish the design of its organization. Their observance will insure habits of ATTENTION, PUNCTUALITY, REGULARITY, and SELF-CONTROL, that are an essential part of a good education, while their neglect will certainly entail a life of mortification, annoyance, and failure. Mention has already been made of attention in Chapter XX.

Punctuality—Anecdote.—General Washington was remarkable for his promptness. It is related that at a meeting of his military family, for a council of war, one of his aids-de-camp was tardy. They had been waiting some time before he arrived. When he came, the general remarked, watch in hand, with some severity, "Sir, you may waste your own time, but you have no right to waste ours." The officer excused himself by throwing the blame upon his watch, which, he alleged, had gone wrong. The general replied, "Either you will have to get a better watch, or I shall have to procure a more punctual secretary."

The general expressed the feelings of every successful business man. He was struggling under responsibilities of the gravest character, and could neither permit his time to be wasted by others, nor suffer others to be put to unnecessary inconvenience and loss on his account. The habit of procrastination, which is strengthened by frequent tardiness at school, is one of the most serious hindrances to success in life, and no one who desires to be esteemed by men of character and influence will permit himself to be overcome by its temptations. The tardy pupil becomes the tardy man, and the man who has the reputation of being indifferent to his engagements can not be trusted. This subject has already been alluded to in Chapter XII, under the head of

---

What will their observance insure? Are these virtues essential to the successful pursuit of all kinds of business? Illustrate them. What anecdote is related in Chapter XX? Give anecdote of Washington. Was he right? Is the teacher right to enforce punctuality? Why? What is meant by procrastination? What effect has a reputation for tardiness on a business man? Has a man the right to waste the time of others by keeping them waiting?

promises. A conscientious regard for the rights and feelings of others will compel every one to be prompt in fulfilling every duty at home and at school.

Regularity.—The welfare of the school, the progress of each pupil, and the comfort and success of the teacher depend largely upon the unfailing attendance of every member. There is a moral obligation resting upon each person at school that he shall do nothing to interfere with the rights of his neighbors. It is his duty, therefore, to be present each day, unless prevented by some unavoidable occurrence. The waste of time, the hindrance in study, and the annoyance to teacher and pupils occasioned by unnecessary absence, has ruined many a school; and the habits of carelessness, indifference, and irregularity, arising from the same cause, have blasted the prospects of many a pupil. Self-respect, self-interest, and the love of the right should compel every pupil to spare no effort to secure a constant attendance.

Self-control.—The ability to exercise self-control over our thoughts and actions is a rare and valuable accomplishment. The following story may not be strictly true, but it carries a moral that is certainly worthy of serious consideration. Plutarch, an ancient writer, says that the geese of Cilicia, when they fly over Mount Taurus, being afraid of the eagles by which it is frequented, carry small stones in their mouths, to prevent them from indulging in their propensity to gabble, and attracting the notice of the eagles.

The propensity to indulge in unnecessary and annoying conversation, so frequently exhibited in church, and in the concert-room, has its origin in the bad habit of talking in school. Dr. Hart, a gentleman of great experience, thus

Why is regularity necessary in school? What is the moral obligation in this matter? What effect have tardiness and irregularity upon a school? What is meant by self-control? Give the story of the geese of Cilicia. What is the moral of this story? Might young folks in school not profit by such an experiment? What does whispering in church arise from?

writes on this subject: "If there could be such a thing as an innocent crime, I would say it was that of talking in school. There can hardly be named a more signal instance of an act so perfectly innocent in itself, becoming so seriously blameworthy purely and solely by circumstances. I believe I express the common opinion of all who have had any experience in the matter, when I say that three-fourths of all the intentional disorder, and at least nine-tenths of all the actual interruptions of study, grow out of the practice of unlicensed talking."

If these statements are true, and no one will deny them, upon what principle can the practice be defended by young ladies and gentlemen? To attempt to prevent so signal a cause of mischief is the manifest duty of every teacher. Every consideration of right, duty, kindness, and politeness should compel obedience to the rule of total abstinence from all such interruption. It may be answered that a little talking will do no harm. How much? "What right have you to talk that is not enjoyed by your neighbor? If one may talk, so may all; if one does it unchecked, so will all." Nor does it matter what is the subject of conversation: it is just as great an interruption of the school to talk about grammar as it is to gossip.

Little things.—It is sometimes objected that school laws are little things, and of comparatively trifling importance. Nothing should be considered trifling which has so essential an influence in the molding of character. The violation of law is not a little thing, as the following incident will prove:

Mr. —— was a bright New England boy, of good family, who graduated from college with much credit. He studied law, and was finally admitted to practice in the courts of his native state. No young man had finer prospects; none

What does Dr. Hart say on this subject? What does he mean by whispering being innocent of itself, and yet wrong? Is it morally right for pupils to interrupt others in this way? How much talking is right? Is it better to interrupt the school about grammar or gossip? Is any wrong a little thing? Give the anecdote.

could look forward to a life of usefulness and honor with a better hope of success. A client put a note into his hands for collection, which, though long overdue, had been neglected. It was dated some time during the year 1857, but it was found, on examination, that the period had expired within which it should have been paid.

The note was really worthless, but the young lawyer saw that by a very slight change in the figures it could be made to appear good. So he took his pen, and altered the 1857 to make it read 1859. The mere change of the figure 7 to a 9 was a "little thing;" it only required an instant to do it; but, unfortunately, that little thing was a crime. The judge and jury called it "forgery," and that young man expiated his violation of law in the state prison. The habit of perpetrating wrongs at school, such as forging notes from parents, etc., leads to the commission of great crimes. He who acts conscientiously as a boy, will not violate the law when a man.

CHAPTER XXX.

"The good needs fear no law,
It is his safety, and the bad man's awe."

THE LAW OF THE SCHOOL.

The morality of the school.—All that has been written in the preceding pages upon the subject of the moral law applies with special force to the pupils at school. If they

---

Was it right to send a young man to the penitentiary merely for changing a 7 to a 9? Are little wrongs justifiable because they are little? Is forgery at school a moral wrong? Why? What may it lead to? Why? Can a liar, a forger, or a law-breaker be a good member of society? Of school?

Why need the good man fear no law?

will practice, conscientiously, the principles set forth, they will acquire such habits of gentleness, kindness, truthfulness, honesty, and charity as will make them loved and respected in after life. The immoralities of school are exhibited in many ways, such as profanity, immodest and unchaste language, the willful destruction of school property, the defacement of school furniture, and the abuse of the school premises.

We involuntarily form an opinion of a family from an inspection of the premises on which they reside. May we not judge unerringly of the moral character of a school in the same manner? If the school-house and its surroundings are marred by the knife, and marked with chalk and pencil; if the gates, doors, and passages are dirty and disfigured, is it uncharitable to say that the school they represent is vicious; that the boys are vulgar, the girls impure, and the teachers unrefined?

We have already learned that, "*A good man, out of the good treasure of the heart, bringeth forth good things; and an evil man, out of the evil treasure, bringeth forth evil things.*" "*By their fruits ye shall know them.*" If these evil indications are pictured in, on, and around the very building devoted to moral and intellectual culture, we are forced to conclude that the minds and hearts from which such vandalism springs must be evil. It may be, and probably is true, that there are refined, virtuous, and pure-minded individuals in such a school, but it is evident that they are in the minority, and that their influence for good, either has not been exercised, or has failed to accomplish a reform.

The reform.—If a school-house presents these shameful signs, which reflect so severely upon the moral character

---

What evil practices are indulged in at school that may become habits? What impression do we receive of a family from the appearance of the premises? Is the school subject to the same principle? May we judge of the value and virtue of a school by the condition of the premises? Why? What does the text say? Is it right that all should suffer because some are vicious? How may a reform be worked out?

of teachers and pupils, it need not, and should not remain in that condition. Every refined teacher, every virtuous girl, and every boy who has a respect for his sister, will unite in an effort to effect the moral purification of the place. Soap and water, brush and sand-paper, scraper and jack-plane will be brought into use, and all will join to redeem the place from pollution and themselves from the shame. if not of perpetrating, at least of permitting such a scandal. Shame on an institution of learning, whether college or common school, that will suffer such glaring indecency to shock the sensibilities of refined people. The moral sense of every school should revolt at such a condition of things, and if it does not, it is a sad illustration of the law of habit, which, by such evil associations, makes them tolerable.

But when the sensibilities of the scholars are so stirred as to require a purification of the premises; when soap and sand, paint and putty have removed as far as possible the foul blemishes that disfigure the place, the question will arise, how shall it be preserved from future injury? How shall the majority control those who have no sense of delicacy or refinement; prevent the repetition of such acts, and vindicate their title to purity? This question will be answered in a subsequent paragraph of this chapter.

Erroneous ideas of honor.—As has already been stated, the precepts of the moral law do not permit us to do wrong, or connive at wrong. Dr. Hart says: "There is a practice common to school life everywhere, known by the not very dignified name of cheating. There is," he continues, "among young people, generally, while at school, an erroneous and mischievous state of opinion on this subject. An ingenuous youth, who would scorn to steal, and scorn to lie anywhere

Who should unite to effect the reform? What is necessary to purify a polluted school? If teacher and pupils unite, may not the school premises be as pure as a private house? What is said by Dr. Hart about cheating? Is it true that boys think they may honorably lie to a teacher?

else than at school, makes no scruple to deceive a teacher. Cheating at school blunts the moral sense; it impairs the sense of personal honor; it breaks down the outworks of integrity; it leads by direct and easy steps to that grosser cheating, which ends in the penitentiary." Not only is this dishonesty seen in the recitation-room, but it pervades all the actions and all the associations of school life. In some schools it is understoood to be a point of honor to lie, to conceal thefts, frauds, trespasses, and personal injuries; and so strong is this immoral idea of honor, that public sentiment will control and compel the pupils, on pain of insult and abuse, to violate their consciences, the law of the school, and sometimes the law of the state.

Anecdote.—Thirty young men, ranging from seventeen to twenty-five years of age, were assembled to recite in college, and while the professor was arranging his desk, they amused themselves by tossing an old wig, which one of their number had stolen, as a joke, from the room of its owner, backward and forward across the room. By an accident, it fell into the professor's chair. On turning to sit down, he saw it, and, happening to be bald himself, supposed it was put there purposely to insult him. Being much mortified at the supposed rudeness, he asked, with some excitement of manner, who did it.

It would have been an easy matter, under ordinary circumstances, for any one in the class to have said that it happened as a piece of boyish fun; that it was an accident, and that no insult was intended, which would have been strictly true. But, unfortunately, the standard of manhood, of real honor, was so low that not one of the number dared to tell, as long as the person who did it kept

---

Is a lie at school of less importance than a lie elsewhere? Will habits of lying in school not become habits at home? Can an honorable boy tell a lie anywhere, under any circumstances? Review the chapter on veracity. May an honorable pupil be dishonorable in school? Are pupils driven to do wrong by the wrong sentiment of the school? Give the anecdote.

silent. The professor asked each member of the class separately: "Did you do that?" "Do you know who did?" and every one answered in the negative. Although the plain statement of the fact would have been satisfactory, yet they all dared to tell a deliberate lie, and that, according to the code of the college, was esteemed an exhibition of honor. The good old professor was grieved at what he was forced to believe was a cowardly insult to himself, perpetrated by the entire class.

Moral sentiment corrected.—When the moral sentiment of many of the pupils is not good, the remedy is difficult, for bad habits are hard to overcome; but those who possess the true principles of real honor, and the moral courage to do what they think is right, can effect a reform. There are several influences which, if united, will accomplish this result. The chief of these are personal persuasion and example, the union of the good, and information.

The union of the good.—As combinations are sometimes made to defy the laws of the school, and to conceal lying, stealing, vulgarity, and destruction of property, under false notions of honor; so combinations may be made to sustain the right by those who wish truth, justice, and morality to prevail. No honorable youth can associate on terms of intimacy with a liar, a thief, or a libertine. "In union there is strength," for good, as well as evil; and, if the virtuous will associate together, and refuse to recognize those who are viciously inclined, morality will become popular, and will in the end prevail. When the general sentiment of the school condemns all kinds of deception, and all dishonesty, those who are addicted to such practices will find the strongest and best inducements to reform—or leave.

Did those young men do right? What would have been right? May a moral reform in school be made? Is it desirable? How may it be effected? Is it right that a few shall give a bad reputation to a whole school?

Information.—School laws, like the laws of every community, are necessary to promote the welfare of all, and of course each pupil is under a moral and legal obligation to render them obedience. It can not, as was said of civil government, be left to the discretion of any one to obey, since the good alone would do their duty. As in the civil court, it frequently happens that information or testimony is necessary to be given in reference to those who transgress the laws. The office of a witness is by no means a pleasant one, and yet the giving of testimony is often a necessary obligation.

All the principles involved in Chapters XI, XII, and XIII, have their application in the school, and no one can study them too closely, or practice them too carefully.

The voluntary informer.—By the municipal law, no one is obliged to criminate himself, but the moral law requires an offender frankly to acknowledge his wrong, and to make whatever reparation is necessary to atone for the offense. No honorable pupil will keep silence when his own misdemeanors are the occasion of injury to the good name of any individual, or to the school. It is unjust and cruel that the reputation of a teacher or pupil should suffer by the unwillingness of the real offender to step manfully forth to relieve the innocent party.

There are circumstances in which the voluntary giving of information against others is not only a right, but a duty. If there is a persistent determination manifested by any one to injure, annoy, and insult any person in the school, or out of it, he should be reported, upon the same principle that a cross dog should not be permitted to wrong unoffending people. If any one is guilty of grossly immoral practices,

---

What are school laws for? Should they be obeyed? What is the duty of good citizens when the laws are defied? May a man justly inform on a burglar, an incendiary, or a horse-thief? May a pupil justly inform on a liar, a thief, or a libertine in school? Review Chapters XI, XII, and XIII, and apply the principles to the school. When is it a duty for one pupil to inform on another?

involving himself and others disgracefully, it should be made known to the teacher, upon the same principle that a man having the small-pox should be prevented from spreading the contagion. If the property of the school is defaced or destroyed, it is the duty of the lovers of order to make the offender known, upon the same principle that every good citizen is interested to arrest and punish the burglar and the incendiary. These are outrages that demand the intervention of justice; and yet there are breaches of school discipline which are not of sufficient importance to justify a voluntary information. These should be left to the discretion of the teacher.

The tattler.—A mere tattler or busybody, who tells the faults of another for the love of gossip, or for the pleasure derived from his punishment, is simply despicable. No more contemptible and dishonorable person exists than he who, through envy, jealousy, or malice, would derive pleasure from another's pain and mortification. The tattler has no good motive, and is entirely unworthy of respect and confidence. A very important distinction should be made between the tattler, who gives information from mean and unworthy motives, and the informer, who is actuated by a desire to do good or prevent wrong. The former deserves the contempt of the good, whilst the latter is worthy of the commendation and regard of every one who appreciates an action done for the benefit of individuals or of the school.

If this distinction is clearly understood, and carefully observed, no one need incur the opprobrious title of tattler while engaged in the discharge of his duty. It is written, "*Woe unto you, when all men shall speak well of you.*" If personal popularity, however desirable it may appear, is

---

Should a man with small-pox be permitted to give the contagion to others? Why? How should this principle apply to one who is morally diseased? What is a tattler? What distinction should be made between the mere tattler and the informer, as spoken of? Why should the moral sentiment of the school despise and condemn the tattler?

to be gained by neglecting the discharge of obvious duty, or by doing what we know to be wrong, it costs more than it is worth. The satisfaction of one's conscience, and the approval of the good, are more to be desired than the praise of the thoughtless or vicious.

It may be urged that the giving of information would be a violation of the "golden rule," and, consequently, wrong. This beautiful moral law was never meant to be a shield for the perpetrators of wrong. It would be a wicked perversion of its spirit that would prevent the exposure of vice and crime, because the informer might possibly, at some future time, be guilty of the same offense. This rule only applies to actions that are right, and it is only in the performance of such actions that we are required "to do as we would be done by."

The involuntary informer.—It is the duty of the teacher to investigate carefully all charges which affect the interests of the school and the welfare of his pupils. To do this successfully, he may with propriety call upon the pupils to give him such information as they possess; and it is their duty to tell the truth, frankly and fully, and not to attempt by any indirection or evasion to conceal it. It may be unpleasant and mortifying to tell, and yet the interests of the school demand "the truth, the whole truth, and nothing but the truth." When it is a recognized principle of honor that every pupil will tell the truth when called upon, the perpetrators of mischief and the violators of law will soon desist from their evil courses, and the school will become what it should ever be—the model of good society.

What is the duty of every one when called upon to give information? What would be the effect if it is understood that every pupil will tell the truth when called upon? Does the golden rule mean that if you lie for me I ought to lie for you? What does it mean?

PART III.

SOCIAL LAW, OR POLITENESS.

CHAPTER XXXI.

CLEANLINESS.

Social law may be defined as a rule of action prescribed by good society, commanding what is right and prohibiting what is wrong in the intercourse of its members.

This law is sometimes known under the name of politeness, and is based upon the principles of the moral law. The "golden rule" is the governing motive of good society, influencing all its thoughts, modifying all its speech, and controlling all its actions. True politeness requires that we shall exercise our faculties to secure the approbation, and, if possible, the admiration of all with whom we come in contact. Good manners are habits of mind and body, derived from right thinking and acting; such thinking and acting as shall afford us the greatest happiness, and at the same time preserve the rights and feelings of our neighbor. These habits are acquired by observation and study, and by association with persons of refined taste and elegant culture.

The neglect to learn and practice the rules prescribed by good society for the regulation of social intercourse brings

---

To what does Part I refer? What is the subject of Part II? What of Part III? Define social law. What is it sometimes called? What is true politeness based on? What does it require? What are good manners derived from? How are they acquired? What punishment applies to those who violate the social laws?

with it its own punishment. Those who are rough, coarse, and vulgar do not merit the respect of well-bred people, much less can they command any good social influence. It is the duty of every one to gain friends by making the best impressions possible, provided it can be done without any sacrifice of principle or honor.

We shall endeavor in the following pages to give such rules of action as will enable the young to enter good society, with pleasure to themselves and satisfaction to their friends; and yet we do not claim to have exhausted the subject. Sufficient will be presented for the consideration of young people to enable them, by a proper use of their faculties, to appear to advantage among persons of refinement and culture.

First impressions.—The following incident, taken from the "*Little Corporal*," is very suggestive of the importance of trying to make pleasing impressions:

"A gentleman advertised for a boy to assist him in his office, and nearly fifty applicants presented themselves to him. Out of the whole number, he, in a short time, selected one, and dismissed the rest.

"'I should like to know,' said a friend, 'on what ground you selected that boy, who had not a single recommendation?'

"'You are mistaken,' said the gentleman, 'he had a great many. He wiped his feet when he came in, and closed the door after him, showing that he was careful. He gave up his seat instantly to that lame, old man, showing he was kind and thoughtful. He took off his cap when he came in, and answered my questions promptly and respectfully, showing he was polite and gentlemanly. He picked up the book which I had purposely laid on the floor, and

---

What is the duty of every one in society? Give the anecdote. How many reasons were there why that boy should have been preferred? Tell the allusion to his feet, the door, the old man, his cap, his answers, the book, his waiting, his clothes, his hair, his teeth, his nails.

replaced it on the table, while all the rest stepped over it, or shoved it aside, and he waited quietly for his turn, instead of pushing and crowding, showing that he was honest and orderly. When I talked with him, I noticed that his clothes were carefully brushed, his hair in nice order, and his teeth as white as milk; and when he wrote his name, I noticed that his finger nails were clean, instead of being tipped with jet, like that handsome little fellow's in the blue jacket. Do n't you call those things letters of recommendation? I do; and I would give more for what I can tell about a boy by using my eyes ten minutes than for all the fine letters he can bring me.'"

Most persons are influenced in their estimate of strangers by the impressions received at their first meeting. As these impressions are difficult to remove, it is desirable that they be not unfavorable. They are derived chiefly from the circumstances of neatness, cleanliness, dress, countenance, voice, and manner, together with the time, place, and company in which these peculiarities are exhibited.

Cleanliness.—The preservation of health and comfort, good taste, and the approbation of friends, require cleanliness of person and dress. As we ought not to offend the sensibilities of any, by neglect in this particular, a few hints may not be unseasonable to those who aspire to be gentlemen and ladies.

Hands and face.—The hands, face, neck, and ears should be thoroughly washed every morning in soft water, and then briskly rubbed with a crash towel until they are dry and warm. There is nothing that preserves and promotes personal beauty like this; it gives softness and pliancy to the skin, and imparts a beautiful glow to the cheek. The hands

---

Why were these things in his favor? Why were these things better than letters of recommendation? What is meant by first impressions? Why is it important that they should be favorable? What are they generally derived from? What reasons are there for cleanliness? Why should we wash every morning?

and wrists sometimes require to be washed more frequently, as they are more liable to be soiled. The nails should be pared to correspond with the tips of the fingers, being neither too long nor too short, and should always be scrupulously clean. Dirty hands and nails, especially in school, are marks of extreme vulgarity.

Chapped hands.—Some persons' hands are liable to chap and become sore in bad weather. When this roughness appears, it may be removed by bathing the hands with soft, warm water at night, and rubbing them gently, but thoroughly, with corn-meal and soap. After the skin is softened, and the rough cuticle is rubbed off, they should be anointed with sweet oil, glycerine, or lard ; a pair of gloves should be put on, or stockings, if nothing better is at hand, for the night. On the next morning the oil should be washed off with tepid water and soap, and the hands wiped thoroughly. If, after this process, they be kept dry and clean, they will become smooth and soft.

Clean person.—Good health requires that the whole body be frequently and thoroughly bathed, an operation that some persons neglect entirely in winter. The skin is full of minute pores or openings for the escape of insensible perspiration, and if these are obstructed, they can not carry off that waste matter which should pass from the body in this way. Not only does the skin become rough, dry, harsh, and covered with pimples, but unpleasant odors emanate from it. These odors impregnate the clothing, and become very offensive. The remedy is the bath.

All the appliances needed for bathing are a tub of soft water, some soap, a sponge or cloth, and a crash towel for

---

How should the nails be pared and cleaned? What must be said of those that are habitually dirty? What are chapped hands? How may chapped hands be cured? How, then, may they be kept cured? What does good health require? What is said of the skin? What is the cause of rough, coarse skin? Mention the things needed for the bath.

drying. These things are not expensive, and are found in every house. If the weather is warm, the bath should be taken in the morning, the water being warm enough to take off the chill. The skin should then be rubbed until it is all in a glow. If the weather be chilly, to avoid the danger of taking cold, the bath should be taken before going to bed, the water being as hot as can comfortably be borne. It is not well to remain too long in the water; ten or fifteen minutes at most being quite sufficient. After a thorough rubbing, put on clean clothes and retire. This is a simple luxury, and at the same time a necessity. Those who try it, will not need to be urged to its repetition.

The hair.—For some time it has been the fashion to cut gentlemen's hair short. As a matter of convenience and cleanliness, it would be well that so sensible a fashion should always prevail. The fashion for ladies in this respect has been neither convenient, comfortable, nor healthful.

The head should be thoroughly brushed every morning, that all impurities may be removed from the scalp. Occasionally, also, it should be washed with soft water, in which a little common salt has been dissolved; then it should be carefully combed and dried.

The use of pomatums, or oils of any kind, assists in retaining the dust upon the head, especially of those who attend school where chalk is much used. Such greasy preparations should be avoided, as the natural oil of the hair is sufficient to preserve its glossiness, if the head be kept clean. When the hair is light, and easily disarranged, it would be prettier and cleanlier to inclose it in a net, or to encircle it with a comb or ribbon, than to attempt to plaster it to its place by such sticky applications.

How shall we avoid taking cold? How long should we remain in the water? Explain why the bath is beneficial. How should gentlemen's hair be cut? Why is the fashion for ladies not so good? How should the head be treated? What is said of pomatums and oils? When the hair is light and short, how should girls arrange it?

The teeth.—One of nature's most beautiful gifts is fine teeth. The laws of health require that they be kept in good order, and social law demands that they be preserved clean, pure, and sweet. Unsightly and decaying teeth are very offensive. If they are disfigured by tartar collecting near the gums, it may easily be removed by applying a preparation of pulverized charcoal and common salt, with a soft tooth brush. Tartar is an injurious and disagreeable substance, which will soon destroy the teeth, if permitted to remain. If the teeth are decaying, they should be examined by a dentist, that the decay may be arrested. A daily brushing will prevent unpleasant odors in the breath, and tend to promote health and comfort. A wooden or quill toothpick may be used, without injury to the enamel, to remove the particles of food that may have remained in the mouth.

Clean clothes.—All linen and cotton clothing should be frequently changed and washed. Dirty collars, wristbands, and shirt fronts are intolerable. Woolen clothes should be regularly brushed and dusted, that all particles of dirt may be removed. If accidentally soiled at the table, or elsewhere, by grease, the cloth should be cleansed at once with benzine or turpentine. Spots of grease upon the clothing indicate a great lack of neatness in the wearer. Every young gentleman and lady should be provided with a handkerchief, which should be so frequently changed as to be disagreeable neither to themselves nor their neighbors. A clean handkerchief is one of the prime evidences of gentility.

Boots and shoes should be kept so neat and clean as to show that their owners are not lacking in good taste.

What is said of the beauty of the teeth? Why should they be preserved? How may tartar be removed? Why should it be removed? If the teeth are decaying, what must be done? What will correct unpleasant odors? What kind of toothpick should be used? Why? What kind of clothing shall be washed? How shall woolen clothes be treated? If greased? What is said of the handkerchief? What is said of boots and shoes?

Odors and perfumes.—Some persons are gifted with a very delicate sense of smell, which they gratify by the use of sweet perfumes. To enjoy this pleasure, they scent their boxes and bureaus with odors, which are thus imparted to their clothing. But all persons are not alike in this respect; perfumes that are agreeable to some are highly offensive to others. It is not in good taste for any person to use such an excess of perfume that they who pass them on the street, or sit or stand near them, shall observe it, and possibly comment upon it. There may be a suspicion that the musk or other odor is used for the concealment of some scent that is supposed to be less agreeable or reputable.

True politeness would suggest that we shall not be perfumed with cologne or musk, onions or tobacco, the odors of the hen-house or the barn.

CHAPTER XXXII.

DRESS.

The dress is one of the prominent indications of character. In the early history of this government, there was a marked distinction between the grades of society in this respect, but through the influence and by the example of such men as Dr. Franklin and President Jefferson, republican equality was at last indicated by a uniformity of dress.

Do all persons enjoy the same perfumes? Shall we offend others to gratify ourselves? How shall perfume be used? Why should it not be used in excess? What kinds of odors are perfumes used to destroy? What does true politeness suggest? Why not eat onions in company?

What is the subject of Chapter XXXII? What is said of Franklin and Jefferson?

Anecdote.—It is related that on the second visit of General Lafayette to our country, at the time he assisted in laying the corner-stone of Bunker Hill monument, on the 17th of June, 1825, an immense crowd was assembled to give him welcome, and witness the ceremonies. A French gentleman being present, who had not been in the country before, observing so large a concourse of people, all dressed like gentlemen and ladies, asked with surprise: "Where are the peasants; why are they not here?" He did not know that in the United States, even the president would not be distinguished by the style of his clothing from any well-dressed gentleman.

Young people, of course, are largely under the direction of their parents in the matter of apparel; still, as tasteful dressing is one of the accomplishments of society, it is not inappropriate to treat of it as a necessary part of a polite education.

The objects of dress.—There are two primary ideas connected with dress. The first is the preservation of health; the second, the prevention of immodest exposure: the former conducing to our physical comfort, the latter to our moral influence. In addition, and secondary to these, is the cultivation of taste in the selection of suitable materials, and in their adaptation, by a proper selection and arrangement of colors and style, to the age, complexion, and form of the wearer.

Healthfulness of dress.—There is a tribe of Indians in the North-west, who, when their children are infants, place a pressure on their little, tender heads, which gradually flattens the skull, producing a terrible and disgusting distortion. From this general custom, they derive the name of Flat Heads. The same people, and other tribes of the same

---

What anecdote is related? What are peasants? Why were there no peasants present? How do the peasantry dress in Europe? How do noblemen dress? Why is the president not distinguished by his dress? Are there any principles to be learned concerning dress? What are the objects of dress? What are the secondary objects? What is said of the Flat Heads?

race, cut slits, sometimes an inch long, in the lobes of the ears, and also bore holes through the cartilage of the nose, above the upper lip, in which they insert feathers, strings of beads, and rings of brass wire or bone.

Fashionable Chinese women have feet only three or four inches long. When infants, their feet are confined in shoes that prevent their growth. This is not a very painful operation, for the compression is so gradual that the child becomes accustomed to it, and by the time its growth is attained, the feet are the perfection of style, and the women, scarcely able to walk, hobble along, rejoicing in the fact that art has made them so beautiful.

The "New American Cyclopædia," speaking of the Flat Head Indians, says: "The flattened skull must be classed among the strange whims of nations, with the small feet of the Chinese, the perforated ears and lips of savages, and the tapering waists of Europeans." But are we exempt from the follies, in this respect, that distinguish less favored people, who have never heard that the body is a temple for the spirit, whose perfect beauty consists in its fullest development of health, strength, and natural growth?

Anecdote.—A few years ago a remarkable woman died in the Massachusetts Insane Asylum, from the effects of tight lacing. Possessing, naturally, a very fine, well proportioned form, she attempted to improve it, as she supposed, by contracting her waist. In spite of the most watchful care of her keepers, she persisted secretly in the practice, and finally died from its effects.

Lacing.—If all the women insane on this subject were in the asylums, the acommodations would have to be largely

---

Of the Chinese? Why do these distortions not produce much pain? Why do these people deform themselves? Do you think these Flat Heads pretty? Why? Why should we not confine babies' feet like the Chinese? What is said of these things in the Cyclopædia? Are we exempt from similar folly? How is our folly displayed? What is said of the woman in the asylum?

increased. The habit is a general one, and very injurious. A good authority says: "It has been found that the liver, the lungs, and the powers of the stomach have been brought into a diseased state by this most pernicious habit. Loss of bloom, fixed redness of the nose, and irruptions on the skin are among its sad effects. If prolonged, there is no knowing to what malady tight lacing may not lead. Its most apparent effect is an injured digestion, and consequent loss of appetite. Of this, however, it is often difficult to convince the practiced tightlacer, for vanity is generally obstinate. But, looking at tight lacing without consideration of its effect on health, and merely as its tendency to improve or to injure the appearance, nothing can be more absurd than to believe that it is advantageous to the figure. A small waist is rather a deformity than a beauty. To see the shoulders cramped and squeezed together is anything but agreeable. The figure should be easy, well developed, supple. If nature has not made the waist small, compression can not mend her work."

Boys and men lacing.—But it must not be supposed that the female sex alone is guilty of this folly. There are a great many young men and boys who seem desirous of emulating their sisters in this absurdity. All that has been written above will apply with equal or greater force to those who neglect to wear suspenders. The shoulders of both sexes should perform the office of supporting the clothing, and any other method is unwise and injurious.

Modesty of dress.—The second question to be decided in the selection and adoption of any kind of dress is, "Is it modest?" Good taste and morality require that, "*Women*

Is this deforming practice common? Why? What does a good authority say of it? What maladies does lacing produce? What are the most apparent effects of lacing? Does lacing improve the form? What does it produce? Why do Chinese deform the feet? Why do American women and men lace? Why should boys wear suspenders? What part of the body should support the clothes? What is the next idea connected with dress?

adorn themselves in modest apparel, with shame-facedness and sobriety," which means that no manner of dress shall be used which suggests ideas of indelicacy. The modest woman seeks rather to escape than to attract observation, and would assume no form of apparel with the design of notoriety. No woman need ever complain that she is made the subject of remarks that are suggested by her own imprudence in this particular. There are some styles that the morality of good society can never justify. If it be considered impolite, as it is, for a gentleman to enter ladies' society, or to sit at table with his coat off, even on a very warm day, it may, for similar reasons, be a question whether a lady may appear in a gentleman's presence with no covering upon her neck and shoulders and no sleeves at all. Whatever may be thought of appearing at home in such undress, no lady who has given the subject the consideration it merits, will permit herself or her daughter to be seen in public in such a condition.

Appropriateness of dress.—The next question that arises concerning a form of dress is, "Is it suitable?" As there are different styles of personal appearance, it is evident that all will not appear equally well in the same costume. One is tall, another is short; one thin, another robust; one straight, another droops; one is fair, another dark; one is young, another is middle-aged; and still another is old. It is plain, then, that the dress should be adapted to these natural conditions, in order to make each individual appear to the best advantage. And yet no person of good taste and modesty desires to appear singular by not conforming somewhat to the customary style. "To adopt the prevailing

How shall women adorn themselves? Why should immodest women not complain? Why is it impolite for a gentleman to enter a lady's presence or sit at table in shirt sleeves? Why should ladies do the same? What shall be thought of a woman who appears without covering her neck and arms in public? What is the next question about dress? Why is the same kind of dress not suitable for all? What should the style of dress be adapted to?

fashion, but not to carry it to excess (provided it can be done without injury to health and morals), seems the most suitable course of conduct."

Dr. Johnson, in praising a lady for being very well dressed, remarked: "I am sure she was well-dressed, for I can not remember what she had on." The doctor's idea was that the appropriateness of her dress prevented the diverting of his attention from herself, which was certainly a high compliment to her good taste.

The fashions.—The principle which should actuate American youth is to dress neatly and appropriately; always having reference to health, comfort, and modesty; to age, form, and complexion; to time, place, and circumstances. Our boys and girls should glory in that health, strength, and activity which will fit them for a life of comfortable usefulness. Nothing ought to tempt them to impair their efficiency as men and women, for the mere gratification of a perverted taste. When fashion demands that they shall injure their own beautiful hair by any process; that they shall restrict the fullest capacity of their lungs; that they shall contract the natural growth of their shoulders; that they shall give an unnatural curvature to the spine, or inclose their feet, Chinese fashion, in improper shoes, they should dare to assert their common sense by refusing to obey the tyrannical decree. All honor to the boy and girl who have the independence and moral courage to follow the dictates of wisdom, rather than of folly, in conforming to unreasonable and oftentimes injurious fashions.

How far shall sensible people follow the fashion? What was Dr. Johnson's remark? Why was Dr. Johnson's remark a compliment to the lady? What principle should always govern American youth in regard to dress? What should they do when injurious fashions are in vogue? How may the hair be injured? The lungs? The shoulders? The feet? Whether is it better to have corns with small shoes, or larger shoes with sound feet?

CHAPTER XXXIII.

DRESS. (Continued.)

Home dress.—Some persons take special care to appear well dressed everywhere but at home. This is a great mistake. The home should be a pleasant place, and its attractions should not be marred by a want of politeness in manners or by slovenliness in dress. Our garments should be always suited to our work, but when our employments do not require it, we should lay aside the homely or rough clothing, and assume that which carries with it more pleasing impressions. Respect for our own influence, among the members of our own family, requires neatness and tidiness at home as well as abroad. When the young ladies of a household appear habitually in presence of father and brothers in dirty and unbecoming attire, with unbrushed hair, unhooked dress, or unlaced shoes, they need not complain of the coarse manners and uncivil address of the male members of the family. To be polite only in presence of visitors is a poor compliment to those whom we should respect and gratify at home.

Street dress.—The dress for street wear should always be suited to the condition of the weather. The Queen of England very sensibly introduced the "balmoral skirts" and heavy walking boots, for ladies' use when out of doors.

What is the subject of Chapter XXXIII? Why do some persons appear badly dressed at home? Is it a duty to appear neat and clean at home? Why? To what snould the dress be adapted? Why? When work does not require the rough clothing, what should we wear? Why? Why should persons be neat and tidy? What effect does carelessness of dress have upon the home? What should be the street dress?

Such fashions are worthy of imitation, as they combine both beauty and comfort. The street dress should never be of such peculiar material as to attract attention by the gaudiness of its colors, the extravagance of its trimmings, or the oddity of its style. No truly modest woman can consent to become the gazing stock of a crowd of vulgar idlers.

There is a class of men and women who dress on purpose to attract attention, who walk the streets to be seen; but these are not members of that good society whose claims we advocate. The moral law places an estimate upon the value of such, when it declares, "*As a jewel of gold in a swine's snout, so is a fair woman without discretion.*" We admire a finely dressed lady, but she who is attired without discretion and modesty has but little claim to our respect.

As an illustration of extravagance and absurdity, we would call attention to the recent fashion of "the train." Following this ridiculous custom, women appeared in the dirty, muddy streets, dragging sometimes a yard or more of fine material upon the ground, to the intense disgust of all neat and sensible people. Such "style" should receive no countenance from the common-sense ladies of America. Whatever apology may be made for the train in a large parlor, as a question of taste, no one will defend its use in a dirty, crowded street.

Church dress.—A decent respect for the house of God and His worship, requires us to appear there in suitable apparel. It is said to be a distinguishing characteristic of American women to dress extravagantly, in high colors, with laces and jewels, for church. In this respect, they contrast very unfavorably with the ladies of Europe. That

---

What three things should be avoided in a street dress? What kind of people attempt to attract notice on the street? What is said of the woman without discretion? What is said of the train? What excuse is given for such a costume? Is it a modest dress on the street? Why? In what kind of dress should persons appear in church? Why should the dress not be gay for church? Why is expensive and stylish church dress immoral?

it is not in good taste thus to appear, decked out in all the requirements of extreme fashion, seems hardly to admit of a question. When persons attend church to worship, they should appear in such plain, modest, simple clothing as will neither disturb their own thoughts by anxiously taking care of it, nor excite the envy and jealousy of those who may be diverted from the solemnities of the place by gazing at them.

School dress.—As has already been said, the dress should always be adapted to the necessities of our occupation, whether of worship, business, or pleasure. As the school rooms are frequently dusty from pulverized chalk, etc., the clothing, whether of the boys or girls, should be of materials that can be easily cleaned, and that do not readily show the dirt. It should be plain, simple, and unostentatious. According to the principles of the moral law, it is wrong to dress in such a manner as to excite the envy, the jealousy, or the covetousness of any who really can not afford to clothe themselves expensively, and yet are mortified to appear meanly clad in contrast with their more richly appareled schoolmates. Many a poor pupil is tortured with his apparent poverty, and by the excess of a false pride is driven from school because he can not compete with those who have more wealth at command.

It would be difficult to suggest any uniform method of dress that could be made practicable for the boys; but it would be very easy for the young ladies in any school to agree upon some general principles by which this difficulty could be overcome. An inexpensive material might be selected that is of a subdued color, is easily cleaned, and yet is genteel and pretty. This might be set off with a plain linen collar and cuffs; the former fastened by a small plain

What passions does it excite? Is it right to excite such feelings in the minds of the poor? What should be the school dress? What should be the character of the school dress? Is it wrong to excite envy? Why? Why are some people so sensitive? What is said of a uniform school dress?

pin, and the latter by pearl buttons. If, for example, the madder-colored calicoes were chosen, and trimmed with simple braid, they would fill all the conditions of a neat, cheap, comfortable, and becoming school dress—"cheap enough for the poorest, and good enough for the best," and with a considerable variety for the exercise of good taste in the selection. Such an arrangement is entirely practicable, and has been adopted in some schools where simplicity of manners and goodness of heart were the prevailing traits of the lady pupils.

Jewelry.—A profusion of rings, chains, pins, charms, and gilt gewgaws is not in good taste among well-bred people. Fancies of that kind should be indulged very sparingly. A watch, used as a time-piece, is very valuable to the student and the man of business, but when used as an ostentatious ornament is simply vulgar. In respect to the wearing of jewelry, there should be a marked distinction between the savage squaw and the enlightened lady.

The following incident will illustrate the fact that tawdry finery and the display of jewels is not consistent with the ideas of good society in Europe:

A party of some sixty Americans were traveling for pleasure in Europe. When in the vicinity of Odessa, a city of Russia, on the Black Sea, it was suggested that they should make a visit of courtesy to the Emperor, who, with his brother and their families, were spending some time at their beautiful residences near a watering place called Yalta. The Emperor invited them, with the assurance that the visit would be agreeable to him and his family. As the party was too large to enter the house, the reception was made in the open air, under the shade of the trees. "The royal family came out," writes one of the party, "bowing and

---

State the reasons why such a dress would be desirable. What are the reasons why it would not be desirable? What is said of a profusion of jewelry? What is said of a watch for use and for show? Ought moral people to emulate savages in their tastes? Give an account of the American travelers in Europe.

smiling, and stood in our midst. With every bow, his majesty said a word of welcome. He said he was very much pleased to see us, especially as such friendly relations existed between Russia and the United States.

"The Empress said the Americans were favorites in Russia, and she hoped the Russians were similarly regarded in America. She talked sociably with various ladies around the circle. The dukes and princes, admirals and maids of honor dropped into free-and-easy chat, first with one and then with another of our party, and whoever chose, stepped forward and spoke with the modest little Grand Duchess Marie, the Czar's daughter. All talked English.

"The Emperor wore a cap, frock coat, and pantaloons, all of some kind of plain white drilling, cotton or linen, and sported no jewelry or insignia of any kind. No costume could be less ostentatious. The Empress and the little Grand Duchess wore simple suits of foulard silk, with a small blue spot in it. The dresses were trimmed with blue. Both ladies wore broad blue sashes about their waists; linen collars and clerical ties of muslin; low crowned straw hats, trimmed with blue velvet; parasols and flesh-colored gloves. The Grand Duchess had no heels upon her shoes. I do not know this of my own knowledge. I was not looking at her shoes, but one of our ladies told me so. I was glad to observe that she wore her own hair, plaited in thick braids against the back of her head."

This long extract has been given to show that persons of great wealth, of exalted station and real nobility, can, without any show of humility, be gentlemen and ladies, and these, in our estimation, are their most befitting titles.

Did they act differently from other intelligent people? Did the royal families act differently? How should noble men and women act but as gentlemen and ladies? Do people who affect style always behave so modestly? Describe the ladies' dresses. Describe the gentlemen's dress. What ought to be the difference between the conduct of an emperor and a gentleman? Was it genteel for the grand duchess to wear no heels on her shoes when that was the fashion? Would she have appeared prettier or happier if she had been decked with rings, pins, chains, and bracelets?

In concluding this subject, we offer a few lines from one of our American poets, Dr. Holmes:

"From little matters let us pass to less,
And lightly touch the mysteries of *dress;*
The outward forms the inner man reveal,
We guess the pulp before we eat the peel.
One single precept might the whole condense—
Be sure your tailor is a man of sense;
But add a little care, or decent pride,
And always err upon the sober side.
Wear seemly gloves; not black, nor yet too light,
And least of all the pair that once was white.
Have a good hat. The secret of your looks
Lies with the beaver in Canadian brooks.
Virtue may flourish in an old cravat,
But man and nature scorn the shocking hat.
Be shy of breastpins: plain, well-ironed white,
With small pearl buttons—two of them in sight,
Is always genuine, while your gems may pass,
Though real diamonds, for ignoble glass.

CHAPTER XXXIV.

THE EDUCATED COUNTENANCE.

First impressions are often derived from what we see, or think we see, in the countenance. On entering a school and examining the faces of the pupils, we are unconsciously drawn to some and repelled by others. Whence comes

---

What are the ideas expressed by Dr. Holmes? What is meant by guessing the pulp? Why should the tailor be a man of sense? Why err upon the sober side? What should be the style of gloves? Why? What kind of a hat should a gentleman wear? What kind of breastpin? What kind of shirt front? What is meant by pearl buttons being genuine? What is meant by gems passing for glass?

What are first impressions derived from? What is the difference between the expressions of countenance as seen in school? Why is this difference?

this difference? Looking around, we discover here a face wearing a pleasant, but not affected smile, while there sits one that cultivates a habitual frown, whose mouth and brows are rough, with a coarse expression of unloveliness; here is one that bears a bright, intelligent countenance—he is a student, a thinker; there is one whose face never lights up with emotion—he does not care to learn; here is one that wears a silly simper, that is ready to laugh at the slightest occasion, indicating a vacant, trifling character; there is one who is full of affectation, whose mouth is moving in pretense of study, but whose eye is watching to see whether he is observed; here is one who affects coarseness, who is abrupt and rude, whose manner indicates respect neither for himself nor others; and there is a coward, who takes advantage of his teacher. Injustice may be done sometimes in thus forming an estimate of character from appearances. Yet, as a rule, we may distinguish intelligence, gentleness, and kindness from ignorance, coarseness, and brutality, by an inspection of the countenance. Habits of mind are stamped upon the face. This is true even of animals. The heart and mind educate the features to express what they suggest.

Anecdote.—There was an exhibition of the pupils of the Institution for the Deaf and Dumb, at Jacksonville, Ill. After many curious and interesting illustrations had been given of the methods of training this class of persons, two of the most advanced boys were selected to convey ideas to each other by the changes of the face alone, without the use of the hands. They were placed about ten feet apart, facing each other. The hands of one were tied behind him, and to him were shown some words, written by a visitor on a

---

What may we discover in these faces? May we do injustice in forming opinions solely on appearances? Are opinions and impressions the same? Can you judge of the character of animals by their appearance? Give illustration. What is it that affects the countenance? How do deaf and dumb persons usually communicate? Give the illustration.

paper, which he was expected to communicate to the other. He read the words, and then each looked the other in the face attentively. In a few moments the boy, who read the communication in the other's face, wrote it upon his slate, and handed it to the visitor.

Curious to understand the method by which this was accomplished, the following alphabet of emotions was furnished to explain it. A was represented by Admiration, B by Boldness, Curiosity, Devotion, Envy, Fear, Grief, Humility, Incredulity, Joy, Kindness, Love, Mirth, No, Obstinacy, Pride, Quiet, Recollection, Scorn, Thought, Uneasiness, Vanity, Wonder, Xebec, Yes, Zany. The xebec is the name of a small boat and a vibratory motion of the body, as of a man standing in a boat, passing over the water, expresses the letter. It is seldom needed. A zany is a fool, and a silly expression of countenance suggests it. If the pupil were called upon to spell CAT, he would do so by expressing Curiosity, Admiration, and Thought by his countenance.

While we may not emulate these deaf and dumb boys in their training of the muscles of the face, we may at least educate our faces, that they be not repulsive. It is not claimed that any amount of training can change the form of the features; all that can be done is to let the countenance be the index of a kind, loving heart. Politeness requires that young folks shall learn to express the better emotions in their faces, and, above all, that they shall not frown or scorn, grin or simper, and thus give the impression to strangers that they are habitually cross or silly.

The eyes, brows, and lips are the tell-tales of the affections and passions, as it is written, "*A merry heart maketh a cheerful countenance.*"

Explain how you can spell your name in this manner? May we train our faces to express emotion? What will our face always indicate? Of what is the face the index? How shall young persons always try to appear? What are the better emotions? Name some of the bad ones.

CHAPTER XXXV.

THE CULTIVATED VOICE.

What a wonderful power the sweetly modulated accents of a fine voice exert upon the ear, and with what a charm they invest its fortunate possessor! Good or bad impressions are made upon us, not only by what people say, but by the tones used in conversation. We feel attracted or repulsed by a person's voice before we have heard fully what he has to say. Habits of thought are indicated to a great degree by habits of expression, as he who is habitually ill-natured will give expression to his thoughts in ill-natured tones. Some young people have a fashion of drawling their words; others speak with amazing rapidity; some deliver their thoughts in a high squeaking key; others utter short, low, growling tones. Some speak so soft that they are heard with difficulty, while others are loud, boisterous, and harsh. All these varieties of utterance indicate a want of culture. Good society demands that we make ourselves as agreeable as possible, and nothing serves to make a better first impression than a carefully trained voice. Politeness requires that we speak clearly, distinctly, and always loud enough to be easily heard, without being boisterous and rude. A whispering style of expression is annoying; a boisterous manner is vulgar.

Self-possession.—The conscious possession of a power to restrain our feelings, to master our passions, to steady our

What is the subject of Chapter XXXV? What other way are impressions first made on strangers? Why do we estimate the worth of people by their voice? Is it always correct? How are habits of mind frequently indicated? What are some of the modes of expression? What do they indicate? What does politeness require in reference to the voice? Is it polite to speak in a low, indistinct tone, any more than in a boisterous one? What is meant by self-possession?

nerves, and to command suitable language for every occasion is invaluable. People differ in temperament. One is hasty, impulsive, and rash, likely to say and do that in excitement which afterward may cause regret; another is, apparently, devoid of nervous sensibility, slow, heavy, torpid, never saying and doing the right thing at the right time; a third is timid, shrinking, sensitive, unable from extreme bashfulness to appear well. All these conditions of mind are unfavorable to success in good society. It is true that such habits are difficult to overcome, requiring time, patience, and practice; but that they may be corrected, no one can doubt. An easy, graceful, self-balanced behavior is attainable by every one who will try earnestly and perseveringly to acquire it.

To illustrate the method of securing self-command, the following suggestion is made to those who are quick to exhibit signs of high temper. Persons who are subject to fits of anger, usually speak in a high key and a loud tone. The surest evidence of self-control under such circumstances is to restrain the voice to the ordinary style of conversation. He who can do this is ordinarily safe from the danger of saying and doing angry, indiscreet things.

The introduction.—In polite society it is customary for one person to be introduced to or made acquainted with another through the kindness of a mutual friend. Among good people an introduction is the guaranty of a good character; since it is fair to presume that no one would bring a stranger into the company of his friends who did not possess such qualities as would entitle him or her to their respect and confidence. It is said of the Swedes, who are a very polite and hospitable people, that one person introducing another becomes responsible for his good behavior, as if he

How may it be attained? What differences appear in different individuals? How may persons learn to restrain their tempers? What does a high, loud voice indicate? Why are introductions necessary in good society. What is said of the Swedes?

should say, "Permit me to introduce my friend; if he cheats you, charge it to me."

It is related of a Frenchman that, seeing a man drowning, he refused to render him any assistance, as he had not had an introduction, and could not violate his high sense of etiquette. The story, whether true or false, will show to any sensible mind that there are times when it is folly to observe nice points of formal politeness. "The true gentleman is sometimes quite as well known by the genial and sensible manner in which he waives, as he is by the thoughtful uniformity with which he generally observes proper etiquette." The same may be said of the real lady.

Introductions may be made in person or by letter. If personal, the gentleman should be introduced to the lady, the boy to the girl, the younger to the older of the same sex, and in general the person of less consequence or dignity to the greater. The form is not so much a matter of importance, except that the names of the persons shall be pronounced clearly and distinctly. It is sometimes very embarrassing for people to be introduced without distinctly hearing each others' names. If you wish to make Mr. Jones acquainted with Miss Brown, you may address her, "Miss Brown, permit me to introduce my friend, Mr. Jones." The lady and gentleman will bow to each other, each repeating the other's name. When gentlemen are introduced to each other, it is polite to shake hands, but it is not expected that a young gentleman and lady shall do so. An old lady or gentleman may offer the hand to one who is younger.

Persons who shake hands should always remove their gloves, or make an apology for neglecting the courtesy. It is an evidence of great thoughtlessness and rudeness to

---

What is said of the Frenchman? How is the true gentleman known? How may introductions be made? What is the rule for introduction? How should the names be pronounced? Why? Give the form of an introduction. Introduce a pupil to the teacher. What is said of shaking hands? What is said of the gloves? Why not squeeze the hand?

squeeze the hand of another with a grip like a vice. Such conduct is sometimes painful, as well as mortifying.

When a letter of introduction is given, the envelope should not be sealed, as the person introduced may not wish to carry it unless he knows what it contains. That the receiver may know the character of the letter, and the name of the person delivering it, before it is opened, there should be written on one corner, "Introducing Mr. —— ——."

If the person introduced has any peculiarity of form or feature, it is exceedingly impolite to appear to notice it. It is bad enough to be unfortunate in having a defective eye, a crippled hand, or a club foot, without the additional pain of being an object of vulgar curiosity. It may be agreeable for Tom Thumb and the Irish Giant to be gazed at, especially as they are paid for it, but it is extremely indelicate to refer to the size, form, or personal appearance of those whom we meet. People generally are extremely sensitive in regard to their personal peculiarities, and we have no right to offend them.

Language the medium of thought.—The fable relates that, "An ass, having put on a lion's skin, roamed about, frightening all the silly animals he met with, and seeing a fox, tried to alarm him also. But Reynard, having heard him attempt to roar, said: 'Well, to be sure! and I should have been frightened too, if I had not heard you bray." The moral is very obvious. Vulgar persons may put on airs, and attempt to imitate well-bred people, but the counterfeit is readily detected in their language. Nothing so surely exposes ignorance and vulgar pretension as the improper use of words.

It is becoming in those who aspire to be recognized as gentlemen and ladies to pay particular attention to the cul-

---

How should the envelope of a letter of introduction be treated? What should you do if brought in contact with a cripple? Why? Is it polite to stare at any person? Why is it proper to stare at Tom Thumb? Should any reference be made to the size or form of any one, if peculiar? Why? What is the fable? What is its moral? How may vulgar people be detected? What is meant by good language?

tivation of accurate and elegant forms of expression. It must not be inferred that by elegant language is meant "big words" or stilted forms of speech. The best English is expressed by simple words in an easy and natural arrangement. The subjects of profanity and impurity have already been alluded to in Part I, as violations not alone of good taste, but also of the moral law.

Indelicacy is often manifested by an affectation of purity. The woman who talks about the "limbs" of the table and the "bosom" of the chicken is unrefined, and exposes herself to merited ridicule and contempt.

"A young woman, with a number of others, who were injured by a railway accident, was carried to a hospital. The surgeon came around, and said to the young and fashionable miss: 'Well, miss, what can I do for you?' Said she: 'One of my limbs is broken.' 'One of your limbs?' said he. 'Well, which limb is it?' 'Oh, I can't tell you, doctor, but it's one of my limbs.' 'One of your limbs,' thundered the doctor, out of patience; 'which is it—the limb you thread a needle with?' 'No, sir,' she answered, with a sigh; 'it's the limb I wear a garter on.' The doctor attended to her, and then said: 'Young woman, never say limbs to me again in a hospital; if you do, I shall pass you, for when a woman gets so fastidious as that, the quicker she dies the better.'"

The affectation of modesty and delicacy is easily discovered by the language. Such a pretense of refinement is disgusting to persons of good taste. But there is an opposite extreme of vulgar frankness that is equally to be avoided. Persons of good culture never offend, either by the roughness and coarseness of their language, or by the use of terms

---

What is meant by big words? How is indelicacy often manifested? What effect does an affectation of delicacy produce? Repeat the anecdote. Why should the doctor reprove such a person? Are such people really modest? Why? What does fastidious mean? How is the affectation of modesty discovered? Is real coarseness at all preferable to affected modesty?

that clearly discover the immodest ideas that are passing in their minds.

Slang.—Slang is defined to be, "Vile, low language: the cant of sharpers or vulgar people." A lady of good taste thus speaks of this kind of intercourse and of those who indulge in it: "But habitually to use slang, and know it, is a sign of coarse association, or poverty of language, or a gross mind, or a bad heart." A book might be filled with cant phrases which are in use in various parts of the country among the illiterate and vulgar. Such a publication would only be valuable as a means of bringing more forcibly to the minds of those whose language is generally good the use of some words or phrases which they have unconsciously adopted. As some persons use profane language without really intending to swear, simply from force of habit, so they may, without reflection, adopt such expressions as "I 'll bet," "You bet," "Dry up," "You 've barked up the wrong tree," "He 's in a bad box," "He made tracks," "He forked over, "It 's mighty nice," "I 'll be blowed," etc., etc.

As correct habits of conversation are generally formed in youth, this subject is commended to the attention of such as desire to excel in all the qualities that distinguish well-bred people.

Define slang. What does a lady say of the use of slang? Are we always conscious when we use slang? How shall we be cured of such a habit? Why is it desirable to cure it? May we unconsciously adopt forms of speech that are inelegant? Do refined people indulge in such language when it is pointed out to them? In what society may we learn slang? In what society is it never used? When are correct habits formed?

CHAPTER XXXVI.

CONVERSATION.

People of cultivated minds enjoy each other's society in proportion as they are able to receive and impart instruction. Ignorant persons talk, and chatter, and simper, but those who possess intelligence engage in conversation. Between these classes there is a very wide difference. The owl is more likely to be esteemed wise, on account of his silence, than the parrot by his extreme loquacity.

Subjects of conversation.—Politeness requires that the subjects of conversation be selected with reference to the tastes of the company. That which is interesting to one may afford no pleasure to another, and it is rude to inflict a disagreeable topic upon any one. We should be unselfish, and adapt ourselves, if possible, to the tastes and wishes of others, that they may have a chance to converse as well as to listen. People often win friends by being able to listen gracefully and patiently.

Egotism to be avoided.—Be careful not to make yourself the topic of conversation. Your joys and sorrows, griefs and fears, exploits and experiences may be very interesting to you, but possibly not to your acquaintances. If there be anything interesting in your personal history that others desire to know, it may be imparted with such a

---

What is the subject of Chapter XXXVI? What is the difference between talk and conversation? Why is the owl the emblem of wisdom? Of what is the parrot the emblem? What kinds of subject should be selected for conversation? How do people sometimes make friends? Should we make ourselves the subjects of conversation? Why?

degree of modesty as good taste requires. Above all things, never attempt to exhibit your learning for the sake of showing yourself. You may be vastly more learned than the company, but any anxiety on your part to make it manifest would be justly esteemed an offense. If the company is desirous of knowing your opinions upon any subject, or of securing your advice, it is proper that you should accede to their request.

Discussion.—In social company avoid, if possible, all discussion with those with whom you may not agree, especially of politics and religion, as your differences are probably too decided to result in a conversion of either side; better choose some more profitable topic, in which your disagreement is less marked and more readily reconciled. If a member of any particular religious faith makes the fact of such membership known, you can state the denomination or sect to which you are attached, if any, and thereby prevent anything being said which may cause offense.

If a discussion appears distasteful to the company, seize the first opportunity to change the subject for one that will give more satisfaction. There are some persons who seem to be so constituted that they can never receive a simple statement without manifesting a disposition to doubt and discuss. They want everything proven. Such persons render themselves very disagreeable, since they do not seem willing to give their assent to anything. Such a habit of disputing is rude. Always argue for truth rather than for a victory.

Attention.—Polite people always look the person, to whom their conversation is addressed, in the face, and he, to appear respectful, must look directly at the speaker. It is

---

Should we parade our learning? Why? What may we do when our opinions are asked? Why avoid discussion in company? Why not discuss religion and politics? If a subject is not agreeable, what is to be done? Is it polite to dispute? What shall we argue for? What shall we do when people address us? Why is it a slight to appear inattentive?

very unbecoming in any one to appear inattentive, even if he is hearing closely all that is said. Such appearance may justly be regarded as a slight. "True politeness," says some one, "consists in making everybody happy about you; and as to mortify is to render unhappy, it can be nothing but the worst of breeding."

Secrets.—If you are in possession of any knowledge that you do not wish generally known, do not impart it to any person. It is only safe, absolutely safe, as long as you keep it. Be exceedingly careful in the selection of those whom you would make your confidants, if you must have somebody to help you preserve your secrets. As a rule, the truest, safest, and best confidants are the mother, father, and teacher, for the reason that they, above all others, are best qualified to impart true sympathy and wise counsel. Exercise great prudence in permitting others to make you their confidential friend. It may appear very complimentary to be chosen to help keep other people's secrets, but it may become a very disagreeable honor. It is generally safe to decline to be the repository of anything which you are not at liberty to use or repeat at your discretion. If your friends can not trust you that far, they should not endeavor to impose a burden which they find is too heavy to bear alone.

Intrusion.—Do not intrude upon those who appear to be engaged in any conversation which they may be unwilling for you to hear, nor seek to know the topic, as it may not be agreeable for them either to communicate it, or to appear rude by refusing. Never listen to overhear conversation that is not intended for your ear. Eavesdroppers rarely hear anything pleasant of themselves.

Of what does true politeness consist? If you have a secret, what should you do with it? Why is it dangerous to impart your secrets to others? Who make the safest confidants? Is it safe to be the keeper of others' secrets? How shall we avoid being the confidants of others? Why is it impolite to intrude when others are talking in secret? Why are eavesdroppers detestable persons?

Whispering in company.—It is exceedingly unbecoming in persons to whisper in company, since it is not unreasonable to suppose that some one present is the subject of their comments. Every one has reason to be offended by such conduct. Nor is it polite to laugh when the company is not aware of the cause. If there is some mirth-provoking joke to tell, let all have the pleasure of the laugh; but if the joke be inappropriate for the company, it should be reserved to some more suitable occasion.

Interruption of conversation.—It is not polite to interrupt a person in speaking, without his consent. If he misstates what he supposes is a fact or a truth, do not deny it roughly or coarsely, nor in such a way as to wound his self-love, but rather convince him, if possible, that he is in error. Never arouse the prejudice of an individual whom you wish to convince. It is also a great rudeness to attempt to assist a person in expressing his ideas by suggesting words, for the inference is that you think him incapable of carrying on his share of the conversation, and that you wish to help him.

National vanity.—Foreigners who come to our land find a great many things better, and some which they think are not so good, as those in the countries of their birth. It is natural that they should love their old homes, and that they should criticise many things in the new; but it is a sign of great weakness in any American to take offense at such criticism. Nor, on the other hand, should Americans wound the feelings of those who come from abroad by unkind and unfriendly allusions to their manners, customs, or language. It is uncivil. It is also rude to smile at the inaccuracies of a foreigner's language. If he does not speak English as

---

Why is it impolite to whisper in company? Why has the company a right to be offended? If there is a proper joke to tell, what shall we do? Why is it impolite to interrupt a person in speaking? How shall we correct an error or misstatement? May we assist another to express his ideas? Why should we not take offense at the criticism of foreigners? Should Americans offend foreigners? Shall we smile when a foreigner does not pronounce well?

well as he might, he certainly does as well as he can, and it is extremely impolite to appear to be amused by his blunders.

Witticisms.—"Never say an ill-natured thing, nor be witty at the expense of any one present, nor gratify the inclination, which is sometimes very strong in young people, to laugh at and ridicule the weaknesses or infirmities of others, by way of diverting the company." Those who are fond of exercising their wit at the expense of others, as a general rule, are extremely sensitive to ridicule themselves, and are very quick to take offense. Such persons should constantly be on their guard, that they may neither wound others, nor suppose, unnecessarily, that others intend to wound them. Wit is a very dangerous instrument. Unless handled with extreme prudence, it is injurious alike to the one who uses it and to the one who is made to feel its sting. Witty persons rarely have very warm friends, as a man may forgive a blow, but rarely can forget that he has been made the subject of ridicule.

Noise not argument.—Persons should remember in conversation that noise and assertion are not sense and argument. If they would command respect, it must be by courtesy. To call hard names, therefore, or use offensive epithets, does not indicate the wisdom or the good taste of the speaker, nor give force to his reasoning.

Truth not always to be spoken.—Nothing but the truth should be uttered. Coarse, uncultivated natures sometimes delight to say an unkind thing, and then defend their rudeness by affirming its truth. It may be true that a man's son is a thief, or that his wife is insane; but that is no reason why he should be reminded of it unnecessarily. It is bad

---

May we be witty at the expense of others? Why? Why are witty people usually very sensitive? Why do witty persons have few friends? Why is it hard to forgive a joke? Is it right to say hurtful things simply because they are true?

enough that it is true, but we have no right to add to his suffering by putting him in mind of it. Nor should we ever say anything for politeness that we do not mean; better not speak at all than convey an impression which is not the truth. It does not follow that when you meet an acquaintance you must say: "I am very glad to see you," when you are not; nor, on the other hand, is it necessary to say: "I am not very glad to see you," although it is truly the fact. Never be coarse and rude; but never, as a pretense of politeness, permit yourself to say what you do not mean. Such conduct is "hypocrisy," of which no member of good society should be guilty.

Correction of speech and pronunciation.—We have already alluded to the subject of bad English, as used by a foreigner. Never presume to correct the pronunciation or false syntax of those whom you meet in company, unless you are upon the most familiar terms, and even then it should be done with extreme delicacy and in private. To persons who are older, such rudeness would be extreme.

A graceful no.—Sometimes it becomes the duty of every one to do or say something in opposition to the interests, views, or pleasure of his friend, or to decline to accede to his requests. When such an unpleasant occurrence arises, the refusal should be made kindly and gracefully. Very often it is extremely difficult to say no, but there are so many instances when it is necessary, that every person should learn to say it, so that, if possible, it should not offend, and at the same time should carry the conviction that it is useless to attempt to get any other answer. To be able to refuse a favor gracefully is a very desirable accomplishment.

Is it right to say an untruth for the appearance of politeness? Does truthfulness require people to be rude? What is hypocrisy? Should we correct bad English or pronunciation in company? If done at all, how may we do it? How should we endeavor to give a refusal? When may it be necessary to say no? Is it polite to tease a person to change his mind?

CHAPTER XXXVII.

BEHAVIOR ON THE STREET.

Young people often seem unconscious of the fact that their behavior on the street attracts the attention of older people, and impresses them with favorable or unfavorable ideas of their character. We have already alluded to the modesty that should be illustrated by the "street dress," in Chapter XXXIII. The same propriety should govern all street behavior. Polite people never do anything on the street to attract attention; they should neither talk in a loud, boisterous manner, nor laugh uproariously. Conversation that is so noisy as to attract the attention of the passing crowd is either the result of ignorance or of a petty effort to secure a little vulgar notoriety.

The rights of the sidewalk.—It is not courteous for young persons of either or of both sexes to have long conferences on the street, as they may obstruct the sidewalk, and at the same time excite both critical and unpleasant remarks. Every person is entitled to his share of the sidewalk, and this right should always be respected. It is only the rude, low-bred woman and the blustering bully that assert their vulgarity by refusing to give the half of the pavement. As a gentleman or lady can never afford to come in collision with such people, it would be better they should even leave the sidewalk than be jostled. To assert our real or fancied superiority by depriving others of their rights is rude and vulgar.

What virtue should young people always illustrate by their dress and manners on the street? How do polite people act on the street? How should they converse? Why not stand long on the street to talk? What are our rights on the sidewalk? Is it worth while to quarrel about the sidewalk? Why?

Persons passing.—When persons pass each other on the pavement, they should observe the same rule that drivers do on the street, in order to avoid the inconvenience and danger of a collision. Each should keep to the right. When a gentleman and lady walk in company, he should walk at the lady's left, in order to prevent those passing from running against her. There is no necessity for the gentleman to change his position at every corner, in order that he may be on the side next the street. She will be protected better if always at the gentleman's right. Persons walking in company should always keep step together.

Street crossings.—When a gentleman and lady cross the street in company, and the crossing is narrow and muddy, requiring them to go singly, delicacy requires that he should precede her, for the same reason that he should be the first to go up stairs and the last to come down.

Friends meeting in the street.—Persons should not be so engrossed in conversation as to pass their friends upon the street without notice, if it only be a slight inclination of the head and a pleasant smile. Serious offense may be unwittingly given to those whom we should have recognized, but seemed to forget. Such apparent neglect is very trying to the self-love of sensitive people, and may be mistaken for intentional rudeness.

Washington's politeness.—"Captain Stephen Trowbridge, the oldest male inhabitant of Milford, N. H., tells the following incident of Washington's visit to that village in 1790: While the latter was walking about the town, attended by a number of his officers, a colored soldier, who had fought under him and lost a limb in his service, made

---

How shall persons pass each other? On which side of the gentleman should the lady walk? Why? How should persons walk together? How shall a lady and gentleman cross the street? In what order shall they ascend and descend the stairs? Is it polite to pass an acquaintance without recognition? How may we offend sensitive people? What is the anecdote of Washington?

his way up to the general and saluted him. Washington turned to this colored soldier, shook hands with him, and gave him a present of a silver dollar. One of the attendants objected to the civilities thus shown by the President of the United States to such an humble person; but Washington rebuked him sharply, asking if he should permit this colored man to excel him in politeness."

The veil.—When a lady appears on the street with a veil over her face, it may sometimes be a sign that she does not wish to be recognized, and an acquaintance may pass her as a stranger, without either giving or taking offense. If the lady, on approaching, shall remove her veil, it indicates that she wishes to be seen and known.

Street recognition.—Young people should always be prompt to acknowledge the politeness of those who notice them. They should never speak to their superiors first, as it might be construed as a mark of pert familiarity, but when a lady or gentleman wishes to salute them, they should respond with a pleasant "good morning" or "good evening," as the case may be, accompanied by an agreeable smile. It is expected that a lady will always recognize the gentleman first; a girl the boy; and, as a rule, the superior the inferior in age or station.

The polite bow.—When young men or boys meet their superiors in age and station, or those of the other sex who recognize them, they should always lift their hats politely, and make a respectful bow. This salutation is very graceful, and ought not to be omitted. If a boy passes a gentleman, and the latter indicates by his eye that he intends to speak, the boy, if on the right, should lift his hat with his

What principles does it illustrate? What does the veil indicate? Shall we notice a lady with a veil? Why? Which should speak first on the street, the superior or the inferior? Why? How should the inferior respond? Who speaks first, the lady or gentleman? The boy or the girl? When boys are recognized, how should they act? How shall they make a bow?

right hand; if on the left, with the left hand, and make a slight inclination of the head. There is sometimes a false idea of personal independence among boys, which prevents their making a polite bow, or giving a civil reply; but it is a very vulgar independence that disregards the laws of good manners.

Smoking in company.—In some parts of the country, gentlemen are never seen smoking on the street, and it would be well if the rule were universal; but there is no exception to the rule that prohibits gentlemen, everywhere, from smoking when in company with ladies on the street. Even if the lady assures him that smoking is not offensive, he has no right to presume on her forbearance in that manner, and give the impression to those who pass that they are both devoid of the culture exhibited by well-bred people.

The graceful gait.—The manner of walking is a matter of more importance than some might suppose, without reflection; and yet the impressions that we derive from seeing a stranger walk are not without their significance. A gentleman never puts on a pompous manner, and a lady never struts. The style of walking should be easy and graceful. The toes should be turned out slightly, the step should be firm, decided, and moderately long. A slouching, irregular, unsteady gait is very ungraceful, while the mincing, wriggling, affected style adopted by some women is as uncomfortable to themselves as it appears ridiculous and unnatural to those who see it. Dr. Dio Lewis, in his charming book, "Our Girls," gives a rule for elegant carriage that is worth practicing. He says: "Whoever carries the chin close to the neck is all right from top to toe, and will walk well." There seems to be philosophy in the suggestion, for if the

---

Is it true independence to disregard the rules of politeness? What is the rule in reference to smoking? Is it important to learn to walk gracefully? Why? What is meant by strutting? How shall the toes be directed? Describe the step. What shall be said of wriggling? Give Dr. Lewis's rule for graceful walking. Why is this rule a good one?

chin lies close to the neck, the head will be erect, the shoulders back, and the chest full. The recipe is worth a trial.

In walking, the breath should be inhaled through the nose, and not by the mouth, which should be kept shut. The "uneducated mouth" is one of the indications of bad breeding.

CHAPTER XXXVIII.

BEHAVIOR IN CHURCH.

It is presumed that young people know and are willing to respect the usages of the church which it is their custom to attend; but as it may not be so clear what politeness requires of those who visit churches of other denominations, a few words may not be inappropriate upon the subject. As has already been indicated in Chapter XXVI, the right of worship is one of the inalienable rights of every man, and it is one of the glories of our republican government that it assures to every man the full enjoyment of this right in the erection of houses of worship, and in the exercise of any forms of religious service.

Differences in worship.—There is a marked difference in the forms of worship in the synagogue, the cathedral, the church, and the meeting-house, and if the Jews, the Catholics, the Episcopalians, or the Friends will open their doors, that we may witness their ceremonies, the least that we can do in accepting their invitation is to behave in a becoming

How shall the breath be inhaled in walking? What is an uneducated mouth?

What is the subject of Chapter XXXVIII? Why are suggestions made on this subject? What is our duty if we visit the religious services of those who differ from us in faith? Why?

manner. No more serious offense can be committed than to show disrespect to any person's religious faith, especially in the house dedicated to the worship of God. As our attendance there is an entirely voluntary matter, we shall be inexcusable if we injure the feelings of any by an apparent disregard of the sanctities of the place.

Punctuality.—Mrs. Chapone was asked why she always went so early to church. "Because," said she, "it is a part of my religion not to disturb the religion of others." Appreciating this idea, we should be punctual to the hour appointed for the services to commence, or, if by accident, we arrive too late, we should wait at the door during the opening exercise, and enter when there is a change in the service.

A respectful entrance.—The entrance to the church should be in as noiseless a manner as possible, and with as little clattering of shoes or rustling of dresses as can be made. Such exhibitions as are sometimes given of new fashions by those who enter late provoke criticisms, not only unsuitable to the time and place, but also very uncomplimentary to the exhibitors. Refined people never display such extreme vulgarity. If we are not acquainted with the usages of the place, an officer or person appointed for such duty will conduct us to a suitable seat. If invited to follow him, we should do so, taking the place he assigns, and thanking him quietly, at least by a smile, for his courtesy.

Cleanliness in church.—It is the custom of the Turks, when they enter a mosque, which is a Mahomedan place of worship, to take off their shoes, that the sacred place may not be defiled. There are those in this land who, when they enter even their own church, not only do not remove their

---

Why is it insulting to behave badly in church? What was the remark of Mrs. Chapone? If late at church, how shall we act? How shall we enter? When the usher takes us in charge, what shall we do? How do the Turks enter their mosques? How should Christians enter their houses of worship?

shoes, but fail also to clean off the mud that adheres to them. A decent respect for the usages of good society might prompt such people to practice the external rules of politeness, even if no higher motive should influence them. The same lack of culture is manifest in those who enjoy the luxury (?) of tobacco chewing during the church service, and use both pew and aisle as a great spittoon, to the intense disgust of those who love cleanliness; to the annoyance of such as possess a refined taste, and to the mortification of those who venerate the place dedicated to the service of God.

Conduct in church.—If the services are such that we may properly join them, it is our duty to do so. It is rude to sit when the congregation stands, unless we have some conscientious scruples against standing. If there be anything strange or peculiar in the ceremonies, it is the grossest rudeness to express any marks of disapprobation or contempt by talking or laughing. Such misconduct is inexcusable. Nor is it proper to read a paper or book during the service, as it appears disrespectful to the minister, the choir, and the congregation, by an implied indifference to the sermon and the services.

Do not appear to be inattentive, nor look at your watch, nor yawn, nor sleep, nor be in an unbecoming haste to leave when the exercises are over. Unless sickness or some imperative call compel you to leave the house, you should remain until the close of the service. When the congregation is passing from the house, do not crowd and jostle, as if you were in a hurry to leave. Be calm, decorous, and dignified. If a young gentleman, and you have a lady in charge, do not stand outside the door till she arrives, but accompany her inside to the door. If a lady, you should refuse to be escorted by one who waits outside for your appearance.

Is it respectful and polite to use tobacco in church? When shall we join the services? Shall we indicate an approval or disapproval of the services? Why? What is it improper to do in church? Is it polite to leave the house during the services? How shall a young gentleman act who escorts a lady? Is it polite to wait outside? How should a lady act toward one who will not escort her in the house?

CHAPTER XXXIX.

BEHAVIOR IN THE CONCERT OR LECTURE ROOM.

When we buy a ticket to a concert or lecture, we purchase a right to all the enjoyment the entertainment affords, subject, however, to the restriction that we do not interfere with the rights of others. We may secure a reserved seat, but have no right to go in at such a time or in such a manner as to disturb others after the exercises have commenced. If the seats have not been reserved, those who come first have the choice.

The tardy.—It is not uncommon to see men and women enter the hall after the exercises have begun, who seem utterly ignorant of the proprieties of the place, or indifferent to the rights of all present. Oftentimes they take no care to come in gently, and manifest no desire, apparently, to avoid the disturbance their entrance occasions. It is such women that push up far to the front, and stand at some gentleman's side, who has come early and secured a seat, in the expectation that he will surrender his place. Gentlemen are thus sometimes deprived of their rights by the coarse manners of an unfeeling selfish woman, who has not even the politeness to acknowledge the courtesy.

A lady should feel a great reluctance in depriving an acquaintance, and much more a stranger, of a seat to which she has no claim. Any gentleman who surrenders his seat under such circumstances does it out of pure gallantry, and

---

What is the subject of Chapter XXXIX? What rights does the purchase of a ticket give us? Have others a right to disturb us? Have we any rights that others have not? Have we a right to come late? How do rude people act? Has a woman a right to a choice seat when she comes late? If a gentleman gives her his seat, how should she act?

any lady who receives such a favor should feel under special obligations, and promptly return her thanks to the donor. The neglect of such an acknowledgment is a mark of very bad breeding.

The talkative and restless.—The signs that distinguish rude pupils in school are the very same that mark the impolite at the concert. They talk and chatter and simper, to the intense disgust and annoyance of the really discriminating and intelligent portion of the audience. Well-bred persons pay more respect to the rights and feelings of their neighbors than to indulge their own selfishness in that manner. The cracking and eating of nuts, and the rustling of fans, programmes, and dresses are all exhibitions of thoughtless rudeness, and are unbecoming in a place devoted to literary or musical culture.

The opening.—Young folks, on such occasions, are sometimes excited. They lose their self-possession, and become impatient for the exercises to begin. Feeling in this condition, they offend against good taste by whistling, cat-calling, and shouting. Such exhibitions of vulgarity do not distinguish refined and polished people, and always give offense to the better and more cultivated portion of the audience.

Approbation.—If the sentiments of the speaker or performer are agreeable, we may approve them by the clapping of hands for his encouragement, but if they do not meet our approbation, we need not offend others by hissing or giving other evidences of disapproval. We must bear in mind that every man and woman has a right to express opinions in this country, and if we do not like them we are not compelled to hear them ; but if we go to learn, it is our duty to

---

How do rude people act during the exercises? Do bad school habits lead to impoliteness elsewhere? How do well-bred people act in this respect? How should young people act before the exercises commence? How shall we approve the exercises? If we can not approve, have we a right to offend by our disapproval? Why?

listen patiently and forbearingly. Stamping is a very objectionable form of applause, since it usually raises a dust, that is very disagreeable to the audience.

Going out.—It frequently happens in concerts and other entertainments of a similar character, that the programme is divided into two or three parts, in order to rest the performers, or to give the audience an opportunity to talk and shift their seats. This relaxation is enjoyable in proportion as the attention has been closely riveted upon the performance. At such times it is very bad taste for young men to get up and leave the room. The impression will be left on the minds of many that they are going out to get some stimulus, which will enable them to endure the remainder of the programme. If the conjecture is true, it is not to their credit that they can not sit a few hours without drinking; if untrue, the appearance of such indulgence will be prevented by their retaining their seats.

Company.—It is one of the rudest breaches of politeness for a lady to intimate to a gentleman that she would be pleased to have him escort her to any public entertainment, especially where tickets are to be purchased. Such conduct would place her under a very unpleasant sense of obligation, and may be the cause of much embarrassment to the gentleman. He may have other plans which will be disturbed by such an invitation, or, if he be in limited circumstances, the loss of the money may prove a serious inconvenience. If he gives the lady an invitation, it rests with her to accept it, or respectfully to decline.

No young lady will accept such politeness without the approbation of her family and friends, since it is probable that they have better opportunities of knowing whether all

---

Why is stamping objectionable? Why is the programme divided? Why should young men not go out? Is it polite for a lady to hint to a gentleman to attend her? Why? Why is it well for a young lady always to consult her friends before accepting an invitation?

the circumstances are suitable. Before the hour appointed, the young gentleman should call at her residence, when she, anticipating his coming, should be ready, without delay, to accompany him. Sometimes young ladies are very inconsiderate. Although they are aware they will be called for, they postpone their preparation until it is so late that they lose much of their pleasure in their hurry, or mortify their friends by coming late.

If a lady declines to accompany a young gentleman, she should not mention it under any circumstances. It is very unbecoming, when he is so polite as to offer her a kindness, that she should add an insult to the refusal by telling it. A real lady is never boastful of her ability to win admiration, and, much less, should she be willing to triumph over those whose attentions she has declined. On entering the place of amusement, the gentleman should precede the lady, secure a seat for her, and not let her hunt one for herself. It is extremely indelicate for a lady ever to suggest that a gentleman should make a purchase of any luxury, as fruit, nuts, or refreshing drink, although it would be proper to request him to procure a glass of water. The latter, generally, could be easily obtained by a little personal effort, which he would gladly make; while the former might cost what he could ill afford to spend.

The return.—When the exercises are over, the gentleman should accompany the lady to her home. If the hour is suitable, the lady may invite him into the house; but, if it is too late, she should say, very frankly: "It is too late to invite you to come in, but I shall be pleased to have you call again." It is very unbecoming for young people to

---

Why should the young lady always be ready at the time appointed? If a lady declines an invitation, why is it impolite to mention it? Has a lady a right to wound the feelings of one whom she may not admire? Does a lady ever boast of her admirers? Why should the gentleman always secure the lady a seat? Should a lady suggest the purchase of any luxury for herself? May a lady ask for a glass of water? When may the lady invite the gentleman into her house?

stand at the gate to converse, and may give rise to unpleasant remarks. No young lady can be too careful to prevent the appearance of any familiarity that may not seem to be sanctioned by her parents and friends. If the gentleman enters the house, he should be too prudent to prolong his stay beyond a proper hour, and thus "wear out his welcome." Such thoughtlessness may interfere very seriously with the arrangements of the household, and prove a real trespass upon the time and good nature of the lady herself.

CHAPTER XL.

GALLANTRY.

One of the distinguishing features of our times is the respect that is shown to woman. The lowest civilization exhibits the female as degraded and oppressed; treated like a beast of burden, and made entirely dependent upon man; while the condition of society in which we live is made remarkable by the fact that she is recognized as the equal of man, socially and religiously, and fit to be his trusted friend and counselor. Her claims to the best education are respected, so that she may become intellectually as great as her industry, her capacity, and her ambition will allow. There is no limit to woman's influence for good or evil. What she is fitted to do she may accomplish, and every day her ability is demonstrated in new and hitherto untried fields of exertion.

Is it polite or prudent to stand outside? How long may a gentleman remain?
What is the subject of Chapter XL? What distinguishes this age from former ages? What is the condition of woman with us? What is said of the education of women?

Home.—The place above all others in which woman's inspiration is happiest and best is as wife, mother, sister, or friend, at home. It is there in these relations that we learn to know her best and love her most. For young men to reverence the sex is but to pay a tribute of love to the influence of their own mothers. The highest compliment that can be offered a young man is that he is a tender, devoted son and brother, and the worthiest sentiment that can be uttered in praise of a woman is that she inspires a son or a brother with such respect and affection.

The roughs.—There is a class of young men who affect a contempt of the female sex; who speak disrespectfully of their mothers, and treat their sisters with derision. The condition of such persons is not to be envied, as they are losing the happiest, purest, and most elevating influences of life. A brother and sister whose ages are nearly equal should always associate together. It ought to be a matter of principle with them that one should never accept a social invitation which had not been extended to the other. Each will be a protection and an assistance to the other. Each should defer to the other's comfort, convenience, and tastes. Common interests and desires would make such companionship a source of constant and unfailing happiness. Happy the brother who has a gentle, kind, devoted sister, whose confidence is his safeguard, and thrice happy the sister who can command the affectionate attention of an honorable and virtuous brother.

The gentleman.—A gentleman is always distinguished by his respectful attentions to women. He never utters a word concerning the sex which his own mother would blush

---

Where is the place in which woman's influence is best felt? What is the highest compliment that can be paid a young man? What to a woman? Who are they who speak disrespectfully of women? How should a brother and sister treat each other? Why? What influences may brother and sister exert over each other? How is a gentleman always distinguished? In language? In manners?

to hear, and he never willingly listens to anything that an honorable man would be ashamed to speak. He has no slights for the aged grandmother, whose eyes are dim, whose steps are feeble, and whose hands are weak. No rude jest escapes his lips in ridicule of the decaying beauty of a maiden aunt. He feels that he should be the protector and friend of those who are weak and helpless. His gallantry does not consist in dancing attendance upon his own particular friends for a selfish gratification, to the neglect of every one beside.

The hoiden.—The hoiden is defined to be a rude, rough, romping girl. The term will apply to such as are not restrained by the rules of polite society to be courteous and civil, but are continually planning and performing unmaidenly actions. A kind of independence which asserts itself in always doing right, is not the kind that charms the hoiden. She delights to indulge in violations of propriety, which sometimes shock and always annoy her more discreet companions. Such a character is not the one that wins commendation, much less admiration and respect, from good society. Young men may appear to enjoy her company, but she can never be regarded with that high esteem which arises from confidence in her modesty and reliance upon her good sense.

The prude.—The prude is defined to be a female of extreme reserve, who affects peculiar delicacy and coyness of manners. This character is cold, dignified, and unsociable; always fearful of compromising her reputation; always sensitive, censorious, and apt to misinterpret the words and actions of others. It is difficult to determine which is the least entitled to respect, the hoiden or the prude; both are unlovely and unwomanly.

What is a hoiden? How does she act? Does such a person win respect from any one? Why do young men appear to enjoy her company? Do they regard her with esteem? What is a prude? What is the difference between the hoiden and the prude?

The sociable.—The place above all others in which these peculiar and striking phases of character are manifested is in the sociable or small party. The excitement incident to such an assembly tends to exhibit the natural dispositions of each individual. Some, and this applies to both sexes, are noisy, rude, thoughtless, and inconsiderate; while others are cold, formal, and constrained. To neutralize these diversities, and enable all to contribute to the enjoyment of the occasion, games and amusements of all kinds are brought into requisition.

Indoor recreations.—The subject of amusements has already been considered in Chapter XXII. There is a great diversity in the forms of recreation which may be enjoyed by the young indoors. Some of these are ingenious, amusing, and instructive. Every one in the company should join in any diversion which does not violate his conscience or his sense of propriety. Any play that is rough and rude, in which there is danger of injury to persons, to furniture, or to clothing, ought not to be tolerated in the house. Such exercise is for the open air and the lawn. That amusement which permits any improper familiarity between the sexes is not in good taste. If the game requires the boys to catch, and struggle, and wrestle with the girls, or even to put their hands upon their persons, or to kiss them, it is of very doubtful propriety. Such freedom is not consistent with that respect which the sexes should cultivate for each other.

Familiarity.—No girl should permit a boy to be so familiar as to toy with her hands, or play with her rings; to handle her curls, or encircle her waist with his arm. Such impudent intimacy should never be tolerated for a moment. No gentleman will attempt it; no lady will permit it.

How is character displayed at the sociable? Why are games and plays introduced? What games are unsuitable for indoors? What is said of boys and girls wrestling? Can boys and girls respect each other when they permit such improper familiarity? How must a girl conduct herself to be respected? Should a gentleman ever lay his hands familiarly upon a young lady?

The witty reproof.—That was a witty reproof administered to a thoughtless young man by a young lady. As they were sitting together on the sofa, he carelessly extended his arm upon the back of the seat behind her. "Does your arm pain you?" said she. "Why, no," he replied; "but why did you ask?" "I thought it must pain you, for I observe it is badly out of place."

CHAPTER XLI.

HINTS FOR VISITING.

Courtesy to strangers.—When strangers enter a community, either to make a visit or to secure a home, politeness requires that those who desire to make their acquaintance shall manifest their disposition to be sociable, by giving them the first call. The moral law, no less than the social, requires that we shall treat them with courtesy and kindness, as it is written, "*Be not forgetful to entertain strangers.*" As a general rule, nothing is more grateful to a person of refinement, in a strange place, than to receive evidences of kind consideration and friendly regard from those into whose midst he is accidentally thrown. When a call is made upon a stranger, he or she should be politely invited to return the compliment, which should be done at the earliest convenience.

The formal call.—It frequently happens that persons have a long list of acquaintances, with whom, on account

---

Give the anecdote. How was the gentleman's arm out of place?

What is the subject of Chapter XLI? When strangers arrive, how should they be treated? Who should make the first call? What does the moral law command? How should we feel, if we were strangers, to receive attention from those we had not known? How shall strangers act when called upon?

of the pressure of domestic cares, or other important business, which demands the greater part of their time, they can not be on terms of intimacy, and yet who desire to cultivate their friendship by the exercise at least of a formal sociability. In order to accommodate this social necessity for recognition, it is the custom to make brief visits or calls, at such times as are convenient, upon those with whom we are accustomed to associate. As the call is necessarily short, it is not expected that ladies shall remove their bonnets or shawls. When calls of this kind are made, and the same may be said of all visits, the visitor should always enter at the front door, but never until after giving a warning by the knocker or door-bell. The degree of intimacy which would justify the violation of this rule, and especially an entrance without the use of the knocker or bell, should be very clearly established. Such intercourse is too unceremonious to base upon it any reasonable expectation of permanence, since, "Too much familiarity breeds contempt"

When the summons is answered by the opening of the door, inquiry should be made for the person or persons in whose honor the call is made; if they are not in, or circumstances prevent their appearance, the caller may leave a card, upon which his or her name is written, which shows that the call has been made. If cards are not prepared, a verbal message may be left, though it is less likely to be delivered. In such cases, the card or the message stands instead of the call.

When calls are not returned, it is understood that even a formal sociability is not considered agreeable.

The social visit.—The call is a visit of ceremony among acquaintances, but the social visit is the informal meeting

---

Why are formal calls made? Is it expected that ladies making calls shall remain long? Why? At which door shall we enter a neighbor's house? Why shall we knock or ring? What is the meaning of the proverb, "Too much freedom breeds contempt?" When shall cards be used? Why? What is understood when the call is not returned? What is the difference between a call and a social visit?

of intimate friends, who may spend hours in each others' society, with mutual pleasure and profit. Such meetings may be accidental, as when friends drop in to enjoy a pleasant evening with a neighbor, without invitation or previous notice on either side. In these little gatherings, the ceremony and style of more formal visits are dispensed with, and hearty good will and neighborly love and kindness have their freest and happiest manifestations in conversation, music, or other recreation.

If no previous announcement of the visit has been sent, the visitor must not feel hurt if he finds, on his arrival, that a former engagement will prevent his friends from affording him the anticipated pleasure. He should excuse them to fulfill their appointments, and lay his plans to come again under more favorable circumstances.

The invitation.—When an invitation to make a visit is received, we should be careful to be punctual to the hour appointed. It is no compliment to our entertainer to go to his house at nine, when we were invited at seven o'clock. It is fair to presume that we are expected at the time indicated in the invitation, and if we are detained, an apology should be made for the apparent neglect.

The arrival.—When we enter the house, we should always seek the host and hostess, that they may know of our arrival, and they will introduce us to the other members of the family or company.

Sociability.—We should always bear in mind that it is our duty to assist in entertaining and making others happy, and, if possible, in relieving the embarrassment of those who are not self-possessed. Particular attention should be

---

May an accidental visitor interfere with the arrangements of his friends? Why are habits of punctuality desirable? When should we go to visit? What shall we do on our arrival? Do we accept the invitation to entertain or to be entertained? What is our duty? To whom should we show attention? Why?

shown to the aged, the sick, and the deformed; not in such a way as to make them conspicuous, but only to render them happy and comfortable. A kind word and a pleasant smile should be ready for every one. Care should always be taken not to show particular or too frequent attention in company to our favorites, lest it may excite jealous feelings and unpleasant remarks.

Laughing.—Do not simper. If there is anything to enjoy that is worthy of a laugh, laugh heartily; but remember that uproarious, boisterous mirth is exceedingly vulgar. The ruder the people are, the louder and coarser will be their expressions of enjoyment.

Social entertainment.—If a person is requested to divert the company with instrumental music, a song, or a story, we should stop our conversation, and listen respectfully till it is ended. Possibly the entertainment may not be very agreeable to us, but the respect we owe to the company, who, it may be, are very much pleased, and to the performer, who is trying to gratify us, should compel us to be attentive. Loud talking and immoderate laughter are frequently heard during the performance of music from those whose selfishness will not permit them to make any sacrifice of their own pleasure for the gratification of others.

It is very rude for a young person to offer to entertain a company without an invitation. When one has the ability to sing or play well, and is invited to perform, he should do so promptly and gracefully, nor wait to be urged. Young people sometimes expect a great deal of coaxing before they comply with a polite request. When one accepts the invitation to sing or play, he should be very careful not to weary the audience by continuing the effort too long. It is better

---

What kind of a laugh characterizes vulgar people? How should we act when others are invited to sing and play? Should a young person invite himself to sing or play? Why? Should he decline when invited? Should he wait to be coaxed? How long shall one sing?

to err on the safe side by singing too little than to cause annoyance to those who would prefer a change.

We should never ask any person to sing or play unless we are very sure it will be generally agreeable. To give such an invitation as a mere compliment, without desiring to have it accepted, is extremely rude and hypocritical. When a person declines to exhibit his accomplishments, it is not polite to insist, as there may be good reasons for the refusal, which it would be improper to make known to the company.

Practical jokes.—Never engage in a practical joke. In the town of W——, Pa., some frolicsome girls determined to amuse themselves by perpetrating a joke at the expense of Miss S. Dressing up a broom in a white sheet, they made it appear as a tall, ghostly person. As Miss S. was sitting in her room, in the dusk of evening, with her back to the door, the apparition, borne by one of the party, entered quietly, and approached her. The joke was expected to be very amusing, and the girls gathered around the door to enjoy the sport. As soon as the young lady saw the uncouth object bending over her, she screamed with terror, and suddenly became unconscious.

So great was the shock to her nervous system that it was feared she never would recover. Long weeks of illness followed, and during her delirium she would cry most piteously and beg that her friends would take that horrid thing from her sight. Of course, the girls never intended such fun as that; nor do young people generally suppose that their jokes will be attended with serious consequences; but as they always involve mortification or annoyance to some one, they never should be practiced. Generally, such fun is played upon some one who is weak or credulous, and is not

---

Is it right to ask a person to sing merely as a compliment? Should we invite a person to entertain the company? Why should we not insist upon a person's singing? Give the practical joke. Do young persons intend to do serious injury? Is it excusable on that account? What kind of persons are generally made the subjects of practical jokes?

a favorite, and on this account, if for no other reason, no brave, generous, or right-minded person would give it countenance.

Sitting in company.—Gracefulness should be studied in all our actions. In sitting, we should never assume a lounging position. The body should be erect, and yet not stiff and ungainly. The feet should not be extended nor spread apart; nor should they be rested upon the rungs of the chair, since the position is not graceful, and the polished surface may be injured by contact with the shoes. Do not sit astride of a chair, nor tilt it back against the wall or the furniture. Young persons should always give a seat to their superiors in age and station. If possible, we should not sit with our backs to the company.

Standing in company.—Restlessness should not be manifested by continually changing the positions of the feet, and by springing the ankles from side to side. Stand firm and erect. It is not courteous to turn the back toward any of the company, or to pass between them and the fire or stove. If compelled to pass between the fire and the company, we should politely ask them to pardon the necessity Young people should not lean on each other when standing together. For a person to rest the foot upon a chair or a chair rung is very impolite. Boys should not contract the habit of standing in company with their hands in their pockets; it is not graceful.

Annoyances.—The habits of drumming with the fingers on the furniture, beating time with the feet, humming, and whistling, indicate a want of good breeding, and are very offensive to refined people. A boy may, with great pro-

---

Is it brave or manly to frighten the weak and timid? What is the golden rule? How shall we sit in company? How do ungraceful and impolite persons sit? How shall we stand in company? How do ungraceful people stand? What are some of the annoying habits of rude people? Is it polite to whistle in the house or in company uninvited?

priety, entertain himself by whistling when he is alone, but to do it in the house, or in company, without a special invitation, is unpardonable. If the hair is not satisfactorily arranged, we should retire to a suitable place to attend to it. To comb the hair, or scratch the head, or pick the face or nose or ears, or clean the nails, indicates a want of proper respect for the company. Such actions are not in good taste. Nor should we blow the nose without using the handkerchief.

Tobacco.—The subject of habit has been treated in Chapter II, and amusements in Chapter XXII. If, after a conscientious study of these two chapters, any of our boys and girls determine to use tobacco, in any form, it would be folly in us to attempt a further argument to dissuade them. All that can be hoped is, that in using the indulgence, they shall neither interfere with their neighbors' rights nor offend their tastes. Cleanliness of the clothes, hair, and teeth have also been alluded to in preceding chapters. Gentlemen do not spit in company, particularly upon the carpets or on the stove. Some persons put spittoons in their parlors rather than have their floors defiled; but it is a sorry confession that some of their visitors are selfish, ill-bred people.

The handkerchief.—There are some articles of the toilet that are designed especially for the use of the owner, and no other. Every person should have and use his own hair-brush, tooth-brush, tooth-pick, and handkerchief. Never offer your handkerchief to your friend, except it may be to clean the mud from his clothes, or some such purpose. He may not wish to use it, and yet will not wish to offend you by a refusal. If at any time you may be compelled to borrow a handkerchief, be sure to return it neatly washed and ironed.

How shall we blow the nose? If persons use tobacco, in what way should it be done? When shall gentlemen spit in the house? Is the spittoon an elegant piece of parlor furniture? What articles of toilet are always for individual use? If we borrow a handkerchief, how shall we return it?

Parlor ornaments and books.—Some persons are fond of collecting pretty, delicate, and rare specimens of shells, corals, pictures, etc., and are very sensitive about their being fingered by unskillful hands. When such ornaments are placed upon the mantle or table, they are to be seen, but not handled, unless at the invitation of the owner. We may look at them, and admire their curious combinations of color, but if we should ruin a delicate shell or coral by letting it fall, or in some other manner, it will be a poor apology to say that the injury was the result of accident.

The breaking up.—We should not yawn in company, nor consult the watch, as if we were tired. If it be necessary to leave before the proper time arrives for the company to go home, it is better to do so without attracting attention. It is not discreet to "wear out one's welcome," by staying to an unreasonable hour; it would be better to have our friends regret our going than to wish we were gone. When leaving the house of our entertainers, we should always see them and bid them good-bye.

CHAPTER XLII.

BEHAVIOR AT THE TABLE.

Promptness.—When the announcement is made that the meal is ready, every one should be prompt to attend the summons, so that no inconvenience may be occasioned by delay. On the other hand, we should not seem hungry and

---

Should we handle parlor ornaments, etc.? Why? Why not yawn or look at your watch in company? How long shall we make the visit? Why? What shall we do at leaving?

What is the subject of Chapter XLII? Why should persons be prompt at the table? Why not rush to the table?

impatient by rushing to the table; it appears selfish and rude. Young gentlemen will never be seated until the older members of the company and the ladies have their places appointed. As the meal should not be delayed by our tardiness, so we must be careful not to weary the guests by obliging them to wait till we are done eating.

Undress.—Ladies do not appear in elaborate dress for breakfast, nor should they be so negligent as to excite remarks at the impropriety of their appearance. Politeness requires that gentlemen shall not come to the table without their coats, especially if covered with perspiration. The propriety of this rule is very obvious.

The blessing.—It is the custom of religious people generally to give thanks to God for the provisions of the table and all other mercies. If that be the practice of the house, we should give a respectful attention to the service; not only because it is polite to conform to the usage of those whom we respect, but also that we may show we are not unmindful of the kind Providence that gives us each "day our daily bread."

Be patient.—Under ordinary circumstances, we should manifest no impatience to be served, but should render whatever assistance we can in helping others. Nor should we commence to eat before the company are all ready. If we eat and drink in great haste, without some apparent good reason, or seem to be extremely fond of some particular dish, it may appear that we have not been accustomed to the enjoyment of a good table.

Fastidiousness.—The exhibition of fastidiousness is extremely offensive to good taste. Young people should

---

Who should be seated first? In what kind of dress should ladies not appear at breakfast? Why should a gentleman not come to his meals without his coat? What is the custom of religious people generally before eating? How should we act at the table where such a custom is observed? How shall we act when the host or servant is helping the guests?

learn to eat what is set before them, and not be over sensitive and delicate. If there be anything unpleasant in the food, or unsuitable, put it quietly aside without attracting the attention of others. To ask for coffee, when tea alone has been provided, or to make a request for anything that will occasion trouble, and possibly annoyance, is very impolite.

Coughing and spitting at table.—Some persons have so little regard for the proprieties of the table as to clear the throat, and cough and spit upon the floor before commencing to eat. Such thoughtlessness is deserving of the severest censure. If it be necessary to blow the nose or clear the throat, it is the duty of a person to leave the table to accomplish the purpose. If there is occasion to remove cherry-stones, fish-bones, etc., from the mouth, it may be done by using the hand or the napkin, but it is very rude to spit them out upon the plate. When obliged to cough or sneeze, the napkin should be applied to the face, and the head turned from the table. To make a noise unnecessarily with the lips in eating may be disagreeable to those sitting near. It is unbecoming to scratch the head or face, or, indeed, to put the hand to the head, nor is it graceful to sit leaning with the elbows upon the table.

The napkin.—When napkins are not provided, the handkerchief should be used as a substitute; but as there are many articles of food that impart an unpleasant odor to the handkerchief, the napkin is preferable It is to be used, in part, to protect the dress from injury from particles of food falling into the lap, and also as a towel to cleanse the mouth and fingers when they become soiled. It should never be employed as a handkerchief for the nose, or to remove per-

---

How shall we act if we discover something disagreeable to us? Is it polite to give trouble at table? Should persons cough and spit at table? What shall be done with cherry stones and fish bones? When obliged to cough or sneeze, what shall be done? What impolite actions must be avoided at the table? What is the napkin for? Why not use the handkerchief?

spiration from the face. Be very careful not to soil the table-cloth by permitting anything to fall off the plate that will impart a stain.

The servant.—Whether helped by your host or by a servant, always speak distinctly and politely. Good manners at meal-time are always appreciated by a servant. If you wish to be helped, you can ask, "Will you please help me, ——?" or if you do not desire what is offered you, you can say, "No, I thank you." Young people lose their self-possession sometimes, and when asked questions do not speak loud enough or reply in a satisfactory manner. Such diffidence can be overcome by care and practice. In passing the plate to be replenished, place the knife and fork so that they will not fall off and possibly do damage. They should not be laid upon the clean table-cloth. When requested to pass a dish, it is better to lift it politely than to shove it along the table.

The butter-knife and spoons.—There ought to be a butter-knife for every butter-plate on the table, and a separate spoon for each dish, with a carving-knife and fork for the meats. With these precautions, no one should be so impolite as to help himself to butter or sauce with his own knife or spoon. If no butter-knife is provided, each guest should be careful to clean his knife carefully upon a slice of bread, that no stain be left upon the butter. Never return any part of the food that has been on your plate to the dish.

The knife and fork.—In the days of our grandmothers, it was the custom to make the blade of the table-knife curved, so that it would be more convenient to convey the food to

---

How shall we speak to the servant? How should you ask to be helped? How shall you refuse? How will you pass your plate? How pass a dish? What is said of the butter-knife and spoons? Should any one dip his knife or fork into a dish? If there is no butter-knife, how shall we take the butter? Why not return the food to the dish? How were knives made and used formerly?

the mouth. When it was used for that purpose, the edge was turned from the mouth, to avoid the danger of being cut. It is the fashion now to make the knives with the blade straight, and it is not considered polite to use them for any other purpose than for cutting the food or spreading the bread with butter. The forks are now usually constructed with three or four tines, so that they are suitable to eat with. Such things as can not be lifted with the fork may be eaten by the aid of a spoon. Never pick the teeth at table, and much less use the fork for that purpose. That it may be known that the course or the meal is finished, the knife and fork should be placed parallel on the plate—the handles to the right of the plate, that the servant may remove them readily.

The cup and saucer.—It was the custom, formerly, to place a little dish at the side of the plate, for the purpose of receiving the cup when the tea or coffee was poured into the saucer. The liquid was poured out to facilitate its cooling, and was drank from the saucer. The cup-plate was a convenience to prevent the soiling of the table-cloth. Now, however, the cup-plates have gone out of use, and people are expected to drink from the cup, after removing the spoon to the saucer. It is considered very impolite to pour out the coffee or tea, and place the cup on the table cloth. When we drink, we should not gaze around the table.

Table conversation.—The rules already alluded to in Chapter XXVI have their application at the table. We should be sociable, without being forward; polite, but not pert; self-possessed, but not egotistic.

How are they made and used now? When and how shall we pick the teeth? How shall the knife and fork be placed to be removed? What was the custom in the use of the cup and saucer? How is the cup used now? Is it polite to set the dripping cup on the table-cloth? What rules of conversation should be used at table?

Change of service.—If there are several courses of dishes, it is well that we do not keep the guests waiting for us. When the new course is served, the company should commence to eat together.

The close.—When persons are done eating, it is very ungraceful to tip the chair back upon two legs, or place the feet upon the rungs of the chair. Nor is it polite to leave the table before the company rises without making an apology to the host for the apparent rudeness. Never, except at the request of the entertainer, take apples, nuts, or sweetmeats away from the table, as it might be supposed that you are not accustomed to such delicacies, and thought it necessary to lay by a supply for future use.

The evening party.—When young people, who are attending school, wish to give an evening entertainment to their friends, they should select Friday evening, as it will probably be the most suitable time, having reference to the duties of school.

The entertainment.—Do not impress your guests with the idea that the pleasures of the palate are the most important and agreeable incidents of the entertainment, as if eating and drinking were the chief delights of intelligent society. The supper should not be postponed till an unreasonably late hour, as it may occasion impatience among the guests, and at the same time conflict with the laws of health. Headache and sleeplessness are the usual accompaniments of very late hours and heavy suppers.

Seating the guests.—The company should be seated by the entertainer in such a manner as to secure the most

---

How should the courses be served? How shall we sit at table? May we carry nuts, etc., from the table? What is the proper evening for school boys and girls to entertain company? Why? Why should the eating not be thought the best part of the entertainment? Why not have a late supper? How should the guests be seated?

pleasant and agreeable intercourse among all the members. If left to themselves to take seats, the most entertaining people may happen to occupy the same end of the table, and monopolize the conversation and attention.

The carving.—Every young person should learn to carve, so that in case of necessity, no embarrassment may be occasioned by the neglect of so valuable an accomplishment. To carve well requires a knowledge of the anatomy of the fowl or joint, and skill in the use of the knife. Neatness and dispatch are essential to the work, while gracefulness is not without its charm. A sharp carving-knife should always be prepared and ready when wanted; it is very awkward to keep a company waiting until the knife is sharpened.

Helping the guests.—See to it that each person is well served. Be generous, but not profuse. Never force your friends to eat and drink for fear of offending you. Such hospitality is not kind, because it is not thoughtful; and it is very impolite to overfeed your guests. If a guest declines to receive any article of food, it is rude to insist upon it or to make any comments upon the refusal, since there may be reasons which it is unnecessary to make public.

The wash.—It is polite, both before and after the meal, to offer the guest an opportunity to wash. It is a thoughtful attention, and is sometimes very gratefully received.

"The old Indian's rebuke."—John Trumbull, the celebrated American painter, when a boy, resided with his father, Governor Trumbull, at his residence in Lebanon, Conn., in the neighborhood of the Mohegans.

The government of this tribe was hereditary in the family

What is said of learning to carve? Why is it important? What is said of the knife and fork? What is the rule for helping the guests? Is it polite to insist upon any one's eating? Why? What is said of washing before and after meals? Give the anecdote of the old Indian.

of the celebrated Uncas. Among the heirs to the chieftainship was an Indian named Zachary, who, though a brave man and an excellent hunter, was as drunken and worthless an Indian as could well be found. By the death of the intervening heirs, Zachary found himself entitled to the royal power. In this moment, the better genius of Zachary assumed sway, and he reflected seriously. "Now, can such a drunken wretch as I aspire to be chief of this noble tribe? What will my people say? How shall the shades of my glorious ancestors look down indignant upon such a successor? Can I succeed to the great Uncas? I WILL DRINK NO MORE!" And he solemnly resolved that henceforth he would drink nothing stronger than water; and he kept his resolution.

Zachary succeeded to the rule of his tribe. It was usual for the governor to attend at the annual election in Hartford; and it was customary for the Mohegan chief also to attend, and on his way to stop and dine with the governor. John, the governor's son, was but a boy, and on one of these occasions a scene occurred, which I will give in Trumbull's own words:

"One day the mischievous thought struck me to try the sincerity of the old man's temperance. The family were seated at dinner, and there was excellent home-brewed ale on the table. I thus addressed the old chief:

"'Zachary, this beer is very fine; will you not taste it?'

"The old man dropped his knife, and leaned forward, with a stern intensity of expression, and his fervid eyes, sparkling with indignation, were fixed upon me.

"'John,' said he, 'you do n't know what you are doing. You are serving the devil, boy! Do you know that I am an Indian? If I should taste your beer, I should not stop till I got rum, and I should become again the same drunken, contemptible wretch your father remembers me to have

---

What was his rebuke? What did the Indian mean by saying John was serving the devil?

been. JOHN, NEVER AGAIN WHILE YOU LIVE TEMPT A MAN TO BREAK A GOOD RESOLUTION.'

"I was thunderstruck. My parents were deeply affected. They looked at me, and then turned their gaze upon the venerable chieftain with awe and respect. They afterward frequently reminded me of the scene and charged me never to forget it." This rule applies at table and everywhere.

Observation.—The customs of society are constantly changing in reference to apparently little things. Young people, who wish to appear to advantage, will be obliged to be cool and self-possessed in order to observe closely, without appearing to be curious, everything that is passing around. Eyes and ears should be in constant requisition, noticing quietly the language and manners of those who are well versed in the rules of polite society. By neglecting to give close attention to all that transpires, people often make ridiculous and sometimes serious blunders. These may be avoided by tact and prudence. It is never safe to affect a knowledge which is not possessed. If we hear a new word, or receive a new impression, it would be better to ask for an explanation than to pretend that the subject is understood, when it is not. The following anecdote illustrates the danger of such a silly and untruthful affectation:

Anecdote.—In one of the villages of New York, a certain lady thought she would call on her nearest neighbor. She was about entering the door, but hesitated, thinking that the family might be taking their supper. "Come in," said the hostess, "we are having tableaux." "Yes," replied the visitor, "I thought I smelt 'em." She was about equal in honesty and intelligence to the boy who insisted that he knew what sardines were: "It is a kind of fruit that grows on trees."

What must young people do to keep up with the times? Is it right to make a pretense of knowledge? Why? Give the anecdote. What are tableaux? What are sardines? What would have been the better way in both cases? Is it truthful to make pretense in that way?

CHAPTER XLIII.

BEHAVIOR IN TRAVELING.

The facilities for traveling are so great in our country that it is not uncommon for young people to make long journeys in the public conveyances, unaccompanied by their friends. A few hints upon the courtesies which will be expected of them by polite society may assist in securing the greatest amount of pleasure for themselves, and in giving the most satisfaction to their friends and fellow-travelers.

The cars.—The rule which governs in the selection of seats in the car is the same that is adopted wherever the tickets are all the same price: the first that comes has the choice. When a passenger buys a ticket, he or she is entitled to all the rights it affords, and no more. It conveys no privilege to claim two seats, since the use of but one was purchased. It sometimes happens that selfish persons will usurp two full seats, piling their baggage about them in a manner which plainly says that they recognize the comfort and convenience of no one save themselves.

To exhibit such a disregard of the rights of those who are entitled to equal advantage, is impolite and ungenerous. On entering a car, and finding that the seats are occupied by the baggage of those who seem unwilling to accommodate, it is not well to try to force them to recognize your rights. As it is the business of the conductor to see that all are seated, a polite request to him will relieve your em-

What is the subject of Chapter XLIII? Why is it proper to offer some hints on traveling? What is the rule for choosing seats in a car? What rights does one ticket give? How do persons sometimes show their selfishness? If persons are unwilling to give us a seat, what shall we do? Who regulates the passengers on the cars?

barrassment, without the danger of insult or annoyance. Persons who leave their seat temporarily may show that it is taken by leaving a shawl or garment in the place during their absence.

Respect for the aged.—There is something very beautiful in the way in which well-trained youth of either sex look after the comfort of old people in traveling. Many little acts of courtesy and kindness may be performed, which will admirably illustrate the spirit of the moral law, which says, "*Thou shalt rise up before the hoary head, and honor the face of the old man.*"

The Lacedæmonians.—"One of the lessons," says Rollin, the historian, "oftenest and most strongly inculcated upon the Lacedæmonian youth, was to entertain great reverence and respect for old men, and to give them proof of it on all occasions—by saluting them; by making way for them, and giving them place in the streets; by rising up to show them honor in all companies and public assemblies; but above all, by receiving their advice, and even their reproofs, with docility and submission. By these characteristics, a Lacedæmonian was known wherever he came. If he had behaved otherwise, it would have been looked upon as a reproach to himself and a dishonor to his country."

The conductor.—The conductor of a train is usually polite and attentive to his passengers; but he has many annoyances, arising from the ignorance, impertinence, and selfishness of ill-bred people. He can easily recognize the gentleman and lady, and is always willing to treat them with kindness and respect. To secure his attention, it is only necessary to be observant of all the rules of the train;

How may young persons show their good culture toward the aged? What law of politeness does the moral law teach? What was the training of the Lacedæmonians? What were they expected to do? What conditions are necessary that ladies may travel securely?

he will afford all necessary information and assistance to those who politely request it.

Lady travelers.—Ladies very frequently travel without any escort, and they may do so without the least fear of annoyance, provided they indicate by their dress, manner, conversation, and conduct that they are well bred. It is the rarest occurrence that a woman, who is actuated by right principles and good sense, is disturbed in the slightest degree.

It is related of Miss Anna Dickinson, who has traveled thousands of miles through the country to fulfill her engagements as a public lecturer, that she was never insulted but once. Her traveling manager stated that, "While traveling west, she was asleep in a car at night, with her head resting upon her muff, on the back of a seat, when a man sat down beside her, and pressed her foot with his. Miss Dickinson wakened instantly, looked him full in the eye, and said: 'Do that again, and I will call the conductor, and have you put off the train.' The man went into another car." Dignified self-possession and conscious virtue are all that is needed to insure immunity from all rudeness and impertinence.

Traveling acquaintances.—The rules already given for politeness have a special application when traveling. Young people should bear in mind that all well-dressed people are not necessarily members of good society, and while it is their duty to treat every person with civility, they should be extremely careful in permitting any one, whether male or female, to exercise any familiarity not warranted among entire strangers. A respectful reserve should always be maintained, and anything like undue freedom should be promptly checked.

Selfishness.—Everything affecting the convenience, comfort, and health of the passengers is worthy of our attention.

If women act rudely in traveling, who is to blame if they are insulted? What is said of Anna Dickinson? What is necessary to prevent insult and annoyance? Is care necessary in making traveling acquaintances? Why?

We have no right to do anything which may prove disagreeable or injurious to those who have an equal right to be consulted. It may be agreeable for one to open the window, but if those who sit behind are inconvenienced by the breeze, or dust, or cinders, it would certainly be very uncivil to insist that it should remain open.

Patience and good humor.—In one of the crowded eastern-bound trains, the patience of the passengers was very sorely tried by the loud and protracted cries of an infant, which appeared to be solely in charge of a man. After bearing with the disturbance some time, a nervous passenger protested against it, and demanded that the baby should be properly cared for or removed from the car. The protest drew from the gentleman who had it in charge the following explanation: "Ladies and gentlemen, I am very sorry that you have been so seriously incommoded by the cries of this child; but I beg of you to be patient, and I shall explain. It is an orphan; its mother has recently died, and I am taking it East to be cared for by its friends. The little thing is frightened, as the cars, its food, and the care it receives are strange to it. I shall do all in my power to make it comfortable and prevent further annoyance."

The sympathies of the passengers were roused, and they not only showed a willingness to endure its cries, but raised a handsome sum, by contribution, for its support. Forbearance and kindness are divine attributes, and it is our duty to cultivate them under all circumstances. A good-humored acquiescence, and the disposition to make the best out of things that are unpleasant, is the true philosophy. The habitual grumbler and fault-finder will have ample opportunity to indulge his ill-natured inclinations while traveling; but such a person is a very disagreeable companion.

How may persons exhibit selfishness in traveling? How should windows, stoves, doors, and ventilators be used? Give the anecdote of the baby traveler. What is gained by good humor? What is lost by grumbling? What is gained by fault-finding? What kind of a companion does a grumbler make?

The hotel.—Every person, before traveling, should ascertain, if possible, the names of the hotels at which he will stop. If a memorandum be made of the name and character of the hotel, it may save considerable inconvenience and expense. Serious mistakes have arisen from not knowing just where to stop, particularly in a city. If no other source of information can be had, the conductor will tell you, if politely requested, the names and character of the various houses of entertainment. On arriving at the depot, there are generally carriages or omnibuses in waiting to deliver passengers wherever they wish to go. Selecting the conveyance, and giving the baggage-checks to the driver, you will be taken to the hotel designated.

If a gentleman, proceed at once to the office, register your name, and secure your room, to which your baggage will be promptly removed. If a lady, and without company, proceed at once to the public parlor, ring the bell, or send for the clerk, give him your name, tell him how long you expect to remain, and request him to furnish you a room, and have your baggage brought. Any information in reference to the running of cars, or to places of business, can be obtained from the clerk. There are always maid servants in attendance to give whatever information is necessary concerning the meals and ways of the house. If a lady is visited by gentlemen friends, she will see them in the public parlor. On leaving the private room, the door should be locked to prevent intrusion of those who are not authorized to enter. Nothing of value should be left lying loose about the room to serve as a temptation to any one to steal.

The table.—Well-educated persons always behave with the same courtesy and refinement when among strangers that they do among their friends at home; but vulgar people

---

How shall we learn at what hotel to stop? Why make a memorandum of it? What does a gentleman do first at a hotel? What shall a lady do? To whom shall she apply for information? Why? Where shall a lady receive gentlemen visitors? Why be careful about locking the door? How do refined people act at a hotel?

affect a rude, coarse independence in the hotel and at the public table, as they wish to attract attention. Because such people are expected to pay for their entertainment, it is no reason that they should be impolite and vulgar. To be ill-mannered and disrespectful to the servants, to scold them about the quality or preparation of the food, and to boast of good living at home, are the surest indications of a want of good culture. If there is occasion to complain of any want of civility on the part of servants of a hotel, it is very unbecoming to quarrel with them, and secure no redress. The proper way is to speak to the clerk or proprietor, and he will remove your grievances, if they are not unavoidable.

CHAPTER XLIV.

MISCELLANEOUS SUGGESTIONS.

Thanks.—Be careful to express your thanks for every act of civility you receive, even from a servant or a child. Such appreciation of kindness will win future favors and friendship.

Replies.—When asked a question by a gentleman, always answer promptly, distinctly, and politely, "Yes, sir," or "No, sir." When addressed by a lady, say, "Yes, ma'm," or "No, ma'm." Such respectful replies indicate a good training.

How do some rude persons behave? How shall we treat servants? If we have a complaint, to whom shall we make it?

What is meant by miscellaneous suggestions? What is said of thanks? Replies?

Mud.—If the streets are muddy, and your shoes are soiled, be careful to use the scraper before entering the house. Muddy shoes are an abomination to good housekeepers.

Always knock.—Before entering the door of a private house or room, be careful to knock or ring, that you may not intrude upon the privacy of the occupant.

Never knock before entering a store, hotel, public office, or other place of business. Where people are expected, it is not necessary to give any warning at their entrance.

The hat.—On entering a private house, a public parlor, or a church, always remove the hat, as a mark of respect to the people or the place. This should become a habit.

The door.—It is evidence of great carelessness and indifference to the feelings of others to neglect to close a door on entering or leaving a room. If you open the door, be sure to turn and shut it when you pass.

Uniformity in temper.—It is not right to be variable in temper; gay to-day, and sedate to-morrow. To be uniformly kind, courteous, and considerate, is necessary to preserve respect and friendship. Moody people are very trying to their friends.

Eccentricity.—Never affect eccentricity of manner, dress, or language, as the notoriety attained will not compensate for the loss of the respect and confidence of your neighbors

System.—If we wish to incommode ourselves as little as possible, and prevent annoyance to our friends, we will have a place for everything—hat, books, overshoes, and um-

---

Mud? Of when to knock? Of when not to knock? Of the hat? The door? What is said of uniformity of temper? Of eccentricity? Of system?

brella—and take good care to return them to their places, when not in use.

The handle.—In giving any tool or instrument, or vessel, to another, be careful to present it so that he may seize it by the handle.

Help.—Always be ready to lend a helping hand to those who need your assistance. A little act of kindness, bestowed at the right time, is often of inestimable value.

Chewing gum.—There are good physiological reasons why the incessant chewing of anything is injurious, and it certainly is not in good taste to see persons in school or other public places with their mouths full of gum or wax, and apparently in laborious exercise. Such rumination is very unbecoming on the street, and, if observed, would give rise to serious doubts whether the ruminant be a lady or not.

Inconvenience to others.—Never do anything that occasions any person, particularly a servant, unnecessary trouble, inconvenience, or labor, without offering them some special remuneration.

Prices.—To inquire of persons in company the price of their clothes or their ornaments, is extremely impolite; even in private, such questions might be esteemed impertinent.

Impertinent questions.—Do not ask questions out of mere curiosity.

It may not be agreeable for persons to make you their confidents in matters that do not concern your interests.

That was a very unsatisfactory reply which a one-legged sailor made to the inquisitive keeper of a country tavern, who was anxious to know how the former met with his

---

Of presenting objects? Of help? Of chewing gum? What is a ruminant? What is said of inconvenience to others? Of prices? Of questions? What is the anecdote of the one-legged sailor?

misfortune. "I'll tell you," said the sailor, "if you do not ask another question." "Agreed," said the host. "Well, then," replied the sailor, "it was bit off."

After gazing impatiently at the injured leg, the host answered: "I'd give something pretty to know what bit it off."

Politeness.—"*Whatsoever ye would that men should do to you, do ye even so to them.*"

"COURAGE TO DO RIGHT."

"We may have courage, all of us,
To start at honor's call,
To meet a foe, protect a friend,
Or face a cannon ball.

"To show the world one hero lives,
The foremost in the fight—
But do we always manifest
The courage to do right?

"To answer No! with steady breath,
And quick unfaltering tongue,
When fierce temptation, ever near,
Her syren song has sung?

"To care not for the bantering tone,
The jest, or studied slight:
Content if we can only have
The courage to do right?

"To step aside from fashion's course,
Or custom's favored plan;
To pluck an outcast from the street,
Or help a fellow man?

"If not, then let us nobly try,
Henceforth, with all our might,
In every case to muster up
The courage to do right!"

INDEX.

Q.

R.

S.

T.

U.

V.

W.

www.ingramcontent.com/pod-product-compliance
Lightning Source LLC
LaVergne TN
LVHW050512100826
845148LV00002B/309

* 9 7 8 1 4 2 5 5 2 1 8 8 2 *